That Flame In Your Heart? Turn it Into a Blowtorch!

30 Days to Reignite Your Spiritual Life!

DAVID LEIS

That Flame In Your Heart? Turn it Into a Blowtorch!

30 Days to Reignite Your Spiritual Life!

Avantt Press

A Gabriel Press Book
www.gabrielpressusa.com

Direction For Our Times
www.directionforourtimes.com

Published by Avantt Press
Princeton, New Jersey, USA
www.turnitintoablowtorch.com

Copyright © 2014 by David A. Leis

ISBN: 1-941172-02-4
ISBN-13: 978-1-941172-02-5
Library of Congress Control Number: 2014907070
Cover Design: Judy Bullard www.customebookcovers.com
Editor: Sarah Rose
Author Photo: Dan Naylor www.dannaylor.com

All Rights Reserved. No part of this publication may be reproduced, stored in a retrieval system or transmitted by any means, electronic, mechanical photocopying, recording or otherwise without the prior permission in writing of the publisher.

Printed in the United States of America

To Don Leis, my dad, and Fr. Francis Marino, my spiritual father. Your lives were an inspiration to me; the faith which you lived out in your unique vocations has been the platform upon which I have built my own life as a father and man of faith. Your unselfish generosity to everyone no matter his or her status in life is a standard to which I can only aspire to in some small measure. I look forward with great anticipation to our reunion in Heaven! To my mom, Norma Leis. You have lived a life of faith exhibited by continuous service to others that seems to have no limits and for that I am a better man because of your inspiring example. And to Anne, for your faithfulness to God in allowing Him to use you as a conduit for the words from His Heart, which have turned my love for Him from a flame into a Blowtorch.

*That warm flame of love for God
you have in your heart?
He wants to turn it into a blowtorch
of burning love so hot and bright
that everyone who sees you sees Him.
As He does that,
the blowtorch will burn up your
pain, sorrow, defects, weaknesses,
and even your very humanity, purifying your heart,
leaving only Him in its place.
When that happens,
you will know a peace, serenity, and joy within you,
no matter who or what you are,
or what you are going through.
He wants that for you, right now, where you are!
So that others will catch His Fire from you!
And His Peace, Serenity, and Joy will spread like wildfire!*

Table of Contents

Foreword	xi
Preface	xv
Acknowledgements	xvii
Introduction: Laying the Firebrick Foundation!	1
Day 1. Suffering & Fire. Lightning from a Clear Blue Sky!	15
Day 2. Exposed: The Life Contained in Every Tabernacle!	23
Day 3. Forgiveness: The First Lesson in Love	29
Day 4. Self-hate: Destroyer of Your Interior and Family Unity	33
Day 5. Jesus Waiting on Me – With Beer & Lime Chips?!	39
Day 6. The Coming Revelation: Leaving No Room for Doubt	47
Day 7. All Your Decisions Have Eternal Consequences	53
Day 8. I Am Not Disobedient! It's My Freedom! ... Or Slavery	59
Day 9. The Secret Realities of Heaven Disclosed!	65
Day 10. The Real Meaning of "I Am With You"	71
Day 11. Finding a Safe Refuge Despite Turmoil & Pain	77
Day 12. Your Family, The First School of the Heart	83
Day 13. Unrestrained Love Explodes from the World's Tabernacles!	89
Day 14. An Intimate Discussion: The Way You Speak	95

Day 15. How to Please Jesus. (It's Not What You Think.)	101
Day 16. Foundations of Holiness: Protecting Your Soul	107
Day 17. Antidote to a Plugged-in, Hi-speed, Multiplexed Life	113
Day 18. Your Spiritual Growth … at the Speed God Requires	119
Day 19. Live True Inner Peace. You Were Created for It.	127
Day 20. No Gaining Heaven Without This New Language	135
Day 21. Oh! Straight Talk from Jesus: Sexual Purity	143
Day 22. A New Twist: Two Obligations of Love of Neighbor	153
Day 23. A Life Not Examined is a Life Not Truly Lived	161
Day 24. The Secrets to Your True Success Revealed	169
Day 25. Cleanse the Soul, Heal the Heart, Feel the Joy!	175
Day 26. You, a Close, Dependable Friend of Jesus?! Yes!	183
Day 27. You Have Specific Souls You Are to Save!	189
Day 28. The Ways You Need to Prepare for His Return. Now!	199
Day 29. Protecting You from Your Own Weaknesses	205
Day 30. Your Ongoing Conversion. You're Not Done Yet!	209
Reflections on the Process of the Dialogue of the Heart	213
Assessment: The 30 Days of Dialogue	215
Epilogue: Foundations of an Interior Prayer Life	217
Notes on Catholic Theology from a Layman's Perspective	223
Recommended Resources	227
Extract of Messages from Volume Two	229
Bishop's & Theologian's Letters	279
Take Blowtorch! to the Next Level	287
About the Author	289

Note to the reader: This book has been written for all who believe in Jesus, or desire to believe in Him, by a Catholic Christian, so all who wish to begin, renew or reignite their spiritual lives can benefit. Some things contained in the book, therefore, are uniquely Catholic, although you will also recognize the influence of other Christian authors throughout. But 100% of the human struggle is common to all people. And 98% of the content is relevant to all Christians. So taken together, as with any book, while not 100% is applicable, one can benefit from what does apply to each person's situation. I trust you will take from this work that which you need and reserve judgment on the rest as you would with any book.

Peace to you.
David Leis

Foreword

This is not like any other book you have ever read.

If you open yourself to the message of this book, it will challenge your way of thinking and of living. As you turn its pages, you will come face to face with yourself, and then you will come face to face with the Person of Jesus Christ in an intimate personal dialogue.

Blowtorch chronicles the journey of a soul. It is a glimpse into a life of struggle so severe that most of us can only imagine its depth of pain. The author does not dwell there, however. While referencing some of those struggles to give the reader some context, David focuses on the Love and Mercy of our ever-present God who walks with him through each tragedy, through each moment of his personal crucifixion. David is not looking for pity; he is looking to enlighten us all to the Love of the Father, the care of Jesus, and the power of the Holy Spirit.

In this book, you are invited to take a journey. It is not an easy journey, as you will read. Yet it is a journey of hope. David took this journey, and now he is able to say, "God is real. God is Love. He cares for each of us with a depth of mercy and compassion that is so powerful that once you encounter it, once you embrace it, your life will be changed forever." David opens his own life so that we may examine our own. It is God who is speaking through him.

As Rick Warren, author of *The Purpose Driven Life,* says, we are always either just coming out of a problem or getting ready to enter one. If you want the best possible preparation for the next problem or crisis in your life, then I highly recommend *Blowtorch*. It reveals the Love of God in ways you have likely never imagined. If this world with all of its distractions and entertainments leaves you empty leaves your heart hurting for something and Someone authentic, join David in this journey.

On Day 24, David speaks of the emptiness he has felt in his life, even during times of great personal success: "You know the emptiness because You created it in me, just as You have for every soul You have created and will create. This is an emptiness that only You can fill with the joy of Your Presence. The emptiness, the longing You created is meant to cause me to search, to seek You out and not rest until I find You."

Is there a reader who cannot relate to this emptiness? Is there anyone for whom this search is foreign? It is God Himself who created this emptiness and is waiting to fill it. Will you seek Him? Will you invite Him to fill you with His joyful Presence? He is waiting.

God wants to share His Love with you in such a powerful way that it will burn away all of the fear, loneliness, despair, and false gods that you cling to.

It is a revolutionary book, if you open your heart to it.

It can be the most important book you have ever read, if you respond to its message.

Blowtorch is also a journey of the heart. It is in our own hearts that God awaits. He is calling us in a way that is, perhaps, unique in history because these are unique times. If you want to know God in ways that you have never experienced, *Blowtorch* will guide you to Him.

And what you will find is that God desires a heart-to-heart dialogue with us. As you join David, let him be your guide to this heart journey with God. That is the journey that forms the basis of *Blowtorch*.

In that heart-to heart dialogue, you will discover that God desires unity with you, personally. He wants a new and deeper relationship with you. He wants to help you to carry your burdens, to fulfill the desires of your heart, to lead you in ways that you have never gone before. All you need is openness to God's Love and Mercy, to heed the call to meet Him in the depths of your heart, and to allow His healing and compassionate Love to lift you to heights that you have never experienced before.

Will you say yes to Him? What stands between you and unity with God? What is more important in your life than a relationship with the One who created you and who sustains you? It is the Triune God, perfect in communion, who is calling you to unity. How can you turn your back on Him? How can you refuse this gift of gifts that will revolutionize your life? Don't hesitate, don't turn away. It is God who loves you in this moment into a new relationship with Him. Open yourself up to His Love in ways you have never experienced before.

This encounter with God is an adventure that will change you forever.

"Stay with Me." This is God's call. This is the call that Dave responded to and the call that he shares with us in this moving and affecting account of thirty days of heart dialogues with our loving Lord.

At the end of each day's reflection, Dave has provided questions that are designed to help you to reflect deeply on the messages God is communicating. Spend time in prayer and reflection on each one; answer each as honestly and openly as you can – and you will allow God to reveal His Love for you in a new and vibrant way. The Creator of the universe and of your own special uniqueness wants to convey His Love to you; are you ready to listen?

The Church is the instrument God has chosen to communicate His Love and Truth to the world. Every diocese and parish has the responsibility to be true to His teachings and, through their best efforts, to draw all parishioners to Him. *Blowtorch* provides an effective instrument to assist in this call. In addition to the "reflections of the heart," the reflection questions can be used for personal growth and – in the right setting – for sharing with others. God calls us individually and communally; this text assists us in this journey of responding to His Love. I am convinced that any parish or diocese that used *Blowtorch* for a facilitated program of renewal with only a fraction of its members would see the spiritual lives of its participants reignited and the flame of God's Love burn like a blowtorch as it renews them!

This book can change your life and the lives of your loved ones. Once you have opened yourself to the Love of God, you will be better able to share that Love with your family, your friends, your coworkers, and all whom you meet. While this book is for everyone, I especially recommend it for parents. As a parent, I know the tremendous responsibility that God has given to steward His children to holiness. At the end of my life, the measure of my effectiveness as a parent will not be reflected in the material goods I provided my children; it will be reflected in the effort I expended to communicate God's Love to them. If every parent, every couple, read *Blowtorch* and opened their hearts to what God wants of them, it would profoundly change the nature of their relationship and the way they parent.

God's timing is always perfect. He has perfectly timed this moment in which you are holding this book in your hands. Now is the time to turn to Him and to allow Him to heal you more deeply, accept His Love for you more completely, and walk with Him more confidently. You are not alone in this journey. If you allow Him, God will fan the flame of love in your heart into a blowtorch that will consume all your fears, doubts, and sin – and lead you to a more perfect union with the One who loves you more than you can possibly imagine.

This book has been brought to your attention because *God wants your attention.*

If you read it and take its inspiration to heart, you will find yourself on the most exciting journey of your life. How can it not be so, if God wills it?

Edward R. Gaffney
Director of Mission Effectiveness
Diocese of Colorado Springs, USA
Author of *Making Peace: A Catholic Guide to Turning Conflict Into Grace*

Preface

I am honored to have this endorsement from Anne, a lay apostle, from Direction For Our Times:

Blowtorch is more of a journey than a book. One feels as though one can put aside one's own suffering while reading this work to walk with David as he carries his cross.

If that were all, it would be enough. However, the contemporary crosses David carries are relevant to many during this period of financial reverses, marital anguish and single parenting. What is seen at the start, the finish and on each page in between, is the intimacy which can develop between the saved and the Saviour when we remain fixed in honest relationship with Christ.

David has given us a rare gift, indeed. Blowtorch is actually more about the reader's experience than the writer's!

Anne, a lay apostle

Acknowledgements

It took over six years to make this project a reality, and there are too many to thank adequately. The first thank you goes to my daughter, Sharon Marchetti, who had the love, sensitivity, and intuition to give me books, Volume One and Volume Two, which reignited my spiritual life like nothing else I have ever experienced. She also read the manuscript and she and her husband, Frank, encouraged me to publish it. The second would be to John and Joan Bickel who read my early notes and encouraged me to write them down in more detail in the first place, which became the manuscript. And my dear friend Ed Gaffney who read an early version of the manuscript, urged me to publish it, and later did a first pass edit. Without their encouragement I would never have undertaken such a daunting task.

I have been humbled by the love and support of my sons John David and Stephen, who have been working alongside me every step of the way and putting up with the long hours of work on this book project. JD also put up the first website, helped with all the work of creating the manuscript and found innumerable ways to assist. Stephen, dear Stephen, loved me every day and kept me focused on the task by asking me where the book was on Amazon! They both provided superabundant love, hugs, laughs and pure joy the whole time.

During the darkest hours, Jim and Joan Dziedzic were there for me when I needed a conversation or someone else's cooking. And then there are Tony and Maria Marchetti, and their whole extended family who all just adopted me like I was one of their own! To Michael and Jennifer, Antonio and Erica Marchetti, Sharon's husband Frank, John Paul and Angela, Rosa and Frank Federici and Alex, your generosity in including me in all things Marchetti and your spiritual support is priceless beyond measure.

My friend, Maureen McNamara, read the manuscript and provided thoughtful encouragement. At just the right time Mary Lou Gormley Warren came along giving me a major boost to turn it into a real project to get it finished and put the first covers on it and bind it. Sarah (Daley) Rose was extraordinarily patient with me and did a great job editing the manuscript. And the team that delivered the training, consultations, and confidence that I could undertake the authoring and publishing of a book, was Steve Harrison and Geoffrey Berwind from Bradley Communications, along with Jack Canfield, co-author of the *Chicken Soup for the Soul* series. It was Jack who told me he loved the current title! Their Bestseller Blueprint course was invaluable.

My mom, Norma, and brothers and sisters, Mike and Lidiette, Brenda and Larry Jensen, Gail and Dant Lasater, Tom and Jerri, Dianne and Jeff Peier, John and Jill, and Jana and Eric Brey (yes, all eight of them!) and their families supported and encouraged me along the way. And when we were together on occasion, or when they hosted us, were always there through my ups and downs. What a great family I am blessed to have!

Fr. Rick Rusk and the people at St. Rose of Lima Parish and the people from the Anawim Community there provided community and a place of welcome for us as a family. My confessor and spiritual guide, Fr. Paul Ruge, the Chaplain at the World Apostolate of Fatima USA provided many hours of unselfish wisdom and counsel as I walked this path those 6 years; his unwavering support and guidance gave me sure footing when it felt as though the world was slipping from under me. Ann and Bill Dee found a way for us to go to Lourdes for a spiritual refresher when I could not have done it myself.

And finally, Anne, a lay apostle who read it and called me excitedly saying she loved it, and Fr. Darragh Connolly, Justin Sofio, Patrick

Howard and the others at Direction for Our Times who read it and encouraged me to keep going. Their spiritual support has made all the difference.

But first and foremost, I thank God, for His Mercy and Love that knows no bounds! This journey of my life has been wonderful, with all its trials and tribulations, because I know His Love and that is sufficient! He has blessed me in every way with unbounded generosity which humbles me as His unworthy servant. May He be praised forever!

With loving gratitude,

David Leis

That Flame In Your Heart? Turn it Into a Blowtorch!

30 Days to Reignite Your Spiritual Life!

Introduction

Laying the Firebrick Foundation!

Yes, you have a love for God in your heart. Sometimes you can really feel the warmth of it (2 Tm 1:6). Like when you are in church and there is a really moving sermon, or when you see a new baby born, or you are in touch with nature in a particular way, or realize that you narrowly escaped some disaster. In those times, we have all felt the warm flame of love of God. Genesis 1:26 says that God created mankind in His own image. God is Love, so when He created the human heart, He put the stamp of love on it; He filled it with the capacity for burning love. This is how every human heart is made, whether one acknowledges God or not.

I believe we are living in a very special time and that God is now making His Presence known in a brand new way. In doing that, He wants to take the flame of love for Him that is in you and turn it into a brightly burning blowtorch, so bright and hot that it consumes the old you and like a refiner's fire leaves pure gold in its place (Zec 13:9)!

Then the flame will ignite others so that the fire races across the face of the earth like a spark racing through the stubble (Ws 3:7), burning up the old, making room for the new and renewing it! It will leave everyone it consumes with a peace and serenity so deep and profound that it can hardly be given voice; it can only be experienced. But others will see it and know. And catch fire from you!

Why would God start this fire? Out of pure love for you and all His children! He wants all of humanity to experience the peace and joy He originally intended when he created the earth! It is the reason He sent Jesus, our Peace, to redeem humanity (Eph 2:14).

I believe He is in the process of returning even now, at this moment in time!

He wants you to experience deep and profound peace and joy, no matter what your circumstances are in life and have others "catch fire" from you so that every family, every workplace, every school, every community and nation can experience it. How can you spread this fire? Simply by allowing God to fill you with His peace and joy, making you a better leader, parent, worker, business person, spouse, and human being!

All Christians, and even non-Christians, know the prophecy that Jesus will return in glory. Actually, I believe He is in the process of returning even now, at this moment in time. You heard that right. The Second Coming will not be just a one-time event. It will, of course, be the greatest event since the Resurrection.

Jesus is in the process of returning now. He is coming now, ever so lovingly, but ever so urgently! You need not wait, wondering when He will come again. He is returning now, in some extraordinary ways!

Consider for a moment the movement of a great general who is intent on recapturing lost territory. He sends in the advance troops to prepare the way ahead of him and his army. Jesus has not neglected the world until His eventual return in triumph. He has sent many prophets ahead of him, from the saints to Oswald Chambers to Billy Graham to Martin Luther King to Mother Teresa to the Pope and on and on. He has even allowed apparitions by His Mother to warn us to turn away from sin and back to prayer, as she did at Fatima and Lourdes.

INTRODUCTION

And now He is sending his lay apostles into the world ahead of His final appearance in an unprecedented manner. He does not merely send apostles and prophets ahead of Him, however; in these times, He is in the process of coming in a much more profound and personal way: through His very Presence.

For many centuries, He was hidden in the church tabernacles of the world in a very simple and humble way.

No more.

> *Now it is as though all the tabernacles of the world are exploding, bursting with His love and graces in torrents unlike anything that has ever been seen.*

Now it is as though all the tabernacles of the world are exploding, bursting with His love and graces in torrents unlike anything that has ever been seen. This torrent is so powerful that those who spend time adoring Him are causing His graces to spread out from the tabernacle in all directions, like ripples in a lake when there is a splash in the middle. This grace is flowing in waves over all God's children, regardless of their knowledge of Him or the tabernacle. Abundant graces are coming to rest in the hearts of those open to Him, even without their knowledge of its Source!!

For those who choose to follow Him, He is developing a relationship with them far beyond anything known in the past. And soon, for however long that is, whether the final coming of Jesus will occur in years or decades or centuries, when He comes, we shall see Jesus Christ, the Returning King, as He is, undeniably.

This book is a compilation of my dialogue of the heart, my personal conversations with Jesus, the Returning King, but it is also a celebration. It is a celebration of the power of God as He works in the life of a very ordinary, unremarkable, common man with tenderness and love beyond description.

THAT FLAME IN YOUR HEART? TURN IT INTO A BLOWTORCH!

It is about hope and restoration, healing and trust. Our Lord is teaching me the way to peace, serenity and joy no matter what is going on in my life. Certainly, I am not there yet, rather a work in progress like everyone, but I do know peace and joy to a degree far beyond what I could even comprehend before. This peace, serenity, and joy comes from a complete trust in His care for me, which I did not previously have.

I believe He wants that for you, for every person He has created, no matter who you are, where you are or what you are or what your circumstances are. I believe **He wants that peace, serenity, and joy for you even when it seems like the whole world has turned against you, no matter how impossible your situation looks, no matter what your suffering is.** He wants us to have trust in Him; this is the virtue of the saints. I believe He wants a heart-to-Heart dialogue with you. And He wants that for you right now in this moment in a very urgent way. If you allow Him to fill you with His peace, serenity, and joy, you will be a witness of His Love like nothing else can.

I invite you to walk with me on this journey. In it, I recount the dialogue of my heart with the Heart of Jesus. Hopefully, along the way, it will enrich your own dialogue of the heart with Him who greatly desires union with you.

Let me begin with a story. It might not be so different from that of a lot of other people in these very difficult times, but it's my journey through a very dark valley to a place of peace, serenity, and joy. A year after my wife of thirty-four years walked out on me and my two special-needs sons, I was still devastated and struggling with finding the Will of God in my life amongst the ensuing chaos.

Here I was, now a single father, living in a new state, commuting an hour and a half each way (on a good day) to work, one son in high school with physical and mental handicaps and the other son, though autistic, in college forty-five minutes from home. I was relatively new to the area I lived in with no real support systems except for my daughter and her family in a nearby state and a few close friends who came to my

INTRODUCTION

rescue, some who made great sacrifices to do so. Life had gone from being quite good to a nightmare, literally overnight, and with no warning.

With the divorce, all my financial resources were gone, every bit of cash gone, all our lines of credit maxed out, my entire retirement gone, and on top of that, not long after this, I lost my job in a merger. I found a new job, 1,600 miles away, and commuted almost every week for a year until that employer went bankrupt and stuck me with a very large sum in back pay and out-of-pocket expenses.

> *Joy is a net of love by which we catch souls.*
>
> - Mother Teresa

Then, when I landed another job, that employer went bankrupt after only four months. He did the same thing to me for a large sum again, much of which had gone on credit cards, all of which were nearly maxed out. The two bankrupt employers owed me well into the six figures, money I needed to survive on. I had gone from a nice positive net worth to a huge negative net worth in a heartbeat, with no income.

I sent out over a thousand resumes, had a few interviews, but one look at my age, and interviewers who were less than half my age declined to hire me. One investor for a company I was trying to help even said "too much grey hair." I was forced by the circumstances of my son's schedules to get up at 4:30 every morning and normally fell asleep working on the computer applying for jobs, networking, etc.

I was frequently sick with sinus infections, strep throat, and for two years, a case of irritable bowel syndrome that wiped me out for days at a time. I was constantly nauseous with severe intestinal cramping. I lost my health insurance and had no money to go to the doctor, and the hospital turned me down. Both my house and a condo that we had were in foreclosure, so the banks were harassing me like clockwork every week. That continued for years until I lost both the house and condo to the banks in short sales. Being served foreclosure papers was humiliating.

THAT FLAME IN YOUR HEART? TURN IT INTO A BLOWTORCH!

To top it off, the divorce had turned nasty at the behest of her lawyer, so every week there were many hours of meetings, phone calls, digging out old financial records, getting affidavits, and on and on. Then there was the cooking, cleaning, laundry, lawn maintenance, and shopping that were necessary just to live. I took charity from food pantries both at church and public. Collection agencies called me several times a day for years.

The federal and two state governments were after me over late tax filings. Companies cancelled credit cards and lines of credit. I was reduced to borrowing from friends and family until I maxed that out. My son was in 2 accidents and, through neglect, trashed out his pickup and banged it up a few times besides. We went through a multitude of home health aides to be with the boys while I traveled, and some years, that was 5-6 days a week for months on end. By the time I paid for that and our bills, there was nothing left.

All this only scratches the surface; the worst of it I cannot even write about. I could go on, but you get the picture. I went from a pretty good life to a complete nightmare in a heartbeat.

In the midst of all this, I determined early on--as a matter of fact, in the first weeks after my wife walked out--that the stress the boys were under had to come to an end and that they needed and deserved only a joyful, peaceful home. What I was struggling with, how I felt interiorly was irrelevant to their situation. Their need was for love, and especially in this time, it was up to me to make sure they felt love from me. I also had to be sure not to poison the love they felt from their mother, despite her having abandoned

If you are going to be used by God, He will take you through a multitude of experiences that are not meant for you at all,
they are meant to make you useful in His hands to enable you to understand what transpires in other souls so that you will never be surprised at what you come across.

Oswald Chambers

INTRODUCTION

them. It was beyond my human strength, so I could turn to only one Person: God.

For Christmas that first year after my wife left, my daughter gave me Volume One and Volume Two from a set of books which she had been reading as well, recommended to her by her parish priest. Knowing the parish and their fidelity to the Pope and the teachings of the Church, I knew the recommendation would be sound.

They had been written by Anne, a Lay Apostle, a living mystic (see "private revelation" in the notes on Catholic theology at the end of the book). My spiritual life had always been present to some degree, at times a flickering candle and other times, a brightly burning lamp, confident of my relationship with God. Reading these first two Volumes of Anne's turned my spiritual life into a blowtorch, burning more brightly than anything I have ever experienced.

That experience continues to this day, six years later as I write this. No matter what is going on in my life, the blowtorch of the interior life continues to burn so brightly that, at times, it feels like it is burning me up from the inside.

I know this for sure: it is consuming the defects of sin and leaving the bright Light of Christ burning like the sun within me in each area it touches (1 Pt 1: 7). Even as I write this, I am filled with the Spirit, and the tears well up in my eyes and my heart feels like it will burst from gratitude! I am completely caught up in the fire of His Love (Heb 12:29) burning within me! That is what Jesus wants for you!

These are my very personal and private reflections based on reading Volume Two (which recently received the

> *When a person is entirely open to the breath of God's love, he becomes caught up in a spiritual "adventure" far beyond anything imaginable.*
>
> *Like a sail his soul is billowed by the breeze of the Spirit, and God can move it according to the inscrutable designs of his Providential Mercy.*
>
> St. Pope John Paul II

THAT FLAME IN YOUR HEART? TURN IT INTO A BLOWTORCH!

nihil obstat and imprimatur from the Church) by Anne, a Lay Apostle, published by the organization, Direction for Our Times (www.directionforourtimes.org). I had not intended to publish them except for the inspiration of my good friend Joan, and the ongoing encouragement of her husband John and some of my other friends: Maureen, Ed, and a few others.

These reflections are mine and do not reflect the opinions of Anne or to Direction for Our Times. Nor have they been approved by any ecclesiastical authority of the Church, unlike Anne's books which have. They are simply my personal reflections on how Jesus's messages communicated through Anne have impacted me.

I share these reflections with great trepidation because I am just a regular sit-in-the-pew Catholic, without even having the benefit of a Catholic education, only CCD through 8th grade. I am the simple son of a carpenter and farmer from Kansas. I am nothing more than the scribe of what He has placed in my heart and my own thoughts on it.

Anyone who knows me knows I am certainly not holy, though within myself I desire and strive to be so. I am just praying that my heart leads my humanity in that endeavor and that my exterior behavior follows.

My hope is that any Catholic or any Christian reading this book or Volume Two of Anne's will have a richer dialogue of the heart with Jesus than what is found on the following pages.

At the very least, a benefit of reading these reflections might prompt you to read the Volumes, or if you have read them and not had a dialogue of the heart with Him, you might be prompted to do so. In fact, if I were pressed to identify a motivation for publishing this at all, it would be to get every person on the face of the globe to have a dialogue of the heart with Jesus. Pure and simple. For that, I am willing to do almost anything, including exposing my inmost self on these pages, despite my fears of doing it.

If you ignore this book, read the Volumes (all of which received the nihil obstat and imprimatur), and begin the dialogue with Jesus, I have accomplished what I think God has asked of me. If my reflections also

INTRODUCTION

cause you to pause, reflect, and document the impact Jesus's words have had on you, praise the Lord!

But I want more than that for you.

I am counting on Jesus to use these reflections to plant a seed in the deepest recesses of your heart, so deep that you do not even know the place.

And then as you read the Volumes for the first time or re-read them, His words will explode in your heart, mind, and soul like a bomb and ignite an unquenchable fire of love (Dt 4:24) within you that consumes you interiorly as it is doing to me!

That is my prayer for you! He can do that! He <u>will</u> do that if you invite Him!

I can guarantee you this: He does not care what your starting point is as you begin this dialogue. For me, the worse sins I have on my soul, the more urgent He is that I enter into this dialogue with Him.

Sinner or saint, He calls each soul into intimate dialogue with Him because His Love cannot be contained nor constrained any longer as He looks upon the condition of the world and the souls being lost to eternal damnation. Torrents of graces from Heaven are being poured out onto the world in ways never seen before as He urges His children to turn to Him! I do not even need to prove the point: if you open your heart, He will prove it to you Himself. If you do not, nothing He can do will prove it to you. Give Him just a slight chance to prove it! Then be ready!

Do not fall into Satan's trap of judging where you are at the moment. It is irrelevant to a dialogue of the heart with your Creator who wants so badly to dialogue with you!

Within these pages, you will find nearly the full range of human emotions as I only know to be completely honest and transparent in front of Jesus. Since He is fully human, I trust that He will allow me that indulgence and understand it.

Whatever our natures, our dispositions, He will adapt His dialogue to us in order to most effectively communicate with us, just as we adapt ourselves depending on circumstances and whom we are talking to.

THAT FLAME IN YOUR HEART? TURN IT INTO A BLOWTORCH!

That realization has given me great freedom in my dialogue with Him. No pretense required or desired. I hope it will be the same for you.

I suspect that like Anne's Volumes and books, these pages are not meant to be read as it were, but slowly digested, a paragraph or a page, perhaps only a sentence at a time each morning. One can take Volume Two for instance and spend years on it, as I have, moving through it sentence by sentence until Jesus brings a point to my attention that He wants to dialogue about. Sometimes I have spent weeks or months on a single page. So too, you may find certain parts of this work.

After the manuscript was written as my personal meditations, a set of questions for your reflection was added to each chapter. They are called The Point as in the point of the two-edged sword that cuts … to the intentions of the heart (Heb 4:12) or the point of the spear that pierces the heart (Jn 19:34). Hopefully, reflecting on the questions will cut deep, as they do for me, piercing the conscience and the heart. The deeper they pierce, the better. What is there needs to come out. What flows in its place will transform your very humanity. He promises that.

30 Days to Reignite Your Spiritual Life!

Jesus Christ wants to enter into a deeply personal,

loving dialogue with you,

right now,

that you might know

His peace and joy in your life

here and now.

And forever!

THAT FLAME IN YOUR HEART? TURN IT INTO A BLOWTORCH!

There are 30 Days in this book which correspond to the 30 Days in Anne's Volume Two. (Note the small dates in parentheses are keyed to Vol. Two) Each Day can be read on its own, as this book will provide you with what you need to reignite your spiritual life. But better, read it in parallel with the readings in Volume Two (I recommend reading Volume One first if you have not, to give you some background. The book is $5 or can be downloaded for free from their website). Read one Day of each for 30 days, first from Volume 2 and then this book to prompt your own dialogue.

In order to maximize the value of this exercise, I recommend that you do this 30 day program as part of your prayer routine, perhaps even substituting this for what you normally do for the 30 days if you cannot find the extra time in addition to your prayer time. For me, the absolute best time for prayer, and the one advocated over and over again in the New Testament by Jesus's example – "and very early in the morning He went up on the mountain to pray.". See the Epilogue: Foundations of a Prayer Life for some helpful guidance. In fact, I suggest you read all the appendices before you start the Days.

Read the Introduction and The Point exercise; it is your warm up! Answer the questions at the end of each chapter - Day, <u>addressing your answers in a dialogue to Jesus.</u> <u>And then in your dialogue with Him</u>, address one thing that you resolve to change in your life.

It will please Him enormously and, by the end of 30 days, will <u>reignite</u> your interior spiritual life! He will do that for you, I am sure. You cannot open your heart to Jesus in new ways and not be changed.

Be open to what He wants to dialogue with you about. The purpose of this book is to start or enrich your personal dialogue with Jesus on things He wants to discuss with you. He may surprise you as He has done and continues to do with me. He will make it clear, I am <u>sure</u>.

I pray that your daily dialogue of the heart with Jesus will be richer and in more depth than what is found on these pages. May the flame of the Spirit (Lk 3:16) burn ever more brightly within you – so brightly that it becomes a blowtorch! And may your heart be set aflame with love for Him who created You in Love and who desires only one thing: your love in return. And only so that you, His created child will be joyful beyond your wildest dreams! Now and forever!

My prayer for you:

Come, Lord Jesus, fill the hearts of Your faithful! Enkindle in them the Fire of Your Love!

- adapted from Christian prayer

So here is the first set of The Point questions for your reflection. I learned long ago that the best way to benefit from questions like these is to not just read them. Take time to answer each of them, ideally in your prayer journal. (A companion Prayer Journal is available separately that will give you more privacy and room for journaling. See our web site www.turnitintoablowtorch.) You will have the advantage of being able to review them later and perhaps add to them as you probe deeper. As a way to help you enter the dialogue with Him, I have phrased the questions in the first person as though He were talking with you. These are my questions, of course, but I think you can easily imagine Jesus asking them of you. I hope this rather unconventional method will make a one-on-one dialogue with the Person of Jesus Christ easier for you.

<u>Remember, this is your dialogue with Jesus as He addresses these questions to you very personally. So, it is important that you direct your answers to Him, very personally as a heart-to-Heart dialogue</u>. Then watch what happens as He fans the flame within you! Doing this for 30 days will be like throwing gasoline on a fire within! Stand back! The beauty of the inferno will be awesome! And in the center of it will be the purified crucible of gold that is you! (Mal 3:2)

THAT FLAME IN YOUR HEART? TURN IT INTO A BLOWTORCH!

THE POINT: Jesus loves you beyond anything you have ever experienced or can imagine. (As you answer the questions, address your dialogue to Him personally and directly. Answer here or better, in your prayer journal.)

1. Are you truly open to being loved by Me, Jesus, in a totally new way, unlike anything you have ever experienced from Me in the past? How do you imagine that will be?
2. Are you open to loving Me in totally new ways beyond the ways you have before now? Are you willing to let Me show you those new ways?
3. Tell Me, what is your reaction as I say I will challenge you to grow in totally new ways?
4. My child, who are you, as you stand before Me? Do you know, really? Can you look deeply within at the real you as I see you? Are you willing to let Me show you?
5. What do you fear in saying yes to My Love?

Taking Resolute Action: Jesus, this is one thing I need to change in my life, to take action on: (write it down). Please grant me the strength and grace to do it now!

Day 1

Suffering & Fire. Lightning from a Clear Blue Sky!

(August 17, 2003)

Lord, as I pick up this volume and meditate on Your words, I begin from a terrible place. You know well the condition of my heart, which is in stark contrast to Yours. The divorce has turned unbelievably nasty, so much so that it has become a hellish nightmare that I keep thinking could not possibly be real. I keep thinking that I will wake up from this.

How can all this be happening to me? Where did it come from? It has hit me like a lightning bolt from a clear blue sky. On top of that, most of the people I thought were my friends, our friends, have taken her side as she spews out the distortions from her pain while I am essentially silent. I am abandoned by all but a few and I am left with just my daughter and her family, my sons at home, a crushing load of responsibilities, and in financial ruin from the divorce.

I am filled with pain and sorrow as I see the unnecessary destruction of my family and its terrible effects on relatives and friends. It is clear to me that while abortion is the worst moral scourge on earth, divorce is the second worst.

My heart is in a pathetic state. I stand at the edge of a terrible precipice. I fear to the core of my being that I could go from here to ending up a bitter old man, hardened and cynical because of all this. Lord, help me! No! Please, God, no! The thought of becoming that kind of person terrifies me!

But what will become of my heart? It is shredded to bits, torn and trampled. Temptations of anger, revenge, and spite continually assault me. Jesus, tears pour down my face as I give You my heart broken to bits, all scraped together like remnants of a shattered jar, and ask You to care for it, as I am unable. I am unable to care for it myself. I cannot heal it or mend it. No human heart should ever experience this. Ever. It is not what You created our hearts for.

Thanks be to God for my two sons who are here at home with me, who deserve none of this, who are two beautiful, innocent souls. It is their presence each day that calls me forth to provide an environment of peace and joy at home. No matter what is going on in my life or within me. They do not need or deserve any share of the turmoil and conflict.

To You I have had to turn daily for the grace to maintain this happy environment for them, even though I'm exhausted and worn out, barely able to function at this point. I pray that peace and joy may be mine within me as I grow in this dialogue of my heart with Yours, my Jesus.

Into this condition of terrible suffering and turmoil, come these Volumes – another, but more beautiful lightning bolt from the clear blue sky! And they have ignited a fire that was only a flame before! You know that You alone have sustained me to this point, but now Your sustaining has taken on a new dimension!

Without You the few family and friends who have supported me would have been insufficient because they are only human, as loving and helpful as they have been, and as thankful as I am for their incredible

DAY 1 SUFFERING & FIRE. LIGHTNING FROM A CLEAR BLUE SKY!

generosity toward me and the boys. But You have come in a shocking new way, more personal and intimate than anything I could possibly have imagined!

My Jesus, as I read these words coming from You, I am convinced it was no accident that I ended up with them. My heart is filled with wonder and love; my eyes begin to well up with tears as the words penetrate ever so deeply! I can feel the sharp pains in my chest as they pierce, ever so sweetly and gently, but it causes my heart and breathing to slow as I sense You within. I am reading them because You intended them for me specifically, personally, and directly.

As in Scripture, Your word goes forth from Your mouth and does not return without doing what it was sent to do. Now You have ignited a roaring fire within me so intense that I am shocked by it. It burns with the heat of Divine Love that I could not have put there; only the Creator of the universe could have! It burns with the heat of a blowtorch!

Now You have ignited an roaring fire within me so intense that I am shocked by it.
It burns with the heat of Divine Love that I could not have put there,
only the Creator of the universe could have!
It burns with the heat of a blowtorch!

As I read these words, I read them with complete openness of mind and heart and they sink to the core of my being. I have dropped all my defenses and stand before You reading these words, completely vulnerable, intentionally. They penetrate the layers of façade that cover my inmost self to touch my heart with a tenderness and love that attract me so powerfully, I cannot put them out of my mind. An excitement washes over me at this moment to ponder these words coming from You as I sense I am being filled by Your Spirit.

Come, Lord Jesus! Fill the hearts of Your faithful! Enkindle in them the fire of Your Love! And You shall renew the face of the earth! Amen!

THAT FLAME IN YOUR HEART? TURN IT INTO A BLOWTORCH!

Jesus, as I ponder the words that come from the depth of Your Eucharistic Heart, I think: "Here is my Lord, speaking so directly, clearly, and forcefully as never before about what He wants from us, from me, in a remarkable way." You want me to know You, to reveal Yourself in the Eucharist in a new way. Am I open to it? I do know Your Eucharistic Heart, though only ever so slightly, because I receive You each time I go to Mass.

But now, You have my attention as You speak from the depths of Your Heart. I am attentive. How can I not be? And what is the first thing You say? You want my love as never before! You have it, my Lord! I do love You as never before – I affirm that to You now. With all my mind, heart and being! How could I answer otherwise? Is there the possibility of another answer? A lukewarm OK?? No! Only a heartfelt "Yes!" is possible. Yes, my Lord, I do love You! *Lord, you know all things. You know that I love You* (John 21:17).

Here I stop for a moment because the very next thing You say is that You want to protect me as never before. I have come to realize that I need protection by You as never before, from the world and from my weak human nature that leads me to sin.

And so my prayer lately has been: "Lord, protect me," even though I was only vaguely aware but not certain what I needed protection from at the time, though You did. I have witnessed You moving with incredible power and speed in response to that prayer, although at

> *If God causes you to suffer much it is a sign that He has great designs for you and that He certainly intends to make you a saint.*
>
> *And if you wish to become a great saint, entreat Him yourself to give you much opportunity for suffering;*
>
> *for there is no wood better to kindle the fire of holy love than the wood of the cross, which Christ used for His own great sacrifice of boundless charity.*
>
> - St. Ignatius of Loyola

DAY 1 SUFFERING & FIRE. LIGHTNING FROM A CLEAR BLUE SKY!

times it was accompanied by painful changes in my life. Still, my soul was protected.

Jesus, You want us – me – to know Your Presence, especially in the tabernacle, but also in the world as never before. I see Your fulfillment of that as I look around me and see Your hand at work in Your people.

You say You are doing something completely new. Am I open to it? Or do I prejudge this work and Your words to me? Am I so proud and so wise that I trust my judgment over Your new way of intervention in the world? Was that not the sin of those who persecuted the prophets, Jesus and his Apostles and disciples throughout the Bible?

Lord, open my mind and heart to Your Spirit! Open my mind and fill my heart each day, and each moment in each day, to the new ways You mean to intervene in my life and in the lives of others through me as I open my heart to You and to them in love!

You want to teach me things that until now were the secrets of Heaven?! But how can I or my humanity receive such a gift? Only with Your grace, my Jesus! Otherwise, the knowledge of Heaven's secrets would be wasted.

Prepare my soul for such a precious gift, Lord, for I cannot hope to contain what You desire to teach me – those things that before now You waited to reveal to a soul until it reached Heaven. There must have been a reason for You to not reveal Heaven's secrets to mortals until now. Therefore, my soul could not possibly have been ready for it without special grace from You! Open my heart, Lord! Fill it with Your grace!

Through Your grace working in my weak and insignificant humanity, I will keep my heart open for other Christians who You say are part of Your tidal wave being raised up to wash away the evil in the world. And I am but one molecule in that tidal wave. You place each soul in my path for a reason, Lord. Therefore I will pay attention to the whisper of the Spirit in my mind and heart and act accordingly, connecting to the other molecules around me! What a delight it is to be your servant in this way!

THAT FLAME IN YOUR HEART? TURN IT INTO A BLOWTORCH!

I sense that the knowledge, wisdom, and love You are bestowing on me is transforming me in subtle but significant ways with every breath I take! I want so much to yield completely to You in every way, that You might transform me completely. Jesus, fan the flame of Your Love in me into a blaze. May the blaze of the fire of Your Love become a blowtorch and burn out every impurity in me!! I feel now the heat of the flame within!

May I receive You in a new way, such as I have never done before, that I may love in a way that I have never loved before! May I love as You Love! Thank You, Father, for all that You are doing in the world, for Your Son Jesus and all these graces.

"My God, I believe, I adore, I hope, and I love Thee! I beg pardon for those who do not believe, do not adore, do not hope, and do not love Thee!" (Fatima Prayer, World Apostolate of Fatima)

THE POINT: Jesus is ready to speak to you in very intimate ways from the depths of His Heart. (As you answer the questions, address your dialogue to Him personally and directly. Answer here or in your prayer journal.)

1. Are you ready to listen to Me as I reveal Myself to you in a completely new way?
2. Are you ready to speak to Me from the depths of your heart? What do you want to say?
3. Do you have a completely open mind and heart for Me at this very moment?
4. Can you drop all your defenses and pretenses to be vulnerable to Me right now? What are those defenses and pretenses? Why do you hold onto them in our relationship?

DAY 1 SUFFERING & FIRE. LIGHTNING FROM A CLEAR BLUE SKY!

5. Are you ready and open to receive the secrets of Heaven I am so eager to show you?
6. What is holding you back, My little one?
7. What else have you learned about your relationship with Me?

Taking Resolute Action: Jesus, this is one thing I need to change in my life, to take action on: (write it down). Please grant me the strength and grace to do it now.

Day 2

Exposed: The Life Contained in Every Tabernacle!

(August 18, 2003)

As I begin this meditation and feel the heat of the flame of love for You, Jesus, growing in me, I wonder what Your love must feel like to You. What an awesome thought! The Perfect Love who loves me, who loves all His creation with a passion no human is capable of understanding, must have a burning Love beyond the brightest sun, beyond human comprehension! So great is the Father's Love that He sent You, His Son, to redeem us. Generosity beyond imagination – it fills me at this moment so much that it causes chills down my spine and my head to want to explode!

Your generosity in residing in the tabernacles of the world is a generosity beyond understanding! You, the living Christ, want to be with us, Your people, so much that You confine Yourself in that way. You want to be available to me, Lord, to make it easy to be in Your Presence. That

THAT FLAME IN YOUR HEART? TURN IT INTO A BLOWTORCH!

Your perfect Presence is there, and mostly ignored is only a sign of Your devotion and patience with us.

Yes, Lord, I want to know You more as a Living Person in the tabernacle. Help me to know You in that way! The fact that You would bestow great holiness upon those who adore You in that way is generosity beyond my comprehension! I trust in Your promise to lead Your children in a more enhanced way by revealing more of Your Life to us.

Somehow, I have to break into my life in such a way that I can be present to Your Presence in the tabernacle more than just when I go to Mass. For that does not leave me the time or space to get to know You more intimately. I do know You want me there. Please, Lord, the weaknesses of my humanity and the tumult of my life need Your grace to achieve this.

Your stark warning about the occult and magical powers that permeate our culture brought me up short. All the popular movies and literature are filled with them. Your language about this could not be more forceful or direct. Any power that is not from you is evil and needs to be removed from our lives. You warned that they open a door to our souls that we do not want open. This warning stung hard because I fell for that once with horrific results that lasted for years. My memories of that are too terrible to ponder. Hideous beyond belief. There are no harmless or innocent "powers." I have gone through the house and will do so again with renewed vigor to destroy anything that is even close to that.

But there You are in the tabernacle, the source of all power in the entire universe! And it seems to me as though every time I walk into a church and see the tabernacle, I sense it is exploding, exploding in love that cannot be contained any longer! As I walked into Mass today, I knew, I felt Your Presence, Your Person. How close You are to me! It is almost unbelievable that You make Yourself available and known in this way.

To be so specific in Your guidance about what is desirable and what is unacceptable is awesome to me! You know I need Your loving direction and correction because in the weakness of my nature, I so easily wander.

DAY 2 EXPOSED: THE LIFE CONTAINED IN EVERY TABERNACLE!

Even when my relationship with You is alive and active. Perhaps even more so then, I need it, if you are to form Your servant for service.

...every time I walk into a church and see the tabernacle, I sense it is exploding, exploding in love that cannot be contained any longer!

Every human knows the feeling of having their love tossed back at them, and knows the hurt. I cannot imagine the feeling of sacrificing Yourself on the Cross out of Love and looking down through time seeing that Love so frequently and casually rejected by so many. I know what it has felt like when my love was tossed back at me, but Lord, how <u>You feel</u>?!! Wow! I am trying to grasp that!

It so easily escapes me that You are completely both God and Man. The Person of Jesus Christ <u>feels</u> the hurt of rejection. I have to stop and consider that statement. But then again, we were made in Your image and likeness! As I have known rejection myself, and have known and sympathized with my spouse or kids when their love was rejected by me or someone else, so it hurts to know You feel rejection by me, by my brothers and sisters on this earth.

You created humanity out of love and rescued humanity out of love. It is an unbelievable travesty that You are rejected by the majority of humanity who, as You say, flings the gift back at Your feet as worthless. Ah, how painful it is for me to consider that, since I love You so much and share a little of that hurt. What can I do to lessen Your pain, to comfort You or help others not to reject You? How can I console You, my Jesus? I am so saddened as I think about Your pain.

I am stopped at the moment and cannot go on without considering this issue. What comes to me is the consideration that what is life about if not to help change the situation?

How can I stand by and watch the majority of humanity so easily and casually dismiss this profound gift of Your Love? It's easy to ask that question as long as I do not make it too personal. But then I have only to look at my life and see how often I have done exactly that, and perhaps

THAT FLAME IN YOUR HEART? TURN IT INTO A BLOWTORCH!

worse because I did it with full knowledge of who You are. Jesus forgive me. Jesus forgive me. Jesus forgive me.

May I do my small part in helping to rectify this situation, to console You by helping others come to know You. You have asked me to take Your words to them. I have done my part to this point as best I could, but I want to do more. May Your Spirit lead me to the ways You want me to serve.

Jesus, give me the grace to listen for Your every whim and to respond immediately with obedience, beginning now with every small desire You have for me, each day and each moment of each day. Holy Spirit, guide me and help me to overcome my fears, past failures, doubts, and uncertainty that I may persevere in serving the King and the Kingdom of Heaven!

> *"Open wide the doors to Christ!*
>
> *Have no fear!"*
>
> - Pope John Paul II

It is good, I think, that Your words in this Volume draw me out of myself, toward You and create so much love, enthusiasm, and excitement in me! And that is because Your words are sharper than a two-edged sword, piercing the heart and the hidden crevices there, puncturing the shadows and darkness with Your light.

Why are we, why am I so afraid to look deeply within myself? Is it because I will see what I do not want to see, the truth about myself? To see the darkness, weakness, and frailty that I do not want to admit to myself are in there?

There is no turning back. This Volume is leading me there and go there I must if I am to pursue You and the path You have set before me. I plunge forward not knowing where it will lead, but trusting You with my very being! Out of the pain of my rejected love comes the invitation by You to grow deeper in my love for You!

Yes, my Lord, yes! Help me to grow in love!

DAY 2 EXPOSED: THE LIFE CONTAINED IN EVERY TABERNACLE!

THE POINT: He who is the source of all power in the universe, who created the universe out of nothing, has humbled Himself to be confined in the tabernacles of the world, to be readily present to you. To reveal Himself to you in a new way. (As you answer the questions, address your dialogue to Him personally and directly.)

1. Will you be present to Me in the tabernacle? When will you come to see Me next?
2. In what ways do you reject Me even now, My dear little soul?
3. Can you ask Me at this moment to show you the ways you offend Me? Shouldn't that be a part of the dialogue of your heart with Me if we are to have a true relationship?
4. Have you taken those offenses to confession, My dear one? Why not? If you love Me and My Church, why do you ignore what I ask of you through My Church?
5. Are you open to hearing the many ways in which you please Me? Please write down all those ways, because it is a long list, My little soul! Listen as I tell you! Then write!
6. Can you give My invitation to love an unqualified "Yes"? Tell Me about it.
7. What else have you learned about your relationship with Me?

Taking Resolute Action: Jesus, this is one thing I need to change in my life, to take action on: (write it down). Please grant me the strength and grace to do it now.

Day 3

Forgiveness: The First Lesson in Love

(August 19, 2003)

Lord, I think that if You are love and all love is You, then I do not know love very well because I do not know You very well, despite all my years of prayer, study, and attending church. How could I? You are infinite and I am so miniscule and finite.

What I know of love I have learned mostly from the world, and I know, from my reading of the great saints and theologians, that in comparison, I know very little of Your true nature or true love.

What poverty I see within myself! What utter destitution I live in! I am in pain as I consider what pretense I have used to cover my nothingness. How blind and insensitive I have been toward You and others in that pretense! I am humiliated by it, my Lord. It hurts!

But I am delighted by Your promises to instruct me in Your ways of love, and

What poverty I see within myself!
What utter destitution I live in!
I am in pain as I consider what pretense I have used to cover my nothingness.

THAT FLAME IN YOUR HEART? TURN IT INTO A BLOWTORCH!

thus, to know You as the saints have known You. It fills me with excitement and wonder! I feel such urgency to have You help me empty this earthen vessel and fill me with You! It cannot happen fast enough! How I want my nature to be transformed by Your grace! How I desire it with every fiber of my being!

As I reflect on the obligation to love, I know that forgiveness is integral to it, because our humanity is so frail! To love guarantees that we will be hurt and offended. This is because we are all imperfect, and in our weakness, we will hurt and offend each other. It is only natural; therefore, I should expect to be hurt by those whom I love and not be so surprised when offenses come. Rather, I should see it for what it is, just part of the normal human condition, and then persist in my genuine love for the other anyway.

And I only need to consider Your love for me and the millions of times You have forgiven me to see what my own obligation is, if I am to love as You love. Why is it such a big issue when I have to forgive one whom I should love for some little – or even large – thing? I make such a big deal when I need to forgive another, as though the world is just supposed to go my way forever. Help me to see every single instance in my life where I need to forgive someone, and help me to do it quickly and without any hesitation!

How can You forgive me repeatedly when I have hurt You terribly so many times? How is it that You continue to love me day after day, hour after hour, when I am constantly neglecting You? You ARE here with me at this moment in Your Presence, waiting for me to turn to You for wisdom, counsel, renewal, courage, and healing. You stand here with me, but I just go on ignoring You!! Such frailty of my humanity would otherwise cause me to despair if I did not believe that You have promised to renew me and walk with me!

Your promise to give me a new heart capable of love and forgiveness sends chills down my spine as I contemplate the meaning and impact of such a promise! Oh God, how I need that new heart at this point in my life! I am desperately in need of it. Your restoration of my poor heart is

DAY 3 FORGIVENESS: THE FIRST LESSON IN LOVE

Man has two great spiritual needs.

One is forgiveness.

The other is for goodness.

Billy Graham

the promise of the restoration of my whole being! To be made new again, as, in Your original plan, You desired me to be! What a delightful way to be! It is in that way that I can serve Heaven now and be ready to join You there when You call me.

Oh holy Guest of my soul, yes, please come and take up Your residence there. Make my soul Your home, reside within me, my Lord! I anticipate with all my being the benefits of Your presence there – Your promise to heal all the damage from hurt and anguish and sin, to restore my heart completely!

Come, Lord Jesus, come! I throw wide open the doors to my heart and soul! With joy I extend my heartfelt invitation! Even now, I close my eyes and with my entire being, all that I have, I cry out from the depths of my heart, "Come, Holy Spirit, come take up Thy rest in me!"

So now I come to the practical part of this contemplation, the need to practice, first in my head and then in my heart, the words of forgiveness to each of those who have hurt me. And then to ask for forgiveness from those I have hurt.

It is so much easier to just ignore them – to go on my way and cut them out of my life. Forgiveness and repair of relationships is so very hard if I rely on my human nature! But I also know that You have promised to provide the grace for me, and so I trust that I will do it in each circumstance of my life as I need to. Grant me the grace to abandon my self-reliance and instead rely on Your Spirit to forgive.

I am anxious to have that superabundance of love and forgiveness You promise. I will forgive all in my life in order to receive more forgiveness! I want to love without concern as to whether that love was returned or not, whether it was reciprocated or not, whether it was cast aside or not, whether I was taken advantage of or not.

Fill my heart, my Lord; fill it with Your superabundant Love!

THAT FLAME IN YOUR HEART? TURN IT INTO A BLOWTORCH!

THE POINT: Jesus who is Love and the Source of all love wishes to love you, to forgive you and heal you as the basis of bringing peace into your life. (As you answer the questions, address your dialogue to Him personally and directly.)

1. Will you accept My Love in a totally new way, to a totally new depth as I pour My Love out on you?
2. Or do you think you are OK with where you are now with Me? Will you reject these new advances of My Love?
3. Do you know the dimensions of your own poverty? Can you describe it to Me?
4. Do you believe in My promise to heal all the damage in your heart and soul? Can you describe some of that damage to Me now?
5. Whom do I need to help you to forgive in your life? Write them down for Me.
6. Whom do you need to make amends to for having offended them?
7. Can you resolve to forgive and make amends with everyone who has been a part of your life? In what ways can I help you?
8. What do you fear, My little one? Come! Tell Me all!
9. What else have you learned about your relationship with Me?

Taking Resolute Action: Jesus, this is one thing I need to change in my life, to take action on: (write it down). Please grant me the strength and grace to do it now.

Day 4

Self-hate: Destroyer of Your Interior and Family Unity

(August 20, 2003)

Lord, You speak of unity, and the pervasive nature of disunity in the world and, in particular, the disunity within the family. But unity in the family begins with unity with You and Your Will. And so, I find that I am in need of reflection on the ways I am in disunity with You, those ways of resistance, independence, and little offenses against what You are asking of me. As I come to know my offenses, and acknowledge them to You, then I repair our relationship and grow in unity and love.

To the degree I hold myself in contempt and judge myself negatively, and yes, even hate myself for my imperfections, then I fail to reflect Your love and mercy toward me and others. My anger and frustrations with my failures and weaknesses reflect the distance between who I am and who you call me to be: forgiving, loving, and merciful in Your image.

You know what a huge step it is for me to accept myself. I have spent so much time and effort in that struggle because I have spent too much

THAT FLAME IN YOUR HEART? TURN IT INTO A BLOWTORCH!

Let love be sincere;

hate what is evil, hold on to what is good;

love one another with mutual affection;

anticipate one another in showing honor.

- St. Paul, Romans 12:9

time hating myself and being critical of myself for my failures. Your gracious mercy toward me in the midst of the huge struggle that was crushing me twenty years ago shone a very bright light within my soul and illuminated the core of it: self-hate emanating from having allowed others to abuse me in so many ways.

Ah, I can feel it now, the memory of that very deep wound being exposed! Both huge pain and huge relief as it was exposed. And then the heat of healing and restoration!

But You have shone a light within me! I have opened my whole interior to Your love. And so unity with my family and others begins here, in this relationship with You, in accepting Your love and mercy toward me and having that same love and mercy toward myself. Then in abundance, it overflows to others, most especially to my family.

In the last few years, my family has grown in unity and love and peace in very beneficial ways. What I have come to see is that my family, even in our chaotic circumstances can pray together and grow in love and unity. What a delight it has been to me to call many times a day when I travel, and say breakfast and morning, dinner, and bedtime prayers with them! I have seen the fruits of that simple practice grow as we grow as a family! And it has turned into a very enjoyable time for us as well, with laughing, chatting, and sharing after we pray, growing in unity of mind, heart, and spirit.

You asked me to re-examine my activities and priorities, making sure to differentiate between entertainment and duty, between preoccupation and relationship, between diversions and the unity that arises from prayer.

I know that the reason for Your request to examine my life's patterns is not so that I will not enjoy my life. Exactly the opposite is true.

DAY 4 SELF-HATE: DESTROYER OF YOUR INTERIOR AND FAMILY UNITY

It is so that I will be in unity with You and in my family, that joy and peace and harmony can be ours! You only want what is good for me! Therefore, my motivation is to seek Your way, which is perfect for my family.

I struggle with deciding when else we can pray together as we do all the normal prayers of a family and daily Mass, but I hear Your call to look at it with You. I just lead a life with so much disorder in it that praying more seems for now to be beyond me. But then again, when You ask me to re-examine my priorities, I can easily see where I waste so much time on frivolous activities – TV, reading, and computers chief among them.

It is my role as a parent, just as it is for all parents, to raise my children, to guide my family to holiness. To raise my children to be wholesome, engaged, and wise in their Christian obligations as they grow to be saints.

As the disorders of our lives are corrected, we can grow toward focusing more on serving Heaven's goals and less on our own entertainment. I know that our nightly decade of the Rosary is good, but a five-decade family Rosary is possible, even with the limitations of my children, and we will strive toward that end. Your promise to advance the family quickly in these times by our devotion to Your Mother through the daily Rosary tells me I need to involve them, not just pray it myself.

Daily, I need to re-examine my priorities, asking moment by moment what You desire for me, as I know You have a desire for all my activity and dispositions to serve the Kingdom of Heaven. It is my constant prayer and the prayer of my family that keeps us in touch with Your desires and opens us to the graces Heaven wishes to send us to accomplish what You desire. And so my prayer, our prayer, becomes an imperative, constantly throughout the day, to open our hearts and minds to Your Presence and the wishes of Heaven to serve.

It is my role as a parent, just as it is for all parents, to raise my children, to guide my family to holiness. To raise my children to be wholesome, engaged, and wise in their Christian obligations as they grow to

THAT FLAME IN YOUR HEART? TURN IT INTO A BLOWTORCH!

be saints. It is a serious charge You have given me as steward of your children, one that I cannot hope to live up to without extraordinary grace, even at this point in their lives. To the degree I still have any influence with them at all even at this late date in their lives, I must do all I can to encourage them in loving and subtle ways.

You stopped me with a single sentence when You referred to teaching children their responsibilities to others and to God from the secure love source of the family: "I intend for this to be the norm again." I am stopped. Wait. What was that? You do not say anything without meaning. For that to be the norm again implies that You intend to make a huge course correction in the culture of the whole world. "…the norm again."

Wow! What hope!

What joy arises within me when I contemplate that! Your mighty hand at work will be evidenced clearly by many who will take it to heart! What great hope there is in that promise!

Before, I looked at my own family and most families of the world with such despair as I saw our condition. Now, I look and see as I did before the truth of our condition, but I see with a hopeful heart!

Come, Lord Jesus! Fill the hearts of your people! Take away our hearts of stone. Give us hearts of love!

THE POINT: Jesus intends to restore unity in every family, making that the norm again. (As you answer the questions, address your dialogue to Him personally and directly.)

1. Can you look deep within yourself to identify the sources of disunity that alienate you from Me and My creation?

DAY 4 SELF-HATE: DESTROYER OF YOUR INTERIOR AND FAMILY UNITY

2. Can you identify all the dimensions of your disunity – interiorly, with your spouse, your family, your relationships, your Church, and Me, your God?
3. Why do you resist Me, My child? What will it take for you to cooperate with Me, to yield to Me, to restore unity?
4. In what ways, if you look at your own attitudes and behaviors, are you expecting Me to cooperate with your will?
5. Is your daily prayer life where it needs to be? Where I want it to be? Can you reset your priorities as I have asked you? Can you pray the Rosary as I have asked?
6. What else have you learned about your relationship with Me?

Taking Resolute Action: Jesus, this is one thing I need to change in my life, to take action on: (write it down). Please grant me the strength and grace to do it now.

Day 5

Jesus Waiting on Me — With Beer & Lime Chips?!

(August 21, 2003)

Well, my Jesus, Your words this morning, while earnest, caused me to laugh so hard I could not contain myself! It is a serious topic, but the image You asked me to imagine, of You in a tabernacle with the TV or radio was so comical and absurd that I could not restrain myself! I immediately thought I could see a beer and chips by Your couch as You wile away the time waiting for me to show up! I hope you have a good supply because I don't come by often enough, do I?

You know my "irreverent" humor in regards to You is full of love and respect and the fear of God, so You wouldn't be offended if I asked if the chips in Heaven are lime flavored?! LOL! Absurd fool I am! Good thing You have a sense of humor this morning, or I'd be dead, huh?! I have tears of laughter running down my face!

Lord, I really do enjoy Your company on this journey of life! It is a delight to have such an intimate and dear Friend as You so that I can be

THAT FLAME IN YOUR HEART? TURN IT INTO A BLOWTORCH!

completely open and just be me, knowing that You love me as I am! How freeing! I am so peaceful and relaxed in Your holy Presence, even as I strain to grow in holiness and service!

But this is a very serious and holy topic! The follow-up to that ridiculous image, however, is poignant. Actually, it stings a bit. While I am busily preoccupied with my priorities, You spend Your time waiting for me by looking out for me, interceding for me, protecting me, and loving me. Ouch!

Jesus, I can go out from where I am to include You,
or I can go out from You to where I am.
Big difference.
The world calls that a paradigm shift.

The relationship is very lopsided, I think. You get my spare change, as it were, while You seek an active, engaged relationship. You want a relationship where my activity emanates from our relationship, not where my activity just happens to include our relationship. I can go out from where I am to include You, or I can go out from You to where I am. Big difference. The world calls that a paradigm shift.

Jesus, You want me to join You by sitting in Your Presence as You dwell in the tabernacle. You want me to be with Your Perfect Presence there in a particular way, so that we are with each other, person to Person. And each time I take the time, I come away enriched as our love and friendship grows.

It amazes me that You care for every detail of my life! And that You spend Your day looking to every detail of my life and directing all of Heaven's help for me. It pains me that I so easily get consumed with my life that I ignore You and Your concerns. That I so easily skip something so simple as coming to visit You in the tabernacle or go to daily Mass when I have the opportunity.

Why do I seem to only love You or pay attention to You when I need You or when it is convenient for my own purposes? My humanity is so weak and frail! But I do not despair – I am saddened by the failure, yes, and beg Your mercy, but I also see and rejoice in the marvelous work I

DAY 5 JESUS WAITING ON ME — WITH BEER & LIME CHIPS?!

see You are doing in my soul. I know today and each day that You are working to prepare me for the next day – to grow in holiness and serve You.

Jesus, I long to find a place, a space, where I can sit before You in the tabernacle in silence. My life is so hectic, so crazy with the long commutes, being away from home every week, the obligations of being a single parent, the domestic chores, and work. And yet, when I break out of that and sit before You in silent anticipation of receiving the gifts You promise, I am never disappointed. From the smallest whisper in my soul to the experience of Your Power and Presence, You have come to me each time. So often I find comfort and solace for all that I need, in particular for all the hurts in my life. But it is for adoration and thanksgiving that I come, not to receive or benefit.

Your love is so merciful and bountiful that the meager little I wish to give back to You is completely overwhelmed by Your generosity. I feel like a tiny grain of sand on a beach with a tidal wave upon me! You melt my heart with Your love, my Lord! My eyes fill with tears of gratitude!

So small and insignificant is my love, thanksgiving, and adoration of You in comparison to the tidal wave of Your love! How delighted is this little grain of sand! I want to shout out to the other sand so that we may become a chorus of praise, thanksgiving, and adoration! I am overwhelmed with anticipation of being totally consumed by the wave of Your love and being drawn into the ocean of Your love for all of eternity!

Lord, help me to quiet my mind, my heart, and my soul, that I might hear Your voice and be attentive to Your love that is constantly directed toward me. I am trying to silence the noise in my life in every area. It seems that I live in an ocean of noise. The noise is compounded by all the disorder in my life – self-induced chaos – which comes from my weakness. I am so far from living a life of quiet, ordered, and disciplined ways. I know the work You are doing in my soul will bring the results I desire.

The work You have done has made a big difference in these last few years. I can remember how it started. That first year after I had read Your words in this volume, when it came time for Lent, I fasted from all

THAT FLAME IN YOUR HEART? TURN IT INTO A BLOWTORCH!

sources of external noise – radio, music, TV, movies, everything. And the boys joined me in it. The house and the car went silent for six weeks. It was during that time that my meditations on Your words in these volumes really bore tremendous fruits. Actually, in the silence of Lent, the words exploded off the page and pierced my heart! The flame of the Spirit became a blowtorch burning with tremendous pinpoint heat! White hot! Our dialogue flowed more easily throughout the day beyond my morning prayer.

I find now that I am mostly reluctant to turn on the sources of noise except at specific times, mostly evenings around the news hour. Even so, I am sensing I waste too much time with it. Even my good music collection goes mostly unused. For the most part, the house is quiet these days – it has become a place of serenity and peace. In that environment I find myself conversing with You more often, particularly when I notice one of Your images around the house.

As often as I read those words from You, "I love you. I want only your love," I still find that at times, as I turn to You, I do not feel very lovable and, therefore, incapable of returning that love. How could I know true love? That only comes from You. The love I mostly know is that of the world's example, and the closer I get to You, the more I see that the world's love is unmasked as self-gratification.

When one pulls the mask off all the forms of love that I have repeatedly bought into, it is not You and Your example of selfless, self-sacrificing love that I find within me. Rather self-gratification in one of its myriad of forms is there. It is hard to discern – no, impossible – to unmask it without being in dialogue with You. Only then do You reveal the truth of my actions and intent to me in an ever so gentle and loving way. But even in Your gentleness, at times the truth penetrates and cuts to the core of my heart so deeply that it brings me to tears. Hot, bitter tears of sorrow for being so self-centered and selfish!

The truth is that self-gratification, or false love, is theft. I steal from others what is rightfully theirs for my own pleasure. I steal the true love they deserve and substitute a fake love in its place for my own gain:

DAY 5 JESUS WAITING ON ME — WITH BEER & LIME CHIPS?!

self-gratification. My brothers and sisters on this earth deserve only one thing: true love. And that has its origin in only one place: You.

> *The truth is that self-gratification, or false love, is theft.*
> *I steal from others what is rightfully theirs for my own pleasure....*
> *Taken in that light, when did I become such a thief?*

Taken in that light, when did I become such a thief? Such a bold robber in broad daylight? I had such great examples of true love, self-sacrificing love, in my parents, our good parish priest, and so many others. I am filled with painful remorse for my offenses against You and so many of Your children! I want to fall down under the burden of it. How did a good man go so terribly wrong?

The answer strikes like a bolt of lightning from the clear blue sky. It penetrates into the core of my being. I turned there, to self-gratification, from a place of deep hurt. As I was deeply hurt by others outside myself and having an insufficient relationship with You, I turned inward to myself. Though I hated myself for allowing others to hurt me, I sought relief the only way I knew how. And so all the forms of love and affection I displayed had but one goal: my own self-pleasure, reinforced by others, which invariably led to pride. Such a vicious and addictive cycle, so sad a circumstance!

Thanks be to God for Your penetrating light and wisdom! And for Your mercy on me, which gives me hope and freedom! The cycle is broken and I am free! My heart leaps for joy at this moment! I am filled to overflowing with gratitude!

I long to be brought closer to You each day – to know the forgiveness and trust You offer. I do sense the "residue" of sin on my soul, but I know the experience of Your cleansing breath in the sacrament of Reconciliation and the joy I feel from the sacrament. There is a certain "deadness" of spirit that I experience as a result

Free at last!

Thank God Almighty,

I am free at last!

Adapted from Dr. Martin Luther King

THAT FLAME IN YOUR HEART? TURN IT INTO A BLOWTORCH!

of the sin in my soul – a darkness and a veil between us. That remains even though I continue with my life of prayer. Until Your breath blows away that residue in Confession and removes the veil, I cannot fully experience the joy and newness You describe, when my soul will blaze in light and Heaven will fill it!

So today, here I am. Having blown the residue from my soul, the light of Your truth has penetrated the deep darkness of my soul and cut out the cancer. I am free of its grasp enough to be open to Your love. I walk confidently, knowing that as I strive for holiness, You will completely remove the patterns of self-gratification and replace them with Your love.

Truly, my Lord Jesus, I am free! Thank God Almighty!

THE POINT: Jesus promises our happiness, to help us, to solve our problems, and heal our wounds if we will but come to visit Him in the tabernacle! (As you answer the questions, address your dialogue to Him personally and directly.)

1. Will you visit Me regularly to take Me up on My promises? Or don't you need My help?
2. What resolutions do you need to make to take Me up on My offer?
3. Do you know the comfort and peace that comes from being in My Presence before the tabernacle? Describe that experience for Me.
4. I speak softly and gently. What noises will you cut out of your life so you can hear Me?

DAY 5 JESUS WAITING ON ME — WITH BEER & LIME CHIPS?!

5. As you look deep within yourself, do you know the difference between acting in selfless love like Me and loving for self-gratification, for what you can get out of it?
6. What else have you learned about your relationship with Me?

Taking Resolute Action: Jesus, this is one thing I need to change in my life, to take action on: (write it down). Please grant me the strength and grace to do it now.

Day 6

The Coming Revelation: Leaving No Room for Doubt

(August 22, 2003)

Wow! A trite saying, but I do not know how to express my feelings otherwise today as I read Your words, Jesus! Your choice of words "blows me away" as the saying goes. I am excited! "In an unparalleled way, I lavish graces on souls." "I intend to heal your world." "...and I will reveal Myself to you in such a way that you will have no doubts" (p.19, Aug. 22, 2003). Powerful words, my Jesus. Forceful and direct. The implications for my soul, and all those who seek you are extraordinary. "...unparalleled..." You have acted and poured forth grace very dramatically in the past in order to heal our world, so Your promise of action now must be awesome!

This is an extraordinary promise! To reveal Yourself, leaving no room for doubt, tells me You intend to act in an extraordinary way in my soul and every soul that opens itself to You. All I have to do is show up with a simple faith. Bring my presence into Your Eucharistic Presence.

THAT FLAME IN YOUR HEART? TURN IT INTO A BLOWTORCH!

And graces pouring out from Your Sacred Heart will flood into my poor heart, penetrating my doubts, cynicism, fear, mistrust, ignorance, and pride!

Even now, at this very moment, I can feel it as I assent to it! My heart pounds nearly out of my chest each time I read this and re-read it! I can hardly breathe and tears pour profusely down my face.

I can hardly hold this pen to write these words. I am completely overwhelmed by Your love and gentleness toward me! In the last few moments You have done all three things within me: grace, heal, reveal. I can feel the heat in my soul of Your healing touch, of cracks, wounds, and hurts being healed though I cannot name them. The blowtorch of Your Divine Love consumes the defects of my heart, turning it from a heart of stone to a heart of flesh, a heart of love (Ez 36:26)!

Again, wow, Lord. I think you just rocked me to my core. I feel grace and refreshment pouring into my soul at this moment, like cold, clear water on a warm day! I can feel my heart and mind fill with the Spirit!

"...no room for doubt..."

I know You are lavishing graces upon my undeserving soul, and those of others, as never before! I also know that Your Mother Mary plays a role in that as never before. Confession this week was a wonderful experience – it always is – in an unusual way as I had the powerful sense of Mary's presence and her graces pouring down upon me as I examined my conscience and during my confession, enlightening my mind, heart, and conscience with the ways I have offended God. Words fail me describing it.

> *All I have to do is show up with a simple faith. Bring my presence into Your Eucharistic Presence.*
> *And graces pouring out from Your Sacred Heart will flood into my poor heart, penetrating my doubts, cynicism, fear, mistrust, ignorance, and pride!*

DAY 6 THE COMING REVELATION: LEAVING NO ROOM FOR DOUBT

I pray that each day I might wake with the first thought to greet You and all of Heaven and that I might pledge myself to be of service to You and Heaven first and foremost. Help me to bring Your words, not mine, to those who suffer and in doing so, bring them to You. Help me to be an instrument of healing in Your hands as I decrease and You increase in me.

It is only when I lose focus of You – when I am distracted by my own concerns – that I lose the joy of being Your representative. The degree of my joy is a direct reflection of the degree to which I am focused on You. And sometimes that is a very great struggle for me, particularly when I am in so much pain as I am at the moment. I have been sick for a long time, over a year and a half, and being unemployed with no health insurance and having no income and being in foreclosure and on and on, I live in my own pain and fear and despair, preoccupied with my own concerns.

I struggle in these circumstances to stay peaceful and trusting and focused on what You want me to do to further the Kingdom each day. But that is the Way of the Cross, isn't it? Though You struggled under the weight of it, and fell three times, You got back up and continued on. So I can do with Your grace, continuing to love and to serve others with peace and joy even in my exhaustion and pain. Somehow, You keep supplying all I need to do so, such that at times, I can only smile and marvel at Your generosity.

I have come as You have directed "in firmness" to the tabernacle, and have experienced Your Presence in

> *Out of the darkness of my life, so much frustrated, I put before you the one great thing to love on earth:*
>
> *the Blessed Sacrament ...*
>
> *There you will find romance, glory, honour, fidelity, and the true way of all your loves on earth...*
>
> - JRR Tolkien, author, Lord of the Rings, The Hobbit and others

THAT FLAME IN YOUR HEART? TURN IT INTO A BLOWTORCH!

such a powerful way that I could have no doubts on many occasions. The experience of the Trinity in the Adoration Chapel in Knock, Ireland, was unexpected and profound. It was so powerful that I felt my heart stop as I felt the beat of Your Heart. I know the experience of You in the quiet whispers that bring joy to my heart as I sit and contemplate You in the tabernacle or during adoration (holy hours). That is sufficient for me, though I know that "feeling" Your Presence is not requisite to knowing Your Presence in faith.

It is here, in the tabernacle, that You reveal to us the Presence of Your Person in a most perfect way.

More and more I turn toward You and Your Presence throughout the day as I seek Your Divine guidance in all matters, great and small. I know that nothing is too small to seek Your Will, for in seeking Your Holy Will in the small matters, I learn obedience.

Obedience is such a struggle for me because my personality, my nature is so unruly. I determine what I want to do and what I do not want to do, which things to go after and which to ignore. I would last ten minutes in a monastery! To be obedient to the small details of my duties and responsibilities, to be obedient to Your promptings and those of John, my Guardian Angel, that is the biggest challenge I face.

To be obedient takes humility, a virtue I cannot claim to know very well. In my simple mind I see the relationship: pride leads to disobedience (e.g. Satan's fall; Adam and Eve), and humility leads to obedience (e.g. the Saints). Only extraordinary grace will allow me to begin the transition from the former, which I know so well, to the latter, which is foreign to me.

As I grow in obedience, I can hear Your Will in the larger matters and follow Your direction more easily. Lord, help me to be open to the gift of faith that You wish to bestow on me!

As I ponder the day I return to You, I rejoice in thinking about it. Pondering the joyful day of my entrance into Heaven causes me to consider the temporary nature of things here on earth and grow in peace.

DAY 6 THE COMING REVELATION: LEAVING NO ROOM FOR DOUBT

So, as I put myself in Your Presence at this moment in my contemplation, I am able to touch my pain, hurt, and fears which are so near the surface of my being right now. I pour them out to you now and my heart is filled with so much sorrow and pain that I am overwhelmed by it. The hot tears pour down my face unabated. I am tempted by despair and hopelessness as I look at my life situation and see nothing but more of the same, an impossible situation and my total abject failure in life.

My only hope as I come before You is Your promise to do the work in me, to bring me to the place in Your Sacred Heart that is reserved for me, the place You created for me when You created me in the first place. I pray that I might more fully cooperate with Your grace each day that nothing might hinder my journey of return to You in Heaven.

Sing, my heart, sing! For joy at the thought of my return! To the Creator who made me!

THE POINT: The Eucharistic Heart of Jesus intends to reveal Himself in such way that you will have no doubts. He intends to pour forth love and graces on souls who desire it like the world has never seen. (As you answer the questions, address your dialogue to Him personally and directly.)

1. Do you still want Me to reveal Myself to you in unparalleled ways? Why?
2. Will you return to My Presence to receive My grace? Do you want what I offer? How much do you want it?
3. Do you want My action in the depths of your soul to heal you? Do you know the need for healing? Can you describe it to Me?
4. Can you touch all the levels of pain within your heart and soul that need My healing touch, My child? What are they? Tell Me.

THAT FLAME IN YOUR HEART? TURN IT INTO A BLOWTORCH!

5. Do you know obedience in the smallest of matters? Do you understand how much that pleases Me?
6. Are you ready for the day of your return to Me, your Creator?
7. Tell me, child, what do you need to do to be ready if I call you in a few hours?
8. What else have you learned about your relationship with Me?

Taking Resolute Action: Jesus, this is one thing I need to change in my life, to take action on: (write it down). Please grant me the strength and grace to do it now.

Day 7

All Your Decisions Have Eternal Consequences

(August 25, 2003)

What does it mean that You remain a prisoner in the tabernacle, waiting? For what? For whom? Why? So that on occasion I can come to visit You? So much for so little! Forgive my ingratitude! Like a lover waiting for a beloved, You wait, unappreciated, until I appear and then, encountering Your pain of loneliness, I understand what pain I have caused by my self-centered focus and negligence. As I understand the pain I have caused, it hurts, Lord, and today it hurts deeply. But Your love and mercy are not deterred by my failings, station, and duties. Rather, there You are constantly, waiting for my visits with Your graces.

More and more I see Your hand in my life and in the lives of those whose hearts are open to You. As I contemplate that, I know that my life, and each action in my life, has eternal consequences for good or evil. In accord with Your Will or not. I cannot gloss over a single day or even a single thought, word, or deed. Each has eternal consequence. And so I weigh each, attempting to seek from You the holiest way in each moment of my day.

You have chosen to call out to all people in a determined fashion, to get their attention, much as You have done with me in the past when I was more purposeful in my choice to ignore You. I pray that, through some little means or crack, they will allow You entry into their heart, just I did with You. Their circumstances and choices are not unknown to me – I made many of those same choices in the past as well, so I am confident that, given just a small opening, You will succeed with them as You have with me.

I know now that my days are carefully numbered by You and that I must decide once and for all how I will use them. I can no longer waver and delay the choice as if I have all the time in the world, because I do not. I do not know the number of days or hours allotted to me and the work you have planned. I only know that the work You have assigned to me has the salvation of a certain number of souls attached to it.

Therefore, let me choose Your work before mine daily! What could be more important? Certainly nothing attached to this world or my own concerns! So it is with joy and anticipation that I wake each day, greeting You as my first conscious thought, and offering to serve You with my day.

I do not think You mind my informal greeting when I say, "Good morning, Jesus and Mary! How are you today?!" I always laugh at myself for such a lighthearted, foolish greeting! I hope You enjoy it too!

Most days I do not see the results of my "work" – my love, sacrifices, and prayers. But sometimes, in the midst of my day, You break in and I have to laugh because I realize that some small conversation or exchange I had earlier was directed very pointedly by You! Then we share joy, gladness, laughter, and humor over the small situations that I realize bring You joy. Your Presence was brought into the situation with such subtlety that, even though I was intent on serving You when the day started, I completely missed seeing it when it happened! Pretty funny! Even better because I know You are laughing as well!

DAY 7 ALL YOUR DECISIONS HAVE ETERNAL CONSEQUENCES

How interesting that is to consider. I know that You are True God and True Man. You are a True Person. My love for You delights You and my neglect hurts Your feelings. You feel and have emotions as a Person. I can please You or displease You with my thoughts and actions. Be careful, my soul, as I act deliberately or even without thought or consideration, not to offend, but to please, just as I do with others in my life.

I do know the joy within my soul of serving You and the work of Heaven. The most rewarding times of my life have been when I felt Your smile interiorly and knew I had served You well in a particular moment or situation. As I recall those times, I think I was responsive to the Spirit and allowed You to point the way, though I did not know the way myself or where it was going, necessarily.

My circumstances are so much different now. Then I felt as though I was on the front lines, a part of the team contributing to the mission of Heaven. Now, in these last few years, it seems that others have taken my place and are doing great works for the Church and the Kingdom.

And where am I? Nowhere. My life is full of chaos, duties, and the pain of rejection and failure. Everything I touch fails. And just when I think my situation can't get any worse, it does. The peace You offer is elusive. At times it appears that I am about to turn a corner with my situation, and things will get better. But then I only meet yet another disappointment.

Why do You not reach out with Your mighty hand and change things? You have moved so very powerfully in my past life. When I was in despair, You rescued me, sometimes in spectacular ways. What are You waiting for, my Lord? My situation is impossibly difficult. I have lost everything and my life is a total failure. Do

Consult not your fears, but your hopes and dreams.

Think not about your frustrations, but about your unfulfilled potential.

Concern yourself not with what you have tried and failed in, but with what it is still possible for you to do.

Pope John XXIII

THAT FLAME IN YOUR HEART? TURN IT INTO A BLOWTORCH!

You not see my pain and suffering? Some days the pain of it all is so much that it overwhelms me and I can only cry and beg from a very small place within me, the place of a helpless child. Begging for Your mercy to strengthen my faith and trust. To grow in humility. What can I demand from You? Nothing. Only beg as creature to his Creator.

Even as I give voice to the pain within me, I turn interiorly to You and You immediately fill my soul with Your Presence! My peace is regained, and the despair evaporates like smoke.

In all things, Lord, Your timing is perfect as You are perfect.

In all things, Lord, Your timing is perfect as You are perfect. And so I work at resolving the situation in my life, trusting that You will provide Your grace to sustain and guide me, awaiting Your perfect timing of assistance to me.

Lord, I trust You. I am at peace with that as I rest in You. May You fill my heart with joy from the well of salvation!

May Your peace take its place in my heart and reign there!

THE POINT: Jesus knows exactly how many days and hours you have left on this earth and the work He has designed for you which will save souls. Now you realize that Jesus and you will see all your thoughts and actions and their consequences, no matter how insignificant, together when you come before Him because they are the fabric of you. (As you answer the questions, address your dialogue to Him personally and directly.)

1. How do you intend to spend the precious few days left to you, which I have numbered?
2. Yes, I know you have a family, work, and responsibilities, because I gave them to you. But whose work will you attend to, yours alone or Mine, which includes your family?

DAY 7 ALL YOUR DECISIONS HAVE ETERNAL CONSEQUENCES

3. What is the focus of your living for the time I have given you that you have left?
4. Are you open to a new way of living the life I have given you?
5. Can you go about your vocation and responsibilities with a new purpose, My purpose, burning within your heart and mind?
6. What do you need to change to let My purpose dominate your very being? What stands in the way?
7. Do you consider the eternal consequences of all your thoughts and actions? In what ways do you need to change, My little one?
8. Do you see also that the eternal consequences of your smallest kindnesses and generous acts will be celebrated for eternity? Tell Me how that makes you feel, My child.
9. What else have you learned about your relationship with Me?

Taking Resolute Action: Jesus, this is one thing I need to change in my life, to take action on: (write it down). Please grant me the strength and grace to do it now.

Day 8

I Am Not Disobedient!
It's My Freedom! ... Or Slavery

(August 26, 2003)

Oh, Jesus! You say You are obedient to us. You are obedient to us?! How can that be? Your obedience to us, to our requests for protection and assistance, are born out of Your unfathomable love for us! What a stunning and marvelous mystery – that the God who made me and sustains my very life and breath and all of the universe is at the same time obedient?!! To my requests for assistance and perfection in grace?! I am filled with hope and wonder!

Oh, Jesus, may You protect my soul from all evil and assist me in growing in holiness that I may more perfectly serve You and cooperate with Your Will in preparation of my soul for entry into Heaven!

I will endeavor, despite my weaknesses, to respond to Your request to do my part out of loving obedience to You. To be obedient in all things from the largest to the smallest and most insignificant. Help me, dear Jesus, to be obedient as You were to all rightful authority. Help me to

THAT FLAME IN YOUR HEART? TURN IT INTO A BLOWTORCH!

grow in holy obedience, to reject disobedience and rebellion in all its forms in every aspect of my life, interiorly and exteriorly.

What a stunning and marvelous mystery – that the God who made me and sustains my very life and breath and the universe is at the same time obedient?!!
To my requests for assistance and perfection in grace?!

I can look back on my life and see the wages and results of disobedience – from the sin to the pragmatic. How much easier and happier my life would have been to this point had I been obedient! Much of my suffering has been self-induced from my unwillingness to obey You, Your laws and Your kind inspirations. Much of what I wanted out of life – peace and joy – was subverted by my own willfulness. Even in the pragmatic parts of my life, when I look at it and see how You were trying to answer my prayer to reduce the stress, etc., and you sent a solution, but it was not the solution I wanted, I refused to comply.

How much suffering I have brought on myself through willful disobedience! And now, as I look at it and see the resulting pain, suffering, and stress, I can only wonder why You continue to suffer my presence before You. You created me for happiness and joy, and I have caused the misery in my own life. How good and gracious is Your mercy toward me! I am humbled, grateful, and joyful!

Would that I might grow in holy obedience, that my soul might be more perfected, and in that growing perfection, I might serve the Kingdom of Heaven more perfectly. Lord, grant me strength in the discipline of mind, heart, and spirit in obedience, and grant that I may not suffer the undisciplined rebellion and unruliness of my nature.

May I more perfectly serve You and the Kingdom of Heaven and thereby grow in peace and joy. May I grow in obedience to all the teachings and precepts of Your Church here on earth and all its determinations as it guides Your people in this time of upheaval.

This challenges my faith. Do I believe that the Church represents Christ on earth? That the Church is the Body of Christ on earth? That

DAY 8 I AM NOT DISOBEDIENT! IT'S MY FREEDOM! ... OR SLAVERY

the Church IS Christ? If the world has changed and is changing, then must I demand that Christ change to accommodate me? The world has changed; indeed, it has become more disobedient, not more obedient to You. So I demand that the Church which is the Body of Christ change to accommodate my disobedience? Lord, the folly of such illogical thinking!

But I can look back and see that, in subtle ways, I have been guilty of that very thing at times. When I made a judgment about a teaching of the Church with my clearly superior intellect and understanding of the nuances of theology greater than all the 2,000 years of the Church's teachers and theologians put together! Well, of course that is ridiculous, but that is the way I acted when I challenged the Church on something I did not like or understand. What arrogance! It humiliates me to think of it.

No, You are the Way, the Truth, and the Life, the unchanging God of eternity. It is I who must change as You draw me along the path of salvation. You, who prepare my soul for Heaven, which is unchanging. There is only one truth, one perspective, one reality, and that is Yours.

> *Lord, make me a channel of Your peace!*
>
> *Where there is darkness, only light!*
>
> Prayer of Saint Francis

Your promise of intervention to reset our course on earth is remarkable, Lord, in its determination – like nothing else in the past. Help me to open my mind and heart to a greater depth of conversion, and to then change my life accordingly.

In this place, I am in great poverty. I have nothing, own nothing, possess nothing that can get me to the place I desire, that of greater conversion. It can come only from You, my Lord. Yes, I must change, but it is You who are the Source of grace I need to do it. And so You lead me gently along this path, patient with my weakness, but constantly calling me further. Sometimes I grow so impatient with myself and the slowness of my humanity to respond. I want to lean into the direction and make it come quicker.

THAT FLAME IN YOUR HEART? TURN IT INTO A BLOWTORCH!

When I look back at my mistakes as I have tried to pursue this walk, at times I am humiliated when I contemplate them. How could I be so slow, so stupid, so insensitive, so obtuse, so self-centered, so self-willed, so spoiled, so greedy, so lazy? My sin can overwhelm me if I let it.

I need to grow in wisdom and understanding of who I am and who You are, my Jesus, and trust in Your mercy. I cannot fear making a mistake, as that is paralyzing. I cannot fear the humiliation of making another, nor Your condemnation that will never come. Those fears will paralyze my progress of growth in You.

Rather, I pray for the wisdom that will lend itself to an adventurous spirit as I pursue You in new directions and dimensions! And for that I am excited! I pray for an openness and receptivity to the graces You offer in this time of renewal. Help me to hear You as You call me by name, whom You have created, in the unique way you have chosen for me! The thought fills me with enthusiasm for the journey!

You have created me, as You have everyone, for great heights of holiness! The depth of that, the reality of that, I can only begin to grasp. In the silence of my heart, may I hear the Spirit guiding me on the way. Blessed silence. Quiet. To hear the sound of Your whisper. And then to respond with every ounce of strength I have!

The peace I desire so badly, the peace of mind, heart, and spirit, comes only from You. The more deeply I am united to You, the greater the peace in my life, despite all the suffering You send me and my own death.

Lord, You are my peace and joy!

THE POINT: Jesus, meek and humble of heart, was obedient to all rightful authority. He asks the same of you that you might know His joy and peace. (As you answer the questions, address your dialogue to Him personally and directly.)

DAY 8 I AM NOT DISOBEDIENT! IT'S MY FREEDOM! ... OR SLAVERY

1. My dear child, why are you so disobedient? Do you know the ways you are disobedient?
2. In what ways have you killed your conscience and accepted the ways of disobedience?
3. Can you plumb the depths of your being to expose to Me those defects for healing?
4. Do you know obedience down to the smallest detail in your daily life?
5. Do you know My smile within you when you are obedient to My promptings and the promptings of the Spirit and My Holy Angels whom I send to you so frequently?
6. Do you desire an adventurous spirit to pursue Me in new directions and new ways?
7. What else have you learned about your relationship with Me?

Taking Resolute Action: Jesus, this is one thing I need to change in my life, to take action on: (write it down). Please grant me the strength and grace to do it now.

Day 9

The Secret Realities of Heaven Disclosed!

(August 27, 2003)

The knowledge of Heaven as You describe it and the assurance of the presence of some of our family members there fills me with hope and joy! What a marvel to contemplate!

And too, I marvel at Your revelation that those who served You in similar ways enjoy a fraternity that springs from their common service to You. In the same way, common experiences here on earth bring a bond among its participants, no matter in what generation it is experienced, like serving in an elite unit in the army. It is a unity and community that is built here on earth among fellow servants, and continued in Heaven! I never imagined anything like that before. Awesome!

It is such a delightful thought to consider that my human quest for knowledge, which was implanted in my nature by You, will be continually fulfilled in Heaven as I contemplate the wonders, marvels, and generosity of God! I know that in each line of inquiry as I grow in understanding the universe, the source and summit of the beauty of the magnificent revelation will be You!

In knowing Your creation and the depths of Your power and glory, I come to experience joy, wonder, and love for You. The human mind can scarcely conceive of such a thing, much less grasp the smallest part of it. How this meditation fills me with awe and wonder and longing to experience it! As I turn the thought over slowly in my mind and consider the many dimensions of it, I am filled with awe!

There is a little bit of humor here, Lord! I think about the hundreds of times I have said I could not wait to get to Heaven to ask about something! And how You must have smiled telling me to be patient, My son! Sometimes, I think I still have the spirit of an inquisitive kid! I always want to know about everything – from black holes in space to how atoms get their energy.

I wonder that perennial question: why do men and women think so differently? You really intended that? Ha! I am sure You and Your Mother will enlighten me! Actually, I am having a good laugh about that the more I think about it! I suppose I will recall all those funny cartoons I saw that captured some essence of those differences! Seriously, soon I am sure I will be able to answer my quest for understanding.

As You part the curtain that veils Heaven, and reveal the mysteries of Heaven in completely new ways now, as I ponder them, it causes me to stop and consider carefully what You have revealed. May I enter more fully into those mysteries and, in so doing, enter into unity with all of Heaven and You, my God. I cannot simply read with passing interest as I am inclined to do, but rather, I must read and reread, and let the words penetrate my being. In doing so, I grow in unity with Heaven so that Heaven's ends may be accomplished in me, and its domain extended here on earth.

Would that all humanity in each moment of each day were thus united to Heaven! What would earth then be like if each person was in unity with Heaven and conscious of it and its participants each moment of life? If each person walked and worked through each day in unity with

DAY 9 THE SECRET REALITIES OF HEAVEN DISCLOSED!

You and all of Heaven? And so You mean it to be!

Then it comes to death. Death is a celebration of new life, my new life in Heaven. My preparation for that new life in Heaven is to grow in holiness assisted by all those in Heaven who have an interest in our service to Heaven. Whether I am listening to these words or the Gospel, the call is the same. Therefore I prepare now for my arrival in a new life. And if the language of that new life in Heaven is the virtues, then I must practice very hard now because I know so little of that language. But I already know from my small steps that the greater the virtues, the greater the understanding and participation in Heaven's joys and work.

Heaven is connected to me and completely present to my very person in every moment of my existence.

In no other place in this Volume 2 are words underlined except here: "<u>We are linked to you</u>" (p.32, August 27, 2003). It causes me to stop abruptly. <u>We...</u> – You mean all of Heaven – <u>...are linked to me</u>. Connected. Directly. I only need to turn my inner self toward Heaven's presence. And when I do, I sense fully the presence of my Heavenly friends! I know your presence here with me, my friends, I sense it clearly with my soul!

Heaven is not just a place out there somewhere in the sky, some distant place I am meant to enjoy forever without any relationship to my former home on earth. No, You intend with such emphasis to impress upon me just how close Heaven is involved, not just generally, but specifically with me. Here. Now. Continually. Heaven is connected to me and completely present to my very person in every moment of my existence. I am part of a great crowd of friends, who are all eager to help me, even when I am "alone."

The experience on the Feast of the Transfiguration yesterday brought it home to me. I had gone to First Friday Mass, then Confession, First Saturday, and normal Sunday Mass. Monday was the Transfiguration and Mass was like any other as was Communion.

THAT FLAME IN YOUR HEART? TURN IT INTO A BLOWTORCH!

But when I returned to my pew after receiving Communion, I suddenly felt Heaven surging upon me in wave after wave, overwhelming my mind and heart. Both were set ablaze! And then between the surges, each time I felt my soul lunging up and out of me as though it were going to leave and follow my Heavenly friends home! This went on for what seemed like a long time. It was overwhelming but very peaceful. I imagined that if my soul did leave, my body would just crumple there dead, and the coroner would ascribe it to a heart attack! Which in a manner of speaking, it would have been! I am happy about it, even laughing at the potential irony.

O Lord, just as You acted in my life to get my attention so many times, so now You mean to act in profound ways to get the attention of all humanity here on earth. It is a bit of a shock to read that you intend to "make a loud noise, in a manner of speaking" (p.32, Aug. 27, 2003), soon to awaken us. I think it will take nothing less, unfortunately, as I see humanity spiraling downward faster and faster. Lord, make it loud and make it soon! Come, Lord Jesus!

You have taught me and are still teaching me to learn to love and trust You in everything. But many will react with fear to Your acts to get our attention. And so You prepare the vanguard, Your lay apostles who can show the way to those who are caught up in fear. Lord, help me to cooperate as fully as humanly possible with Your preparation of my soul for Your service! Help me so that I can help others, who are caught in fear as I have been, in their hour of need.

In the heart of Jesus, which was pierced,

the kingdom of heaven and the land of earth are bound together.

Here is for us the source of life.

- St. Edith Stein

How good and gentle and forgiving You are, Lord, to all of us who do not deserve Your mercy. What man does to my body, my humanity, is irrelevant. All the rejection, hurt,

DAY 9 THE SECRET REALITIES OF HEAVEN DISCLOSED!

abuse, and even the violence that others heap upon me in this life is surely terrible, but cannot affect my soul, which is Yours.

My soul belongs to Heaven. I will fear nothing with Your grace. Each time I am afraid, I will call on You and Your promise to me to have You supply the graces -- extraordinary graces -- to deal with them. May You manage my fears of the present and the future.

Come Lord Jesus!

THE POINT: The realities of Heaven include the fact that those who are charged with your care are linked to you, present to you, and are "clambering" to help you! Without fail. Always. Everywhere. (As you answer the questions, address your dialogue to Him personally and directly.)

1. Do you have a constant awareness of just how close My Heavenly Helpers are, how present they are to you continually?
2. Are you unmindful of them and Heaven? What are the implications of that knowledge and awareness?
3. If you are now more mindful of the very close link between you and Heaven, what needs to change in your life? When will you start?
4. What else have you learned about your relationship with Me?

Taking Resolute Action: Jesus, this is one thing I need to change in my life, to take action on: (write it down). Please grant me the strength and grace to do it now.

Day 10

The Real Meaning of "I Am With You"

(August 28, 2003)

O Lord, You say, "My children, I am with you." Before now, I knew that I did not understand it. Now I am growing in understanding as You have become my constant companion throughout my day. For whether I am on my knees in the church or on my knees cleaning the kitchen floor, You are there!

But though You are my constant companion, I too easily lose my awareness of Your Presence. How I desire to be constantly aware of Your Presence with each breath I take so that I am aware that I am continually in Your Presence. Lord, may You grant the greatest desire of my heart! And being in Your Presence I may do Your Will in all my slightest actions and with each beat of my heart.

Jesus, I know You are both within me and beside me as my constant companion. You are present to me in every moment. I only need to turn my interior heart and eyes to You to be in Your Presence with my consciousness. Here I am thinking that I need to tell You how I feel, what I think and experience! But You see through my eyes and feel with my

THAT FLAME IN YOUR HEART? TURN IT INTO A BLOWTORCH!

heart and experience with my body all that I experience. You ARE with me, more completely than I can fathom.

You know me better than I know myself! Knowing that, the question becomes, do I live that knowledge? Does each movement of my mind and heart and being reflect that reality? No! Though I strive for it and desire it with all my being. And so I turn to my Mother Mary, who DID live that, and beg for the grace to emulate her. The big secret of Mary is that she alone has lived that perfectly and desires to help all who turn to her to grow in that perfection!

I am torn between straining ahead for that end and retreating in calm and patient anticipation of that gift from her. Is it possible to do both? In my human nature to strain ahead in disciplines and in my spirit to wait on her timing in faith? Help me to be present to You, my Lord, constantly – to walk, talk, act, and be in Your Presence.

To be present before the Presence of You, Jesus, is to be constantly aware of my reliance on You. That awareness causes me to consider how much I trust, because I can easily see how much I distrust, how far I fall short of trusting completely. I contemplate Your Presence in my life, in each moment, here and now, and in doing so, begin to grow in trust a little more.

The desire of my heart is to capitulate completely. To let go of everything, my worry and stress, focus every fiber of my being on Your Presence and trust completely as Your words invite me to do. It is the desire of my heart, mind, and soul.

My poor humanity, my weaknesses and sin, claw at me, trying to drag me back from making that leap of faith for which I cannot see the bottom or the outcome. And yet, it is precisely in faith that I know the outcome in eternity.

What torment! My humanity cannot see the outcome of the leap in faith in this life and so resists with all the deformed nature of my years. My soul, newly discovering You, desires with every facet it has in spirit and nature, to turn to You in love and relief. Such is my trial of torment that I happily bear though it wears on me humanly.

DAY 10 THE REAL MEANING OF "I AM WITH YOU"

I know from the small experiences I have of truly letting go, and not being preoccupied with the worry and stress of this life, that I can focus on what You want by listening to Your direction. It is trust that will lead me to walk away from difficult situations that threaten to entrap me emotionally and detract me from Your Will.

You know the difficult situations of my life are monumental right now. I am massively in debt, owe everyone from friends, banks, credit card companies, the government. I am facing homelessness, divorced, with special needs children at home, working half a dozen jobs, unable to meet my monthly bills, everything broken around me, and chaos in every part of my life from being a failure in every aspect of my humanity.

On top of that, I am a weak and sinful man, filled with remorse over my self-centered nature, which so easily takes to itself what rightfully belongs to You. For me, walking away from every difficult situation is to walk away from my entire life. I am often, when I lose focus of You, completely overwhelmed in pain. But it is in those moments that my contemplation of You gives me joy for I know You have not abandoned me!

I suffer the pain of my situation in life, and yet with all of that chaos happening around me, I can still keep a clear mind, heart, and soul. Clarity of mission. Clarity of purpose. Clarity of presence before You.

And I have the perfect model in You during Your Passion from the Last Supper to the Crucifixion. Was it not the same for You? Accusations, lies, abandonment, torture, and every form of physical, psychological, and emotional abuse? And yet, in Your trust of the Father, You kept Your heart, mind, and soul focused on what He had sent You to accomplish. So I am to model and emulate You, even as I work with every part of my humanity to correct the chaos I am living in.

It is not enough that I ask for the grace to do my duties.
No, I depend on You to supply me with the grace for a peaceful and joyful disposition at the same time.
Not for my sake, but for theirs.

THAT FLAME IN YOUR HEART? TURN IT INTO A BLOWTORCH!

I am often unable to sleep as I work to respond to the demands of my life. I find that even then, in my human exhaustion, Your grace, if I turn to You for help, is sufficient to sustain me to accomplish what I must during my day. Sometimes it comes to the point of begging – begging for the strength to put one foot in front of the other, to put the dinner on for the boys or to bathe my son and say night prayers. Just to get me through the next 15 minutes of my life, because I am so exhausted I can hardly function.

And always, without fail, if I ask, Your grace is there to not just do my duties, but to do them with love, making sure my sons feel loved and are happy. I know clearly that it is only by Your grace that I have been able to make sure that they wake up happy every day, depart for work happy, and go to bed happy. Without fail. That is You, not me.

I realize that I ask a lot of You in this situation, Lord. It is not enough that I ask for the grace to do my duties. No, I depend on You to supply me with the grace for a peaceful and joyful disposition at the same time. Not for my sake, but for theirs. What is going on within me is irrelevant to the moment. They deserve a joyful, peaceful existence at home because they are Your beautiful and innocent children. I look to You to give them that gift through me.

The beauty of this experience is that You have never, not once, failed to come to my aid, even when it was all I could do to utter something as simple as "Jesus, help me!" I get the sense that You uttered the same prayer to the Father on Your way to Calvary as You fell in pain and agony. "Father, help Me!" And He responded in similar fashion! What a stunning revelation that is for me!

All this reveals to me how little I rely on You, really. You say that when I learn to rely on You, my life will become easier and less stressful. I know You do not mean less suffering. And in fact, even as the suffering continues and worsens, I am amazed as I stand back and look at the joy and peace that fills me more and more.

What I see is that, despite my professions of reliance on You, at times I find that as my life has become more and more difficult I fall back into fear and feelings of stress.

DAY 10 THE REAL MEANING OF "I AM WITH YOU"

Why? Because at those times I do not trust. In my humanity, I have "learned" that I could trust no one completely. Even those closest to me have failed me as only human beings can. But I have transferred that to You, for You have never failed me.

This trust issue is a very big obstacle for me, my Lord. All of my stress and much of my sin has its origins here. As the difficult situations in my life have become steadily worse over the last few years, my normal human response has largely been to succumb to the panic, fear, anxiety, and worry. So much so that, many times, it has immobilized me, frozen my mind and heart with sheer terror. I have broken down and cried bitter tears of desperation, condemning myself for being such a fool and a failure.

> ***Oh God,***
> ***come to my assistance!***
> ***Lord, make haste to help me!***
> ***Glory to the Father, and the Son, and the Holy Spirit!***
>
> Adapted from Liturgy of the Hours

Then, in my weak condition, I find myself falling into all sorts of sin as I look for comforts and consolations to help ease the pain and distract me from the situation. I can take my finger and draw the line from most of my sins to their source and the spiral path that got me there, the source so often being lack of trust in You, unwillingness to abandon myself to Your Love and Providence.

Into that miserable place You have entered with such tender mercy and compassion! You have touched my soul and my heart and drawn me up to Yourself, wiping away my tears and filling my heart with love sufficient to drive out the despair. And then, instead of condemning my distrust, You have shown me the way to trust and confidence in You.

It is these little lessons in humility that teach me the value of trust and the absolute uselessness of distrust that leads to fear, anxiety, and stress. How good and tender You are, my Lord and Shepherd! How gentle are Your ways! How You melt my hard heart!

THAT FLAME IN YOUR HEART? TURN IT INTO A BLOWTORCH!

Mary, I pray that you come to my aid; help me to rely completely on your Son, Jesus, and to trust Him completely and consistently!

———————

THE POINT: Jesus is with you, present to you to a degree that the human mind can scarcely grasp. (As you answer the questions, address your dialogue to Him personally and directly.)

1. As I reveal the ways I am present to you, is your heart and mind open to My Presence in You? To My Presence in the tabernacle?
2. Do you have the experience of turning to Me interiorly? Can you stay there? Even as you go about your daily duties?
3. What are the implications of doing that? What are your roadblocks?
4. Can you trace the root of your sin to its source? And the spiral path connecting the two? Describe that to Me in detail.
5. Can you put aside whatever is going on inside you, your struggles, your emotions, how you feel, etc., to serve another with My peace and joy?
6. Can you die to self to give joy to another? Will you let Me help you?
7. What else have you learned about your relationship with Me?

Taking Resolute Action: Jesus, this is one thing I need to change in my life, to take action on: (write it down). Please grant me the strength and grace to do it now.

Day 11

Finding a Safe Refuge Despite Turmoil & Pain

(August 28, 2003 II)

One of the mantras I live by is "In all things, God's timing is perfect." How could it be otherwise? You, my Lord, are perfect; therefore, all You do and all that You allow through Divine Providence is perfect. And so, as I read this particular reflection, I pause to consider how Your timing is perfect as we just started the Novena to the Sacred Heart of Jesus yesterday. Perfect timing to read and contemplate this message about Your desire to draw all souls into Your Sacred Heart.

    You start by saying you want to draw me into your Sacred Heart, into that place of love and security and rest. It is from that place that I can begin to see the world through the eyes of love, Your eyes, with greater clarity that comes as we grow closer in unity. So whether I see things that trouble me or cause me great joy, I beg to see as You see, hear as You hear, and feel as you feel. In that way our unity can gradually grow as I become one with Your Will. And then I can share in Your joy.

THAT FLAME IN YOUR HEART? TURN IT INTO A BLOWTORCH!

You say You are joyful about me? You are joyful as you see me struggling? Because I am trying to do the right things, to be holy? Lord, forgive me, but the struggle is work. It is exhausting and difficult and not so joyful on my end all the time.

I do often feel the graces and little ways of assistance You send from Heaven, but the burden at times is so heavy it feels like I fall down in the dirt and have no strength to get back up. At times my whole being wants to just stay there and give up. Why bother? What is the use? It would be so easy for me, even now, to give in and go with the world's attractions. And it would feel good.

Ah, left there, in that place of cynicism, my heart would grow cold and I would give up. Giving in to my nature, I would pursue a path contrary to Your Will. But my love for You, and Your love for me, causes me to have a very different reaction.

I reflect on the question, and then consider Your reaction: You rejoice at seeing me struggle to grow in holiness and send all kinds of help and assistance. It causes my heart to leap a little with joy to know that my struggles cause the One I love to be joyful.

It is not any different than a normal human reaction when I have been encouraged by similar reactions from ones I love here on earth. They see me struggling with something and working to overcome it, and it causes them joy and they reach out to encourage me. So my struggling is a sign of growth, like exercising that leads to growth through work and pain.

Rather than be left in a place of cynicism, I am left in a place of gratitude for Your joy and encouragement, which cause me to get back up when I have fallen and continue along the path You have laid out for me, more resolute and determined. Lord, You know my desire to serve You totally, without reservation, but You also know my human limitations and the fear, anxiety, and stress I struggle with.

You rejoice at seeing me struggle to grow in holiness and send all kinds of help and assistance.
It causes my heart to leap a little with joy to know that my struggles cause the One I love to be joyful.

DAY 11 FINDING A SAFE REFUGE DESPITE TURMOIL & PAIN

And from this place, which appears so hopeless, when I see people enjoying life, I sense the evil one lurking in the distance, waiting to tempt me to slide into bitterness and resentment, even hatred, towards those who could have rectified my situation or at least reached out to help but did not.

For me, that battle is mostly about my search for employment and the rejection by those half my age whose jobs I could do in my sleep. But what must it be for those who are destitute? Or starving to death? Or homeless? I just want to preserve my standard of living. For others, it is so much more severe, even a matter of life and death. My struggle to love, to be happy and at peace in spite of suffering, is nothing compared to theirs.

I am spoiled and pathetic in my complaining; I have no real reason for bitterness or resentment. Still, I see that path and how easy it would be to go there. My nature is fully capable of going there, though my heart and soul recoil from the thought. My compassion for those who choose that path, perhaps even unwittingly, is so much greater. They do not deserve my judgment, only love. I am not so different from the worst of the lot.

But You offer a different alternative, one that holds out the hope of a more joyful and peaceful path: to take all my emotional and psychological and spiritual burdens to You. And give them to You over and over again each time I encounter them within me, whether weekly, daily, or even hourly. Let go of them. Do not hold onto them. Release them to You. Let You take them all. In each moment of each struggle. That is the path to my growth in holiness. Unburdened, I can easily get back up and continue to climb the mountain of holiness, encouraged by Your joy for me and feeling the helps You continue to send along the way.

Yet even as I see this path before me and know this experience, when I check in with my interior self, I detect the problem: I am so accustomed to living this way, holding onto the negative thoughts, the fear, anxiety, and resentment that to give them up to You is a tearing of the fabric of my being, tearing the spiritual me from the fallen nature of me.

THAT FLAME IN YOUR HEART? TURN IT INTO A BLOWTORCH!

> *We shall steer safely through every storm*
>
> *so long as our heart is right, our intention fervent, our courage steadfast,*
>
> *and our trust fixed on God.*
>
> - St. Francis de Sales

Still, in faith I will keep doing it – giving all those emotional, psychological, and spiritual struggles over to you because I trust in Your word to me. You have bestowed on me the right to give You all those burdens and let it end there – with giving them to You. In return, You promise to give me a portion of Heavenly peace in advance, a concession because of the times I am living in.

So here they are, my Lord! All of them. Take them. I push them like so much garbage out of my interior. May Your peace flow in its place! Fill my heart, mind, and soul, my Lord!

Thank You my Lord! I trust in Your word and Your promise!

Let it be done to me according to Your Will! Amen!
(Mary's response to Gabriel, Lk 1:38)

THE POINT: Jesus reveals Himself, His Sacred Heart, as a place of refuge and safety from everything we struggle with, every storm of life. And He rejoices to see us straining to go there. (As you answer the questions, address your dialogue to Him personally and directly.)

1. Are you aware of the refuge for you within My Heart? How would you describe it?
2. Are you aware of the help I offer with every detail of your life? Describe for Me a time when you perceived My help and what that felt like. How can you grow in that awareness?

DAY 11 FINDING A SAFE REFUGE DESPITE TURMOIL & PAIN

3. What holds you back from a dialogue with Me about every detail of your life? About every temptation you face? About every sin you commit? About every joy you have?
4. Do you think I am unaware of your heart and mind in those situations?
5. What do you think My response will be any time you turn to Me, whether the issue is big or small?
6. Have you ever considered that, even as I am your omnipotent King, I very much enjoy talking with you? Even about the small details of your day?
7. What else have you learned about your relationship with Me?

Taking Resolute Action: Jesus, this is one thing I need to change in my life, to take action on: (write it down). Please grant me the strength and grace to do it now.

Day 12
Your Family, The First School of the Heart

(August 28, 2003 III)

Lord, I cannot start this meditation without wanting to just jump and shout or dance in the streets like King David over how unbelievably good You have been to my family! My gratitude knows no bounds!

What should have been a disaster coming out of the divorce, with the kind of people my two sons and I are, has turned into a very beautiful thing to behold, like a flower garden! OK, maybe a little bit rough 'cause we are guys, so it has the feel of bursting out all over. The three musketeers, maybe?! We watch movies together, play football, cook together, travel and enjoy life together. And we go to Mass, pray together, and serve others together. Our lives are simple, but beautiful, and only You could have done this, could have affected such a beautiful transformation to peace and joy!

But then, I turn my attention to Your heartache. My dear Jesus, my heart aches to know of Your distress at seeing the human family You created being destroyed.

THAT FLAME IN YOUR HEART? TURN IT INTO A BLOWTORCH!

It is properly the first school of the heart, the little church of faith that is being attacked so successfully today, even among the most faithful of your children. My own pain at the destruction of my family, something I thought I would never experience, gives me only a dim sense of the pain You must feel.

Even now, as I consider it, I know the pain of destroyed families so well that if I stop to consider it, it still feels like a terrible wound, a spear thrust into my heart. What must it feel like to You? I had no idea before. I think I must have even sat in some kind of judgment before – and for that I am deeply grieved to the point of shedding tears. Oh yes, I was mostly sympathetic to those who found themselves in that situation, and surely I did what I could to comfort them, but still, in complete honesty, I know that at some level there was judgment instead of compassion.

Jesus, I offer up to You all this pain in my life in reparation for my sins, and those of all my family and friends. Only You can make any good come of this disaster. Just as You grieve for the loss of the family, so I join my own grief to Yours as I see the devastation that is being wrought across the world. My heart is filled with grief and pain now as I think about my situation and all those I am aware of who have experienced similar situations. And then to the whole world.

The family is Your creation, not ours. You are in control of who the members of the family are by Your Divine Providence as You send children into each family according to Your design. It is in this way that You express Your love for each of us and our families in particular: in the uniqueness of our persons and the families You create. What arrogance You must see in our attempts to control this in so many ways, such as cohabitation, birth control, and abortion!

> *The family is Your creation, not ours. You are in control of who the members of the family are by Your Divine Providence*

You say by Your creative act "This is what I want," and we, through our actions shout back in Your Face, "No!" We shout, "No, this is what

DAY 12 YOUR FAMILY, THE FIRST SCHOOL OF THE HEART

I want!" It even becomes vicious as we rebel and attack those who confront us with the truth.

Though Your Will in this matter has been and will be constant and eternal, our disorder and sin is manifested in the kinds of families we have attempted to create today ourselves. Yet even in this situation, Your love is constant for us, always working for the good of our families and each of us in particular. Why You sometimes allow the one-parent situation for Your own good reasons, as in my case, I do not understand but accept as Your Will.

As I reflect on this I know that, in my own situation, being a one-parent family was not Your original intent, that it was only our mutual sin and disorder that brought about this situation. Nor in fact, was this my own will or intent, as I tried everything I could to prevent it, but this was the end result and consequence of the sin, weakness, and disorder in both of our lives.

And yet through all of this You have made such good come of it. I can see the fruits of the struggle and where my children are today as they shine with peace, joy, serenity, faith, love, and budding holiness. Only You could have done that in this impossible situation! Even through all the disorder, pain, and chaos, Your goodness to my family is almost beyond belief! You shower so many abundant blessings down on us, I cannot even begin to keep track. This morning, my son came upstairs as I was getting coffee (yes, I know I am bad – a little piece of oatmeal cookie, too! One of these days I will have to get some discipline and fast from that too!), and he gave me a hug. As I walked back to the living room, I looked downstairs, and there he was in his own "prayer chair" saying his morning prayer! Here is a young man who loves his electronic games, praying! By the time he comes up for breakfast, he will have been at it an hour! A 20-something guy! You, my God, are so very good!

I cannot know Your reasons for giving the responsibility of raising the children to one parent – to me – nor should I, for fear of pride which so readily torments me. My only response can be to accept Your Will and

THAT FLAME IN YOUR HEART? TURN IT INTO A BLOWTORCH!

to fulfill my responsibilities and duties as I strive to grow in holiness and help my children to do the same.

My goal is properly to raise saints, as poor an example and teacher that I am. I cannot make my judgments about why You have allowed the situation. You will show me if You so desire over time, but You do not need to. I just need to keep focused on my responsibilities and leave the wondering as to Your motivations until I reach the Kingdom of Heaven.

To accomplish Your Will in my family means to put away the things of immaturity that occupy my time and attention and seek Your Will in the raising of my children in love and patience. It is my duty that comes first in this regard before all else, including work, play, and even rest.

So we, my former spouse and I, are to be a help to each other – a source of holy help to each other and our children, whether still married or not. We are to continue our responsibility as parents with You as the central part of our triune relationship through which they were conceived and born.

It is the reality of their existence that gives witness to the procreative relationship that was present and therefore the responsibility that exists, no matter what the state of my marital relationship is at present. And even though the marriage was annulled by the authority of Your Church, it does not absolve my responsibilities as either a parent of my children or even as a fellow sojourner with my former spouse toward the heavenly goal, though the nature of the relationship and the help we provide one another is changed.

Lord, make of us one family in Your Heart!

> *The history of mankind, the history of salvation, passes by way of the family...*
>
> *The family is placed at the center of the great struggle between good and evil,*
>
> *between life and death, between love and all that is opposed to love.*
>
> - Pope John Paul II

DAY 12 YOUR FAMILY, THE FIRST SCHOOL OF THE HEART

THE POINT: From the beginning, the original intent of God for the family and its design was expressed by His Divine Providence. The uniqueness of the family was willed by the Creator in who He sends as children if He sends them. (As you answer the questions, address your dialogue to Him personally and directly.)

1. How have you tread on My turf by trying to control the makeup of your family?
2. Is your family a school of the heart teaching obedience and love or one of rebellion and independence? Is it a school that I would approve of? What needs to change, My child?
3. What kind of example are you as a role model for what I intend families to be?
4. What needs to change within you? What else needs to change in your family?
5. What else have you learned about your relationship with Me?

Taking Resolute Action: Jesus, this is one thing I need to change in my life, to take action on: (write it down). Please grant me the strength and grace to do it now.

Day 13

Unrestrained Love Explodes from the World's Tabernacles!

(August 29, 2003)

Your words stop me in my tracks: "The love I feel bursts out from My Eucharistic Heart. I cannot contain it." As I have contemplated You in the Eucharist, at times I have felt the beating of Your Heart, the overwhelming Love pouring forth so strongly, I thought my own heart would stop completely! My heart fills to the point of bursting! My mind is set ablaze!

Oh Jesus, I know only too well what You describe – stumbling through my life, turning away from You and falling deeper and deeper into sin – and in my pain, inflicting that on others or leading them down the same path. How very, very painful that recollection is to me, bringing tears to my eyes for the suffering I have caused You and so many others. Lord, I am so very sorry! Have mercy on me.

But there You are, with a love You cannot contain and a compassion for me, a Heart that hurts to see me err and in pain, a Heart ready to

THAT FLAME IN YOUR HEART? TURN IT INTO A BLOWTORCH!

absorb my sin and pain and rebellion, a Heart ready to heal me if I but turn ever so slightly toward You and accept You! I am stopped by the thought!

> *How could I not turn toward You?*
> *My heart and mind, my very being cries out for relief and peace.*

How could I not turn toward You? My heart and mind, my very being cries out for relief and peace. And yet my will is stubborn in persistence of its habits and ways, seeking the gratifications of the nature it has grown so accustomed to. It is as though I have become addicted to the drug of my seeming independence and freedom to do as my will dictates, and in doing so, I have become a slave to my nature and passions. What a pathetic state of my humanity!

It is nearly incomprehensible to me why You want me back so badly that You are willing to immediately forget all my sins and the punishment I deserve. It is so far from my own nature and inclinations that I have to stop and consider it carefully.

And yet too, I do know that disposition as I consider my love for my own children and my own reactions to them when they have behaved badly and then come to me repentant. It is as though we even deepen our relationship because, in their small act of humility and my forgiveness, we reach a new depth of love and understanding in our relationship. So it is with You if I will but let it happen, as I see with renewed eyes and heart the depth of Your love for me. This is not just a one-time event, but rather a continual journey as I probe deeper and deeper.

You call me to the tabernacle to encounter Your Love and Mercy – to meet You there, specifically and in Your Real Presence. You forgive all my sin and make me as white as snow, as pure as if I had never sinned.

The first tabernacle I must visit is that dwelling place within me where You are – that I may come to know and be conscious of my sin, of my many ways of offending You. Otherwise, it is all an empty gesture – a generalization that I must be a sinner, but no admission of my specific offense, and therefore no admission of the specificity of my culpability.

DAY 13 UNRESTRAINED LOVE EXPLODES FROM THE WORLD'S TABERNACLES!

The second tabernacle I must visit is the tabernacle of Your representative here on earth, the tabernacle of the Confessional to come to terms with my sin and reconcile with Your Body, the Church. Then as I kneel before Your Real Presence in the true tabernacle in church, I come as a leper seeking Your healing touch, and confident that You will do as You have promised!! And so I approach You with confident joy! I am filled with joy at the realization of what a beautiful process this is, a way to peace beyond description! A way to peace that can only be experienced!

The habit of my sinful condition makes my daily struggle against it one of continuous dependence on Your grace. You are right – I have grown accustomed to some of my sins. And therefore complacent in my sinful condition, and so You come to me with great urgency to re-examine my life, repent of the sin, and turn toward You where I will find Love and Compassion, Comfort and Consolation.

Your promise is remarkable – should there be any doubt in my mind, or any inability to face the truth of my behaviors that offend You and separate me from You, You promise if I will but come to You, You will tell me directly. You will communicate with me and reveal those behaviors and offenses specifically. What an amazing promise! It fills me with hope as the burden is not on me for perfection in this, but rather to just trust You and Your promise! Remarkable!

Why would You do such a thing? Why bother with me who am already a sinner and abuser of Your generosity to me? Therein lies the first part of the answer – because my pursuits and abuse have led to pain and suffering that only You can heal.

And the second part of the answer is connected to it – without Your restoration, I risk losing the salvation of my soul which You are so urgently trying to get me to see and respond to. It is the restoration of my being, the healing of my soul, that You so generously offer.

Having thus been restored by you, I can regain the correct perspective on the true purpose of my creation and existence. The gifts of my person were given to be used in the service of the King, as You say, like

THAT FLAME IN YOUR HEART? TURN IT INTO A BLOWTORCH!

those of a loving child looking out for the interests of his father. But how have I used what has been given to me, to what end have I applied the gifts given, what are the fruits of my labors to this point?

The question must be asked in truth, and the answer must be given in complete truth and humility – both the "successes" as well as the failures of my efforts. I can see those times in my life when I was devoted to the service of the King and, much more, the times in my life when I used the gifts to further my own interests to the exclusion of Yours – and the futility of those efforts. The cravings of my sensuous and hungry humanity will never be satiated; they only grow if left unchecked.

The third part of the reason You are so urgently begging me to come to You to be restored is that You need me to help You through my relationships and my presence in the world. You can then be present to others through me in order to bring them to the Kingdom. You tell me that there are souls in the world that can only be saved through me – Your Presence to them through my presence to them!

Stop! I am stunned by the revelation of the huge responsibility – it has eternal consequences. How can I be lost in my own concerns when such a thing is before me? All else pales by comparison. So You must lead me and help me to tune the eyes and ears of my heart to Your Will, to Your guidance each and every day. How difficult that is for me in my humanity. Only by Your grace!

When I awoke this morning my mind was filled with regrets at not having listened to Your very direct Word to me in the past regarding something I needed to do. I ignored it, debated with you, hesitated, and delayed out of fear and confusion.

Do you realize that Jesus is there in the tabernacle expressly for you – for you alone?

He burns with the desire to come into your heart...
The guest of our soul knows our misery;

He comes to find an empty tent within us - that is all He asks.

- St. Therese of Lisieux

DAY 13 UNRESTRAINED LOVE EXPLODES FROM THE WORLD'S TABERNACLES!

And now, five years later, I still am paying very heavy consequences for my inaction. The suffering is extensive in very real ways. Why do I not listen and jump to obedience? Teach me obedience, Lord! To respond to You immediately!

Actually, here comes my irreverent humor again, Lord. I have this image in my head of sitting around a nice table in Heaven after a sumptuous meal with family and friends laughing and recalling the issue. Those who were already in Heaven are telling me they sent every form of alert they could think of that God would allow, almost like clanging fire engines with sirens blowing, and still I ignored the warnings. So they finally convinced You to speak those words I heard clearly that day. You did, I did not act even then, and You just looked at all my friends, smiled, and shrugged Your shoulders! I can be so stubborn, it is comical, if not sad.

All this is good and meant for my instruction, to return to You in obedience. You are begging my return to You with greater love and fidelity, that I might comfort Your Loneliness, the loneliness of a Creator for His creature who has wandered and suffers from not being in the Creator's Presence.

Lord, grant me the grace to respond to Your request, Your begging me; help me to answer: "Here I am Lord, I come to do Your Will." Help me to be present to Your Presence!

Here I am Lord! Is it I Lord? I have heard You calling in the night! (well-known Christian hymn)

THE POINT: Jesus pours out His Love both urgently and profusely upon you. He wants to stop the destruction going on in your soul and bring you peace, joy, and healing. Then He wants you to move quickly to help save others through your relationship with them. (As you answer the questions, address your dialogue to Him personally and directly.)

THAT FLAME IN YOUR HEART? TURN IT INTO A BLOWTORCH!

1. Can you see the destruction in your soul from sin? Are you sensitive to it?
2. Can you see how it accumulates and darkens your soul and intellect so that you cannot be sensitive to My Will for you?
3. Are your ready to receive My healing love and forgiveness?
4. Can you see how important it is to help Me reach others through your relationships?
5. My little one, what are you waiting for?
6. What do you need to drop or let go of, child?
7. What do you need to pick up or grasp?
8. In what specific ways do you need to return to Me?
9. What else have you learned about your relationship with Me?

Taking Resolute Action: Jesus, this is one thing I need to change in my life, to take action on: (write it down). Please grant me the strength and grace to do it now.

Day 14

An Intimate Discussion: The Way You Speak

(August 29, 2003 II)

In being an apostle of Jesus, the Returning King, do I have a vision for what that truly means? Has the genuine desire to grow in holiness settled into my heart and mind? Is my growth in holiness becoming a preoccupation? And if I have that vision and desire to achieve a high level of holiness, then the question is, does my speech reflect that? But more than that, my speech cannot reflect who I think I am at the moment because in my human weakness, I can be discouraged and be less than I am. Rather, my speech must reflect who You call me to be, a holy man.

It brings a smile to my face and joy to my heart that You allow my feelings of a lack of holiness in order to protect my humility! How good You are to operate so delicately within me to protect me. To protect that which I desire but am unable to do on my own.

Some days, the flame of Your Spirit burns so brightly within me that I feel it might consume me! I feel the heat of the blowtorch within me!

THAT FLAME IN YOUR HEART? TURN IT INTO A BLOWTORCH!

Despite my feelings of inadequacy or "un-holiness," You, my Lord, are asking that my speech, my outward conduct, reflect the level of holiness to which You desire for me. Ah, that is so very different. To know Your Heart and to know Your desire for me means I have to listen to my Lord very carefully. And in knowing Your Heart's desire for me, it becomes my heart's desire.

Clearly, I know and feel the light, Your Light, burning brightly within me. Some days, the flame of Your Spirit burns so brightly within me that I feel it might consume me! I feel the heat of the blowtorch within me!

How can I hide such a Light which is You? May it burn so brightly that it DOES consume my very humanity, that all who see me, see not me, but You! The thought of it quickens my pulse and fills me with joy and enthusiasm – a zeal to continue my day in hopes that You might be revealed through me, as poor an example as I am.

But of course, that requires asceticism. I cannot let my feelings or emotions dictate my behavior or conduct. Rather, I need to trust Your Word, Your promises, and act on them no matter what is going on within me or around me if I am to serve You, Jesus Christ, the Returning King. The King must be served by the servant, no matter how he feels or what is going on within or around him, with trust that he is loved and protected by the King.

Stop. Halt. I can so easily blow by that asceticism. To be and act and do, to love and extend compassion and mercy to others, no matter what is happening to me interiorly or exteriorly, because I am a servant of the King and serve Him first and foremost, that is my duty. Surely, a servant of an earthly king is expected to do at least that much. Or else the king will have the servant punished or thrown out and search for a new, more disciplined servant.

Thanks be to God, I do not work for an earthly king who is demanding in that way. No, I serve a compassionate and merciful King, who shows me the way to serve, the Way of the Passion. You served the Father's Will with love, mercy, and compassion, even as You were being abused, tortured, and crucified.

DAY 14 AN INTIMATE DISCUSSION: THE WAY YOU SPEAK

> *All that emanates*
> *from me*
> *must be You!*
> *What else could it be?*

I can put aside what is going on with me to serve You, my King, and Your Will. No matter what. I do not need to wear my interior on my sleeve, for all to see, complaining loudly while I serve. I can just serve.

I am struck by where You take Your message next – to an intimate place of asking me to examine the very nature of my speech! Never have I heard of my God being so intimately involved in my life! But of course it is as it should be. First, I need to make sure it is always You who is conveyed in my speech in every encounter I have with another, beginning with those closest to me. Does the message I convey reflect me or the love of Jesus Christ – who is being reflected in the mirror of my speech?

(The scientific facts are that only 7% of the meaning in communications is in the words; 34% is in the inflection and tone of voice – the remainder in the body language.)

> *...it is a great secret.*
> *The smaller I become*
> *within myself,*
> *the greater You become*
> *within me...*

Thus, it is not just my words but my being that needs to reflect Him whom I carry within. The very tone of my voice You ask that I listen to in order to make sure that I am conveying love, that I am talking as You would talk. All that emanates from me must be You! What else could it be? Jesus, may I decrease that You might increase within me so that all who see me do not see me but rather You in me!

That is not just a trite saying, but rather it is a great secret. The smaller I become within myself, the greater You become within me, and then as I speak and act, the more You are conveyed and the less of my humanity is conveyed. What joy there is in that, to see You at work through me!

So often I fall short of that, my Lord! But I refuse to be discouraged – because that is not what you are asking of me. Rather, You ask me to pick myself up and try again; You would never ask me to do something that is impossible. And so I am encouraged that I can repeatedly come to You,

THAT FLAME IN YOUR HEART? TURN IT INTO A BLOWTORCH!

reviewing my conversations with others constantly, even going so far as to review them beforehand to hear how You want a conversation to go. I trust that You will give me the words.

Many times, while I am on the phone, I turn to an image of You, in particular the Sacred Heart, and beg You to give me the words You want conveyed to the person I am talking to. I find myself smiling because You never fail to answer that prayer, sometimes in absolutely fascinating ways.

This past fall, when I taught the college course, I opened each class with a discussion on a quote that I handed out in class. As I was handing it out, my interior prayer was, "Please, Lord, give me the words these students need to hear today. You alone know their hearts. You alone know what they need to hear through me to lead them ever so gently to You."

The result of those discussions was remarkable as I later found out from a few of them. Not once did I mention God in the classroom, but their hearts were moved toward truth, goodness, and light. The seed planted, it is Yours to nurture.

And so you form and inform my heart with Truth in Love, that I might bring Your Word to them, whomever you direct me to each day, and that I might "speak to them as You speak to me"! But wait! You say it is fitting that I be intimately acquainted with You?!! Would You do that? Allow or desire to be intimately familiar? And then you say, to speak to them as You speak to me?!!!

I am stunned. And excited. My Lord would speak to me in the intimacy of my heart? Of course, I know that and have experienced that, but to have You say it directly to me is overwhelming! Yet, if I pick up this book which I affirm is not by any accident, but by Your design that You have given these word to me in order to speak directly to me, there it is, in black and white! It is unmistakable.

Your words, the way You speak to me, are full of tenderness and mercy, full of Truth in Love, without compromise, but understanding of my sinful and frail humanity. I need to do what You ask of me, particularly in my relationships, without fear, making sure that I am doing exactly as

DAY 14 AN INTIMATE DISCUSSION: THE WAY YOU SPEAK

You ask, no more and no less, and doing it in the way You have asked me to do it. So I must speak the Truth with a sincere and loving heart – in all situations of my life, no matter where I find You have led me each day.

I see a trap into which I have fallen very often as You point out, and that is the spreading of unpleasantness, whether factual or not. That is so very easy and common these days in the era of digital communications when the world is filled with conflict, cynicism, political division, 24-hour news, and on and on. It is hard in that situation not to speak negatively about others and berate them for their actions.

It is one thing to hold a different opinion, to disagree with actions that people undertake that are harmful to the Church or the Kingdom, and quite another to berate them, to speak negatively about them as a person. Your challenge to me: not to speak negatively about another person – because You do not speak negatively about me. Let me pause to consider how I need to change….

You correctly point out the truth: I am sinful enough on my own – what place is it of mine to point out the sins of another? Who gave me the right? Or power to condemn?

My speech needs to be holy speech – full of loving compassion. Leave the rest alone. While I think that is the way I have always conducted myself with those I have known personally, I have not done that in the broader sense with regard to all my brothers and sisters. If I stop to think about it, they are all in the same condition, sinful and needing compassion and love.

Lord, please grant me the grace of being merciful and compassionate in my speech toward and about my brothers and sisters as You, Jesus, are to me, wherever they are on the face of this globe. I will be merciful and compassionate as You are, Jesus, toward others, as I realize the depth of mercy and compassion You have for me.

*If you are silent,
be silent out of love.*

*If you speak,
speak out of love.*

- St. Augustine

THAT FLAME IN YOUR HEART? TURN IT INTO A BLOWTORCH!

How I need to ponder the depth of Your great mercy toward me! Then I will be humbled and joyful at the same time!

Be discriminate, O my soul, so as not to be so indiscriminate in my speech as my nature would have it. My speech should only convey Heaven to others. How far I have to go!

Lord, grant me the grace!

THE POINT: The words Jesus speaks to you are always the Truth, but He speaks with great tenderness and love, no matter how "bad" you have been, no matter how you have treated Him. (As you answer the questions, address your dialogue to Him personally and directly.)

1. My child, is your speech filled with tenderness and love? How do you fail Me in this area?
2. Are you open to how I want your speech to change? To the details of your speech unique to you? What are those ways?
3. Do you think you can be so open to change your thoughts and speech that I would approve of everything that comes from your mouth? What difficulties are you having with that?
4. My child, how do you need to change in order that everything you say reflects Me?
5. In what circumstances do you most often fail Me in your manner of speech?
6. Do you sense My excitement for how you are changing? What is that throb in your heart as you contemplate serving together with Me? Tell Me, child, tell Me! I am listening!
7. What other lessons do you take away from this chapter?

Taking Resolute Action: Jesus, this is one thing I need to change in my life, to take action on: (write it down). Please grant me the strength and grace to do it now.

Day 15

How to Please Jesus. (It's Not What You Think.)

(August 29, 2003)

You ask if I want to know how to please You, Jesus? Yes, my Lord, I do want to know what pleases You and comforts and consoles You in this time of so much rebellion against You.

I look around at the condition of the world and am aghast at what I see, from family, friends, community, church, and nations. All is in turmoil, in a state of division, one against another and the majority against You! How troubled our world is and how it must pain You who gave Your very life to save each of us. Only to have Your gift ignored and in some cases, even attacked.

Certainly this world does not deserve any further mercy from You! How I wish I knew how to comfort Your anguish! And Your answer: humility. Humility? Why humility, Lord?

Humility is contrary to my nature, my broken humanity. I can hardly control my nature that seeks the path of pride at almost every juncture.

THAT FLAME IN YOUR HEART? TURN IT INTO A BLOWTORCH!

There is always some prideful expression that leaps from within me even when I am deeply immersed in doing Your work.

But humility was the original intent: full knowledge of God the Creator. Thus humility comforts Your anguish because it is the assent to Your original intent – assent to the truth of who You are and who we are as creatures. Complete assent to Your power and goodness and omnipotence.

> *But humility was the original intent: full knowledge of God the Creator.*

Pride is the enemy of humility. The original sin. Pride fed disobedience. It is the original sin I am marked with and the sin to which my nature constantly desires to give its assent.

It shall not be! Rather, in my spirit and my will, I give my complete assent to You, my Lord! Though I may fall into the sin of pride even many times a day, still I will not assent to it, but rather to You, my Lord! To You I yield. To You I give my whole heart and all the love it is capable of.

That is my only defense against my nature, to give my love. To love with all I have within me. And to give that love to the one object of my desire my intellect knows is safe for me to love without reserve who I can trust completely: You! All human loves require me to be diligent and watchful that I not be led astray in some subtle fashion. There is no other object of my love that can claim to be completely safe for me to love, and beyond that, to be redemptive of my soul. As lover to his beloved, I give my complete love to You!

There is a great revelation here! My love for You must be so great that it dominates my heart and keeps my love for all those in my life in perspective and measured against Your Truth and Love. Otherwise I am susceptive to being misled in my weakness, much as King Solomon was with his pagan wives.

As I love You more, I come to see who You are more, and then more of who I truly am. As I grow closer to You, the more I see my imperfections and the greatness of Your Perfection. To know myself in reality and

DAY 15 HOW TO PLEASE JESUS. (IT'S NOT WHAT YOU THINK.)

truth begins by knowing You first. I will decrease that You might increase within me.

I do acknowledge that it is directly to me, to my heart, that You speak, my Lord. I am both joyful and overwhelmed – even terrified by this call to holiness and the process of becoming a saint as You say. This is a call to all of us, but now it is more deeply personal as I realize it is addressed to me individually, directly, and very personally. How could it be otherwise for anyone who knows You? To know You is to be called to holiness, to be a saint.

That is my only defense against my nature, to give my love. To love with all I have within me. And to give that love to the one object of my desire my intellect knows is safe: You!

Would You enter into a dialogue with someone without calling them to go beyond where they currently are? Would You enter the dialogue just to have an enjoyable chat? No, any dialogue with You must be a call to come closer to You, because that is what Love does.

A desire for greater intimacy means movement and movement means change and change means friction and friction means heat and heat means something gets burned up. So it is with some aspects of my life. Consumed by the fire of Your love. And that is what I feel is going on within me! It is both terrifying and wonderful as I sense the changes in me. On the outside, I suppose I look and act much the same as before, but within I know changes are taking place as the old is burned up and the new is left in its place!

In love You created me. In love You gave me all that I have in talents and gifts to be used for the Kingdom. And to build the Kingdom, You have specific tasks that You require me to do. What are those tasks, my Lord, and how shall I go about accomplishing them? I desire the answer that only You can supply. I acknowledge that only in You is found perfection; therefore, only in You is the answer and the answer is Your plan for me.

If You have a plan for me and my life, would You want to keep it a secret? No? Would You want to reveal it to me in a way that accounts for all my limitations? But of course! So I trust that for all my limitations, You will make Your plan known to me, and all the gifts and graces needed, You will supply.

To do that, You want my friendship, and You want me to follow Your path immediately. You have my friendship, Lord! Help me with the grace of immediacy of following, as I see that is my weakness – hesitance to follow. Why do I hesitate, even though I know from experience that the hesitance always leads to difficulties in my life? I also know from experience that following Your promptings immediately has always led to good things in my life. So why do I continue to hesitate? Why do I repeat this same mistake time and again? Why am I in despair over my slowness to change?

The only answer I can come up with is fear – fear of the unknown and lack of trust in You. Lord, help me overcome my fear and lack of trust. Help me to conform my will to Yours, and to Your plan. The more I conform my path to Yours, the greater the peace I will know.

Ah, wait! That is an easy thing to say and even to believe, but extraordinarily difficult to achieve. It is one thing to know peace when my life is going well; it is another to be at peace when my life is in chaos and turmoil. I look at Your example, Your Passion, and I begin to understand the degree of peace You promise.

In Your example of remaining peaceful in doing the Father's Will even as You initially prayed to be delivered from it, You showed us the Way, the example for us to follow. You remained loving, forgiving, and conscious of the Father's plan for Your life even as You were mocked, tortured, and killed. What I endure in my life is nothing close to that.

If it were just Your example, then I might be able to excuse my doubt about being able to follow, but there is the witness of the lives of so many Saints who did exactly the same thing as You, under similar circumstances. Could I remain peaceful and forgiving and loving as I was being burned alive or disemboweled in public or boiled or dragged to death through the streets? The lives of the Saints stand as shining examples of how it is possible to be at peace no matter what is going on in my life. None of my sufferings can compare with theirs.

DAY 15 HOW TO PLEASE JESUS. (IT'S NOT WHAT YOU THINK.)

There are so many who revile You or ignore You – it seems Your true friends are few these days. You desire to call me friend? You may, dear Jesus, call me friend! Please do! I am humbled by the term! And excited! I do not take this lightly!

Where there is humility, there is wisdom.

- Proverbs 11:2

When I think about what that friendship means, I think about how lopsided it is. You are the true and unfailing Friend, and I am the fickle, fair-weather friend who has so often abandoned You in Your need. Still, You ignore all my failings as a friend and just keep coming to me, asking me to continue the journey with You. You even go so far as to keep encouraging the weak and intermittent efforts I make.

The affirmation and gratitude I seek to continue this journey, the Way You have shown me, can only come from service to You. I have no power, no strength to make the needed changes to do it, to follow this Way, the example of You and Your Saints. But I do want to allow You to make the changes in me which You promise to make if I will just give my assent, and then let You do the rest. You have it, my Lord.

I am open to making the changes in my life that You want me to make, that I might grow in holiness. Help me to not resist the changes. Give me the graces I need to make them and to be completely open to the Spirit and His promptings.

Come, Lord Jesus, fill the hearts of Your faithful! Enkindle in us the Fire of Your Love!

THE POINT: Jesus desires an intimate friendship with you, to call you His friend. (As you answer the questions, address your dialogue to Him personally and directly.)

THAT FLAME IN YOUR HEART? TURN IT INTO A BLOWTORCH!

1. What will it take for you to accept My invitation to say yes and grow in the friendship you have started with Me, your Jesus?
2. True friendship with the Creator requires saintly humility and obedience. Are you up to that, to My transforming grace to help you grow?
3. Do you desire that level of friendship with Me?
4. What do you fear, My dear little one? Come, tell me; I am listening!
5. Look deeply within yourself: is there a saint in the making? Ah, I will make you into one, if you let Me! Are you letting Me?
6. How does thinking about that make you feel?
7. Do you want to be the saint I am asking you to become? Do you want the changes in your life that entails? Can you trust that I will provide the graces you need?
8. What else have you learned about your relationship with Me?

Taking Resolute Action: Jesus, this is one thing I need to change in my life, to take action on: (write it down). Please grant me the strength and grace to do it now.

Day 16

Foundations of Holiness: Protecting Your Soul

(September 1, 2003 I)

Your constant presence in my life, in the lives of Your children, I acknowledge, as I have been taught that. But the fact that You are directing so much of what is going on in my life that I just miss or cannot see in order that Your Will can be fulfilled in my life causes me to be excited! God cares about the smallest details of my life?!

Wow! I have experienced that awareness at certain times of my life, particularly when I was on a pilgrimage, like the ones to Knock, Ireland, and Lourdes. There I felt that I was witnessing a finely orchestrated event with a myriad of details all coming together beautifully to allow me to experience the fullness of the pilgrimage.

But to know that You are that close and involved on a daily basis, day in and day out, says to me that I need to pay closer attention to my day and Your Presence in my day.

THAT FLAME IN YOUR HEART? TURN IT INTO A BLOWTORCH!

So often in this Volume, You keep coming back to the subject of protection and Your protection over me. As I have given myself to You, so You promise You will protect me. You see what I do not see and am able to anticipate.

I am convinced that You have done many extraordinary things in my life to protect me. I reflect back on the paths I could have gone down, and where they could have led, if not for Your intervention in my life. As I consider Your protection for me, I see that You act even without my asking because of my commitment to You.

But when I pray for Your protection, it is as though You pay particular attention to that request, and at the same time, the prayer changes me – it opens me to be protected by You in a way that I am more conscious of, even when I do not see or anticipate the nature of the threat until later. And I am sure that I am protected from things I will never know until I reach Heaven.

This is a mysterious part of our relationship, this prayer for protection and its effect on my soul. It is an extraordinarily powerful part of our relationship. Even as I consider it now, it overwhelms my mind and heart as I pause to contemplate it. I am filled with the Spirit as I consider its implications!

What is it about a prayer for protection that is so powerful that I sense it gets Your immediate and undivided attention and response? Is it the prayer of a child to its Father, a prayer of the vulnerable to its Protector, the prayer of humility to the Omnipotent, the prayer of the lover to the Beloved?

The simplicity of this prayer and the realization of its profound impact on one who prays it has set my mind and heart ablaze.

I am convinced that if every Christian were to utter the simple prayer, "Heart of Jesus, protect me" each day, the whole world would radically change in a flash. It would change the person who uttered it and the world around them.

The thought stops me. What if only one out of ten did it? What if only one out of a hundred? Or a thousand?

DAY 16 FOUNDATIONS OF HOLINESS: PROTECTING YOUR SOUL

As I am protected by You, You ask me then to turn my attention to Your service. And what is the motivation for my service? Your answer is remarkable in a way, though of course it is not a completely new revelation as it is foundational to my faith.

I am convinced that if every Christian were to utter the simple prayer, "Heart of Jesus, protect me" each day, the whole world would radically change in a flash.

What motivates my service is Your revelation that once I get to Heaven, I will look around and see all the souls that would not be there had it not been for my service! Together we will rejoice and share the happiness at being there together in Your Presence because of Your Providence and my small yes.

The thought of that meeting with another soul causes my heart to leap! What if I had ignored the prompting of the moment when the Spirit caused me to reach out? The joy of their escape from the alternative and their presence in eternal happiness is enough to make my heart pound! So it will be for many, I hope, as I pray to serve You! What an exciting and unbelievable concept!

Please show me how You want me to serve today. Lord, my service is so poor and inadequate when I consider what is needed by the Kingdom to rescue so many souls who are in danger of being lost. Help me to grow in service to You and Heaven. Please hear my heartfelt prayer to better serve You, that I may help in the rescue of souls in the way that You want.

I trust that You will answer my prayer, showing me the way and granting me the grace to be both receptive to it and responsive to You. Then I can walk in the path You show me with the peace and serenity and assurance of being a servant of the King.

What does the King ask of me? It is not the big things, the grand mission or task at all, though eventually that may be needed of me. No, it is the small, mundane little tasks of love associated with my station and vocation in life that You ask of me.

THAT FLAME IN YOUR HEART? TURN IT INTO A BLOWTORCH!

And why? To form my soul in the detailed way that You need to in order to bring me to wholeness, healing, and the perfection which was intended when You created me. My soul is perfected when You heal and restore my soul from the multitude of fractures within it, the effects of sin.

How badly I sense my soul and my very being is fractured as if not the smallest part of me has been left whole or untouched by the effects of sin. I can almost visualize the animated graphics of it as I see me fractured and then fall in a heap on the ground. And then You picking up each small piece and putting it back together, slowly and carefully, and as You do, the cracks disappear and the part is made whole, like new again.

Your way of healing and perfecting my soul is not what I would have expected. Your request is that I pay attention to the small little things in my life and do them all with love and humility. My actions, each and every one, need to be done with love, patience, and humility.

Let me pause to consider how that looks and feels as I work to make that a practice in my life. Love, patience, and humility as I pay attention to the small things in my life, seen and unseen, and cooperate with You as You work inside me. Hmmmm…. Let me pause for a moment… Washing the dishes, picking up the house, listening to my children, talking to a client…

It is in that way that You can move quickly in my soul to bring it to its highest potential. Your way is most remarkable, my Lord!

And yet, if I consider it, that way is quite natural, like the training of an athlete. Once the basic training and conditioning is achieved, then it is in the details of the exercise and practice that excellence is achieved. So too with the soul of the Christian.

> *The Spirit comes with the tenderness of a true friend and protector*
>
> *to save, to heal, to teach, to counsel, to strengthen, to console.*
>
> - St. Cyril of Jerusalem

DAY 16 FOUNDATIONS OF HOLINESS: PROTECTING YOUR SOUL

This causes me to reflect on Your admonition not to rush through my day in a hurry but rather to proceed calmly and patiently. And to pay attention to Your Spirit as You prompt me in the details of my day to ways I can serve You.

Lord, help me to slow down to pay attention to the minute details. To do all with that spirit of love, patience, and humility that You might be given free rein to reform my soul completely and bring it to the perfection of Your original intent.

Yours is the active, mine is the willing heart to the perfection of my soul.

As I stop to consider it, You are right. Much of my suffering, the overwhelming majority of it, is the result of me turning away from You – the result of my separation from You. The pain, the lack of peace in my life, has been the result of my choice, my sin. Now, as I turn back to You by choice, I am confident of Your promise that You will pour grace out on me and protect me.

It is in the small humble acts done with love and patience that You, Jesus, perfect my soul and repair and change it. As the cracks and defects are repaired, my soul becomes capable of containing more grace. And when it contains more grace, it is capable of more.

Come! Fill the hearts of Your faithful! Come, Lord Jesus!

THE POINT: Jesus desires to protect your soul so that you can grow in holiness. As He does that, He forms it in obedience starting with the smallest, mundane things in your life. (As you answer the questions, address your dialogue to Him personally and directly.)

1. Do you desire to grow in holiness more than you desire "independence"?
2. Are you obedient? To the Church? To rightful civil authority? To the promptings of My Spirit? To My Angels?

THAT FLAME IN YOUR HEART? TURN IT INTO A BLOWTORCH!

3. Why are you disobedient? How does that manifest itself?
4. What is the price of disobedience in your life? In your soul?
5. Can you pay attention to the small things I bring to your attention in your life and do those little things with love, service, and humility? Especially at home? And at work?
6. Are you open to the ways I want to heal and perfect your soul?
7. Are you aware of the ways I have protected you? What did or does that look like?
8. What else have you learned about your relationship with Me?

Taking Resolute Action: Jesus, this is one thing I need to change in my life, to take action on: (write it down). Please grant me the strength and grace to do it now.

Day 17

Antidote to a Plugged-in, Hi-speed, Multiplexed Life

(September 1, 2003 II)

Jesus, You want my disposition to be calm, my soul to be calm and peaceful and present to others, present in each moment. That is so unlike me. I know myself to be a "type A" personality, driving hard from early morning until late at night, moving through my highly caffeinated day, accomplishing a myriad of tasks at work and on nights and weekends, tasks of a single dad. And all the while, I am multiplexing a dozen or more major projects.

There is so much to be done, and everyone depending on me to do my part, my duties. Only when my sons are finally in bed at night and are happily at rest can I even think of slowing down, and often not even then. Most of the time, I just keep going until I fall asleep working, and only then do I give up and go to bed. My whole life has been in this pattern, particularly when I am working three or four jobs to keep the

THAT FLAME IN YOUR HEART? TURN IT INTO A BLOWTORCH!

family afloat like I am now. And when I am commuting three or four hours a day for work on top of that.

Making this change may be the hardest thing I have ever attempted. I do not know anything of this new place I need to move into. It is foreign territory to me. Lord, I am open to this change, and do want to change. I think I will need an extraordinary amount of grace for this miraculous change in my life. It is a good thing You are God! Ha! What a humorous but joyful thing to contemplate!

I sense You are laughing and smiling about this great big impossible mountain of a miracle You need to work in my puny little life! Funny, Lord! What am I going to say? "Are You up to it?!" How goofy is that? Ha! Ha! My heart is full of grateful joy and a tear forms in my eye!

Let it be done to me according to Your Will! I know that the reason You want this change is not humorous at all, but for a very urgent and serious reason – that I can be present to You and to others in every moment, guided by a listening heart.

I can best listen if I am intent on hearing in the present. If I move quickly, I am preoccupied by what is next instead of being present in the moment. And then I do not complete the tasks You have given me or I miss the nuance You are directing me to pay attention to.

It is this training of my nature that leads my soul to the place of being present to Your Spirit. I do know the sensitivity of Your promptings and directions to me. So if You do not like to hurry and do not want me to live hurried, then I need to imitate You.

What a remarkable revelation! Where else have I ever heard of such a thing? Perhaps some Saint I have forgotten. The imitation of Jesus includes moving through life calmly, that peace and serenity may follow.

It seems to me that You move steadily to be attentive to me in my humanity! You do not rush by me and on to the next thing at all, but rather You are calmly and patiently present and attentive to me when I am attentive to You and even when I am not. So I need to be attentive to You, and in doing that, I can be present to others whom You are directing me to in order to provide for what they need.

DAY 17 ANTIDOTE TO A PLUGGED-IN, HI-SPEED, MULTIPLEXED LIFE

How lonely and despairing our world is with everyone rushing around, plugged in and connected to everyone else, but ignoring their presence. No wonder the suicide rate of our youth keeps climbing. They are hurting and no one seems to notice or care until it is too late.

I can see that I need to focus my efforts on being present to You so that I can focus on being present to the other. Then our hearts and souls can connect and I can be present to what You want of me in that particular situation.

It occurs to me that perhaps a lot of the rushing and hurrying from one thing to the next is a form of self-centeredness. It is all about me and what I need to accomplish to feel good about myself. Your calling to me, Jesus, is the opposite of that – to be other-focused in order to serve You by serving the other.

So I need to be attentive to the gentle and quiet whispers, the gentle breeze of the Spirit as You, Jesus want me to hear You. If You are present, then even in my suffering there will be Your Heart, Your Love, Your Kindness, and Your Gentleness. And loneliness and despair cannot be where You are truly present, present in me or present in another.

This is a source of great hope! As I work to follow You more closely, to grow in holiness, then I can reflect You more perfectly and in doing so, can relieve those suffering from loneliness and despair, bringing You to them.

Even now, as I contemplate all of this, a feeling of serenity comes over me. I feel more connected to You and to Your creation, to others who cross my mind at this

If I were a physician, and if I were allowed to prescribe just one remedy for all the ills of the modern world, I would prescribe silence.

For even if the Word of God were proclaimed in the modern world, how could one hear it with so much noise?

Therefore, create silence.

- Soren Kierkegaard

THAT FLAME IN YOUR HEART? TURN IT INTO A BLOWTORCH!

moment. Would that I could capture the essence of this feeling and keep it present in my mind and heart! Do you feel this, my soul? Remember it!

But as I turn my attention to the day, my heart feels a stab of pain. O my heart, where is Jesus for me as I suffer? I know I have lost You if there is despair, bitterness, anger, self-pity, and so on. Not that I will not feel those at all, because I am human and will suffer those feelings and the temptations to give in to them, perhaps even frequently as I sometimes do lately given my present circumstances.

But if those feelings and dispositions persist and become my outlook, then surely I know I have lost You and Your Presence in me because those are not of You. Plainly I know I am in need of allowing You to work in my soul through my constant assent to Your Presence.

The changes I face now seem to be overwhelming, insurmountable obstacles. I am faced with huge changes in every area of my life and all of them are very negative from a human perspective. And most of these changes have no good or even feasible prospects of resolution.

My serenity is based on my complete trust in You, Jesus, and Your total care for every aspect of my life. That would be the counsel of Heaven I am sure; therefore, my disposition can be nothing else but trust and serenity even in the exterior chaos and pain.

I have been sick for so long and this pain I am in is so severe that now I am even unable to sleep through the night without getting up and taking more pain medication. Without health insurance, I have been turned down by the local doctor and hospital. Financially, housing, employment, and everything else in my life is in the same condition. Everything I have known and been is coming to an end in a very painful way – literally.

My reaction to all of it has been far from passive. I have taken a very active role in attempting to discern Your Will as I work very hard at trying to resolve all of the issues I am faced with. I am exhausted from the long hours and hard work.

DAY 17 ANTIDOTE TO A PLUGGED-IN, HI-SPEED, MULTIPLEXED LIFE

Despair haunts me like a wolf as I look over my shoulder and feel its hot breath on the back of my neck. My heart trembles with terror at times as it seems I am close to being torn apart by the forces of the world. But I have faith. You are caring for every detail of my life!

Still, I can feel this battle raging in my soul as my humanity cries out for comfort and consolation. Just give up and give in to the sin that tempts me and be comforted even if it is fleeting as a way to ease the pain for a short time. They are the sins I had grown comfortable with before in my life so there is no obstacle to resuming them. In a way, I am tempted with a kind of lust for my old way of life.

Now as I sit here, I come to this quiet moment with You. I know I just need to stay present to You and the moment. "Stay with me" were Your words to me in Adoration. Those words were pragmatic that day, I did stay and everything worked out, but I know Your words to me have a larger context. To stay with You means to stay in Your Presence even as I move through the day, staying in dialogue with Your Heart as You keep me close.

In dialogue with You then, I can in every detail turn to You and trust in Your guidance and providence. My serenity is based on my complete trust in You, Jesus, and Your total care for every aspect of my life. That would be the counsel of Heaven, I am sure; therefore, my disposition can be nothing else but trust and serenity even in the exterior chaos and pain. It is my small portion of Your Passion.

Like the 24-hour news channels, I need to interrupt every hour at the top and bottom of the hour, break into the action, to refocus on You and the broader mission of Heaven. I walk with great confidence and assurance that, abandoned to Your Will, I will be assured of my place in Heaven, my home.

Such peace I feel from You, my Lord! Such serenity is washing over me and my spirit soars! You fill my soul!

Here I am Lord! I come to do Your Will! – Psalm 40

THAT FLAME IN YOUR HEART? TURN IT INTO A BLOWTORCH!

THE POINT: We all want peace in our lives, but for the most part, it is elusive as our lives are characterized by stress, despair, fragmentation, loneliness, emptiness, and on and on. But the life that is conducive to doing God's Will is characterized as calm, peaceful, and joyful. (As you answer the questions, address your dialogue to Him personally and directly.)

1. Are My peace, joy, and serenity what you want for your life?
2. How important is that kind of life to you?
3. Do you see why I want that for your life?
4. What specific changes do you need to make in your life so that it will be more calm and peaceful?
5. How important is it that you do My Will in your life? What are you willing to do for it?
6. Do you trust that the things I, your King, am asking of you are within your capabilities and require only your best effort? Do you trust that I will take care of the rest?
7. Do you think I would ask something of you and then not provide all you need to do it?
8. What else have you learned about your relationship with Me?

Taking Resolute Action: Jesus, this is one thing I need to change in my life, to take action on: (write it down). Please grant me the strength and grace to do it now.

Day 18

Your Spiritual Growth ... at the Speed God Requires

(September 1, 2003 III)

Jesus, how gratifying it is to know You are pleased with my efforts, as poor and imperfect as they may be! I take great comfort in knowing it is You who perfect my will, my efforts, and my soul as I seek to submit them to Your guiding hand.

I also know from Your statement about my struggle with the world and its very strong attractions to me, "until complete union or surrender occurs," I will be unhappy struggling with my sinful human nature until my entry into the Kingdom. "…until complete union or surrender occurs."

> *In Heaven there cannot be two wills, only one, Your Will, Jesus which is the Will of the Father.*

That is the destiny for every soul if it is to be Heaven bound. It could not be otherwise. In Heaven there cannot be two wills, only one, Your Will, which is the Will of the Father. I cannot enter Heaven possessing even the tiniest shred of my

THAT FLAME IN YOUR HEART? TURN IT INTO A BLOWTORCH!

own will. Between here and there, between now and then, I will have to come to complete terms with that, to complete surrender. Or not. It is the choice of my free will now when that will happen, if at all. If not, my place will certainly be of my choosing, even to hell itself. That is the stark reality of my choice and free will.

And so the journey to be taken up is one of complete surrender to Your Will. Now, in this time and place is the space to achieve that to the greatest possible extent that my limited humanity can with Your grace.

Your call is urgent to do so. You are revealing Yourself in entirely new ways at this point in the history of mankind! And revealing the secrets of Heaven which before this were reserved until the soul arrived there!

Why? Because so many of Your children are being lost to hell forever in a torrent, and You are intervening with this "rescue mission" for souls as You call it. And because the souls that only I can touch and throw Your lifeline to are in urgent need of that assistance.

Lord, please help my poor soul to lead my humanity to surrender to You, that our unity might be complete and I might serve Your rescue mission more faithfully.

I can see also the generosity of Your Will toward me and every one of Your children. You choose carefully the crosses for each of us, allowing us to accept them, carry them, and embrace them as Your Will so that, ever so gently, our humanity becomes transformed as we surrender to You.

Even our suffering at the point of our death and the particular way we die gives us each the chance to grow in surrender. For some, it is a long process, and for others, it happens in a flash, but in whatever way, we all have the interior opportunity for complete surrender. Otherwise, should we not choose it sufficiently here on earth, then those souls who are Heaven bound will have the dual opportunity to repent of sins and accept Your Will in purgatory. What a beautiful plan is Your Plan for each of us!

DAY 18 YOUR SPIRITUAL GROWTH ... AT THE SPEED GOD REQUIRES

Purgatory. Where most souls who are Heaven bound will go. It is a place of great sorrow in repentance and a place of great joy in confidence of our eventual destination.

How eagerly we will take up the task of examining the sins of commission and the sins of omission in our lives on earth! How repentant we will be for all the opportunities and graces You showered on us that we wasted. How grateful we will be for those that we did not waste. For those we will have eternity to rejoice with You and those we assisted.

Purgatory. The place and space we will be given to complete our surrender to Your Will so that upon entering Heaven, there shall be but one Will, Your Will. It cannot be otherwise.

But that causes me to reflect on the urgency here and now that I feel to allow You a free hand with my soul. Your mercy is so great and so incomprehensible that I am continually surprised to see another dimension of it – it is wondrously breathtaking!

There are so many souls on the verge of being lost to hell who need just a slight interior turn towards Your mercy to be saved. They will reach You through me. You have said it. There are souls that only I can reach because of my relationship or my work for the Kingdom. Just a nudge will keep them from falling over into the precipice of eternal damnation. Just a nudge. Something so simple and so merciful. And then You do the rest.

I feel sorrow for the souls who have avoided You, who have not desired You and pursued You, but rather have pursued their own gods of pleasure or vice or violence here on earth. They will never know Your mercy because they have turned away from it. Were You to take them to Heaven, it would be against their will and they would be miserable.

No, Heaven is not for those who have shunned You and rejected the great act of mercy of Your death on the Cross. I pray that somehow I can be a part of helping those in that state see a glimmer of light and turn, even if ever so slightly, toward Your mercy.

THAT FLAME IN YOUR HEART? TURN IT INTO A BLOWTORCH!

I also realize that I cannot fool myself. I am fully capable of turning away, so strong is the attraction of sin and so weak is my nature. The pull of the world is bigger than I am without Your grace.

I feel it in my very body even at this moment – the attraction of worldly comforts and pleasure, the desire to escape into them. So sinful is my disposition that I sin in my subconscious where my will is present, even in my near sleep and at times it seems almost with every breath I take and every thought. Is that extreme? No, I think not.

I know the experience of being so consumed by my sin that I am preoccupied by it during my waking hours at home and at work, and when I lie down to sleep, it is present within me, taking up a place in my heart, mind, and soul. To such an extent that even my dreaming is dominated by the disposition I had as I fell asleep, and then when I wake, I am in the same place, only worse, because it has taken even deeper root within me.

Thus, the critical practice of prayer and repentance, which my boys and I do together every night, has become a safeguard for me as we kneel beside the bed. I could despair over my weaknesses and sin.

But You are my hope and joy as I struggle! You direct me toward complete union and surrender. I am drawn to desire this union quickly, though having that desire dominant within me is so distant.

I get caught up in discouragement as I consider the strong pull of my past behaviors and habits. I know the feeling of joy at being filled by You and the profound effect on my being as You capture the essence of my heart. It fills and completes my humanity and my spirit like nothing else could possibly do.

> *Sing, my heart, with joy! Proclaim His marvelous deeds to all the nations!*
>
> Adapted from Christian hymn

And I know the fleeting hollowness of other things I have allowed to capture my heart momentarily. I have used many things to console myself in the past, but they quickly left me empty again, as they must by their very nature.

DAY 18 YOUR SPIRITUAL GROWTH ... AT THE SPEED GOD REQUIRES

Only You, my Jesus, are permanent and everlasting. Only You are the Eternal Joy and Peace my soul was created to desire. No created thing could possibly take that place.

The peace in my soul permeates my being! It gives my soul dominion over my body, heart, and mind. I feel and sense it growing within me, even now. Though this peace is fleeting now, by Your grace it is growing as my soul leads my mind and heart, as it should, according to Your original intent. Peace and joy grow within me, and I feel them settle deeper and deeper within my heart and soul!

As I surrender, my soul is more and more under the dominion of Your watchful Heart. How I wish the surrender and dominion were total! Who would not want You to have total dominion of his or her soul? "God, come to my assistance; O Lord, make haste to help me!"

Help me to ascend quickly, that my assent may be pleasing to You! I am at peace with the speed You have determined. Sometimes. And sometimes I just want to "be there," and at other times, not at all. What a fickle nature I have! And then, as I pause to consider it interiorly, I realize that my emotions, not my intent or will, are fickle.

No, I am delighted to be in Your service and to be trained and readied so quickly, though I feel some trepidation at my inadequacy. Much like I felt during my training as a soldier and officer, knowing that I would be leading other good men into battle and keenly aware that I was undeserving of this immense task I had volunteered for.

In that case, I had but one choice if I was to serve: trust the trainer and the training. So it is with You, my Lord. Complete trust despite my self-doubt.

Holiness, it seems, is daunting, outside the realm of possibility for me. But I trust in Your good Will. If You call me to holiness, then I trust that You will achieve it in me as I seek it. With You, all things are possible, even in my case, which seems to be such an impossible cause.

It is the small acts of faith I make throughout the day, as I continually turn to dialogue with You, that keep me faithful to Your service. I

THAT FLAME IN YOUR HEART? TURN IT INTO A BLOWTORCH!

struggle to turn my gaze to Heaven, but I am rewarded with peace, even as I carry these crosses of fear and doubt.

Yes! I know You are with me! You are with me because You are within me. You see and feel what I see and feel, and You know everything that I think! Intimacy perfected!

If You are in my neighbors, then I must silence my spirit to hear You in them. And if You suffer when they suffer, then I must tend to their needs so that I may give comfort to You. You will tell me how to comfort You by telling me how to comfort them. I must begin by maintaining a quiet, interior peace and a listening heart so that I may hear what it is You want me to hear through those around me.

It is within my power either to serve God or not to serve Him.

Serving Him, I add to my own good and the good of the whole world.

Not serving Him, I forfeit my own good and deprive the world of that good, which was in my power to create.

- Leo Tolstoy, Russian author

You end by telling me to be at peace and by saying that You are pleased. You are pleased?! With me?! How can that be? I look at myself, maybe a little as You see me, and see a poor sinful man who has spent much of his lifetime offending You. And yet You amaze me with that statement and bring delight to my heart!

In my poverty, I am enriched by Your tenderness toward me! My eyes fill with tears of gratitude for Your unbelievable generosity toward me! I am humbled to nothingness. Tears pour down my face to hear You say You are pleased. I am overwhelmed with sorrow and gratitude at the same time!

THE POINT: Jesus is pleased at your efforts to serve Him and He desires to encourage and support you. He wants you to grow in

DAY 18 YOUR SPIRITUAL GROWTH ... AT THE SPEED GOD REQUIRES

holiness – at a pace that might seem quite fast to you. (As you answer the questions, address your dialogue to Him personally and directly.)

1. Are you ready to open yourself to the growth I have planned for you?
2. Are you willing to let Me determine the way of holiness unique to you? At the speed I determine is appropriate for you?
3. What are your doubts and misgivings, little one?
4. What holds you back, My child?
5. Can you let go completely and free-fall into the abyss of My Love?
6. Dear one, do you think holiness is for you?
7. Have you asked Me to take complete dominion of your soul? Can you do that again now, in this very moment, with a new level of sincerity and trust?
8. Have you surrendered all your past, present, and future to Me? Can you do that right now?
9. What else have you learned about your relationship with Me?

Taking Resolute Action: Jesus, this is one thing I need to change in my life, to take action on: (write it down). Please grant me the strength and grace to do it now.

Day 19

Live True Inner Peace. You Were Created for It.

(September 2, 2003 I)

Jesus, You say You want me to be at peace. How often I hear that from You, in the Scriptures, at Mass, from the Pope, and in the whole body of teachings by Your holy Saints.

Peace. It must be very important. Why?

You want peace for me because that is the way You created me. Peace was Your original intent for Your creation. You have not changed. You still want peace for Your creation and for me. And You want me to be a conduit of that peace for all whom You created.

How gentle and personal You are dear Jesus! You are truly my Teacher! I had thought every hour I could stop and rest in You and that would be good, but it seems so long in between. As I close my eyes, I easily imagine You looking at me, and I return Your gaze with love.

The peace of Christ is my desire and focus. These days, in the storm and chaos of my external life, it has become a very difficult thing to hold

THAT FLAME IN YOUR HEART? TURN IT INTO A BLOWTORCH!

onto. At times, it seems I can go for long periods having a peaceful interior disposition despite what is going on around me. But at other times, it proves terribly elusive. I think I am just getting there, and in the next moment, another thing happens that rips it from me, and I struggle to regain my centered, peaceful disposition.

Peace is Your gift. I cannot achieve it. And so I find that I need to turn again and again to You. Sometimes minute by minute. In Your Presence, I rest again in Your Peace. It is in that closing of my eyes for just a moment which You have instructed me to do, and in the silencing of my mind and heart, that I come to rest in Your Peace. Then I can pick up and resume the work of my living.

Lord, I also long for death so I can be born into eternal life! I want with all my heart to be home in Heaven! But I know my humanity is weak, and when I am faced with death in my last moments, it may be a struggle. Mother Mary, I know you can obtain for me from God the grace of a happy death. I trust in that.

Today I look forward to serving You, my Lord, and know that the moment of death is but my birth into eternal life. In an instant, I will be home, my Heavenly home. At rest at long last, and at peace. Such a day for celebration!

In the meantime, I am here on earth, working to live the life I have been given. My lack of peace, my hurried pace in the past, has caused me to miss so much of what You have tried to communicate to me – so many opportunities to serve You – and so many ways You wanted to provide me assistance. So many graces squandered!

When faced with the truth of my past life, I see that externally it appeared I was mostly fearless, but interiorly, I lived in a constant state of fear. How could it be otherwise if I did not know and live the Peace of Christ, letting it permeate every fiber of my being, every moment of my life? Praise be to God, I am touching that Peace now, and You, Jesus, are teaching me to live it!

The greater I fear death, the more I become distracted from living my life as You want me to live it. My life becomes filled with inordinate

DAY 19 LIVE TRUE INNER PEACE. YOU WERE CREATED FOR IT.

The less I fear death, the more I can live the life You have given me. And in living that life, with no fear of death, then life can be lived to the fullest.
There is the source of my joy in living.

activities and preoccupations to preserve it. How I see that the world is caught up in this fruitless pursuit – an endless myriad of pursuits to preserve life, make it better, improve health and all the rest, chasing longer life. All while the poor starve to death every day.

How senseless we are as a people, Lord. Our pursuit has become an obsession with self while those around us are ignored. I am no less guilty than the most obsessed, to be sure, as I have fallen for the allurements myself. Lord, forgive me for my self-indulgences!

The long life I need to be focused on is the long eternal life. The less I fear death, the more I can live the life You have given me. And in living that life, with no fear of death, then life can be lived to the fullest. There is the source of my joy in living.

You want me focused on serving You in all my earthly duties given my state in life. And that is best achieved when I am at peace because then I can be more focused.

What a beautiful plan is Your plan! The peace the world desires that can come only from You comes to the world from Your servants whom You constantly replenish as peace is drawn from them. The peace that my soul craves is the peace every soul craves.

But the enemy of peace lurks near every soul, creating disturbances where our weaknesses are, constantly probing for a place to enter. I know the probes: the temptations, the memories, and allurements. I feel them and at times am tormented by them almost violently. Sometimes I am going about my business peacefully and suddenly there comes a trigger almost from nowhere, and I am caught up in an interior battle.

It happened just today after a short nap. As I awoke, I found myself in a raging battle with the enemy of peace that lasted for hours, even through prayer, domestic chores, and outside activities. Finally, peace

THAT FLAME IN YOUR HEART? TURN IT INTO A BLOWTORCH!

again, as I determined not to give in and prayed for Your protection. Sometimes, I am left shaken in my humanity by it. But I am at peace interiorly.

I know this battle goes on for every soul, my Lord. The enemy of peace prowls the earth looking to devour souls. I want to reach out to those who know this torment, this battle, and encourage them to stand strong in Your protection. Let them draw peace from me as You fill me with peace in overflowing abundance. May I be a true conduit of Your peace to those around me!

My path to peace is from periodic to frequent to constant presence in Your Presence. That is the progression of every soul that seeks You, whether here on earth or eventually in Purgatory on the way to Heaven.

As I pause in Your Presence, the desire to be there constantly grows into a burning desire. It comes not without willing it, but fighting for it. This is not a passive place, rather an active place. A determined act of the will to be in Your Presence even as I am being drawn away from it. I seek to be there and will be there with the help of Your grace.

And yet I have to suffer with a weak humanity that is distractible. So be it. This is not an easy journey, or else everyone would make it. Sometimes it is even arduous, but then nothing of value is ever gained without concentrated effort, pain, and suffering, no matter what it is. Education and sports have taught me that.

Attaining Heaven is no lottery jackpot. Going along and playing the game does not get me a place in Heaven. Good intentions alone will not get me to Heaven. Nor will just being a nice person get me there. Or professing to believe in God. Even Satan believes in God. Even he knows the pleasantries of being nice and even helpful to entice the unwary soul.

Do not lose your inner peace for anything whatsoever, not even if your whole world seems upset.
If you find that you have wandered away from the shelter of God, lead your heart back to Him quietly and simply.

- St. Francis de Sales

DAY 19 LIVE TRUE INNER PEACE. YOU WERE CREATED FOR IT.

No, I will attain Heaven only by the grace of God and by firm decision and action on my part. I must concentrate to evade the allurements that will draw me over the precipice. The stakes are high – very high – eternity.

As I reflect on this, I consider, what must Your perspective be as You see me? I know You want me to see the changes in my soul, to see my soul as You see it, with clarity. In this way, I can draw encouragement from You as I see the beautiful changes You are making in my heart. I know You care about the condition of my heart, my state of mind, and my emotional state.

Still, I am amazed that You care about my human emotions. God cares about my very human emotions? Really? What god is there that does that except the God made Man? And what do You want for me? You want me to feel Your joy and Presence! I pray to decrease quickly that You might increase in me and that I might be a more perfect conduit of Your peace and joy.

You call me to be an evangelist for Your cause now. To be present to all souls as You are present to them, in the way You want me to be present to them. Your strong words get my attention: "If a soul rejects me now, it is finished. You cannot reject your God and claim Heaven as your inheritance."

My heart breaks to read those words. I am terribly saddened to read them because I love Your people, and some of those for whom I fear are my friends. It hurts! I hurt for them!

Lord, help me to help You touch each soul that none may reject You – as I almost did in my foolishness. My view of my brothers and sisters on earth is changing as I see them more and more as precisely that, brothers and sisters, and less like "others" in a detached, isolated way. I begin to see all of "us" as You see us.

I want to share with them the joy of the Good News: that You are here for them if they will but turn toward You. All will be forgiven and forgotten in the joy of the reunion of the soul with its Maker!

With that, I come to the following realization which crystalized within me:

THAT FLAME IN YOUR HEART? TURN IT INTO A BLOWTORCH!

Lord, make us one!

> *What is the purpose of relationships?*
> *The value of relationships is contained in only one thing:*
> *the revelation of Jesus Christ.*
> *Since Christ is present in the other, then my relationship with the other reveals my relationship with Christ.*
> *And my relationship with the other reveals Christ to the other, to myself, and to all who observe the relationship.*
> *While one might not hear His name in every relationship, though that must be the goal and intent, one must always see Jesus Christ revealed in every relationship.*
> *Thus, the only valid purpose of relationships among mankind is the revelation of Jesus Christ present among us.*
> *And the most efficacious way of revealing Christ is through love and service in those relationships.*

THE POINT: Jesus wants you to be at peace interiorly at all times and in all circumstances, no matter what is going on within you or outside you. He wants to give peace, first, as a gift to you and, second, He wants you to spread His peace to all with whom you come in contact. (As you answer the questions, address your dialogue to Him personally and directly.)

1. Do you know that experience of interior peace at all times and in all circumstances? Do you want that from Me?
2. What disrupts your peace most often?
3. What do you need to do to regain it?
4. Do you want and desire to live that life of peace and serenity which I greatly desire for you?
5. What value does peace have for you?

DAY 19 LIVE TRUE INNER PEACE. YOU WERE CREATED FOR IT.

6. What are you willing to let go of, to give up, for peace?
7. What obstacles do I, your King, need to help you overcome to achieve it?
8. If you live with more peace and joy in your life, what will the effects be?
9. Are you ready to be an example of that peace and joy to draw others into My service?
10. Does serenity so permeate your humanity that others notice it?
11. What else have you learned about your relationship with Me?

Taking Resolute Action: Jesus, this is one thing I need to change in my life, to take action on: (write it down). Please grant me the strength and grace to do it now.

Day 20

No Gaining Heaven Without This New Language

(September 2, 2003 II)

Out of love, You have reached out to us at this moment in time in a most unusual way, to turn our hearts toward You and rescue us from ourselves. These words of Yours, these "lessons in love" as You call them, have had a profound effect on my life, my Lord.

I can see that reading and contemplating them repeatedly in Your Presence has transformed my mind, heart, and soul. As with everything, repetition builds competence. Your way of thinking becomes my way of thinking, Your perspective becomes my perspective.

And Your perspective is that love and sacrifice are almost the same thing. To love is to be willing to sacrifice. The gauge of the depth of my own Heavenly perspective is how closely love and sacrifice are connected in my own life. The greater my love, the greater the sacrifice I am willing or even desire to take on.

THAT FLAME IN YOUR HEART? TURN IT INTO A BLOWTORCH!

I find that I cannot just read these words of Yours like a book. Some days, I read only a few sentences and have to stop to contemplate them for long periods. Sometimes for days. Though I have gone through this Volume many times before, each re-reading continues to reveal something new as I descend to greater depths of understanding, or rather, I should say to greater heights of illumination.

But that should come as no surprise. It is the Heart of Jesus which is revealed and the Heart of Jesus that I am engaged in dialogue with! So while I think I could read a short bit of this Volume every day for the rest of my life and be filled by it, I know that in Heaven I will have no need to read. I will have all of eternity to engage in dialogue with the infinite and unfathomable expanse of the Heart of Jesus! The thought fills me with joy!

What does it take to reach Heaven and this eternal dialogue? You point out that, to get there, it will take the acquisition of the Heavenly language, that of virtues. Since I cannot even identify them I have not placed any effort on acquiring them. How can it be that I can claim to be Your follower and not be following Your instructions in this manner?

What is this new language of Heaven that I must learn? What exactly are these Heavenly virtues that You want me to acquire? Unless You identify them to me, I cannot take the next step to desire them. From Your words, You are urging me to plan, work, and sacrifice to acquire:

Love, Patience, Trust, Fortitude, Kindness, Compassion, Humility, Presence to Your Presence, Peace, Joy, Purity, Obedience

These virtues, mostly foreign to me, must become objects of my desire. Therefore, I must keep them ever before me. I am but a common man, mostly lacking in virtue as I have pursued everything but these. The few of these I do possess have come only through great struggle and long periods of pain.

Now, however, You are asking that my disposition toward them change. Now they must become objects of my desire, something that I

DAY 20 NO GAINING HEAVEN WITHOUT THIS NEW LANGUAGE

am willing to work for, to acquire in a proactive way, not just as compensation for loyalty to You during suffering.

Jesus, please place the longing for these virtues in my heart and help me to desire them more. Longing for them will allow me to sacrifice to achieve them, much in the same way as I am willing to sacrifice for the earthly treasures I long for.

Lord, You say that all is going as it should, but at the moment, I see my progress as slow or non-existent, and my offenses are many as I fail in these virtues. Please hurry to teach me these virtues so that I may cease to offend You and Your people. It hurts me to consider the pain I inflict on others by my sin and lack of virtue.

While I accept the flawed nature of my being, it does not make the pain any less. I know that I will offend and hurt those I love most on earth, but that knowledge does not lessen the pain I feel when I hurt another. Please help me to desire these virtues. I know You will not disregard this holy request, and I trust in the timing of Your response.

Your promise that I am destined for great holiness if I remain united to You brings me up short. Great holiness? Who, me? And this promise is for everyone united to you. I hardly know what to think.

Since I do not know the particular way of holiness You have chosen for me, all I can do is keep close to You.

Jesus, I do desire to grow in holiness, but only You can achieve this in me. Since I do not know the particular way of holiness You have chosen for me, all I can do is treasure holiness in my heart and keep close to You. I know that if I stay united to You, doing Your Will in my daily life according to my duties and who You place in my path, You will see to the growth in holiness that You have destined for me.

Therefore, keep me close to You and protect me as You would a delicate growing flower. I trust in Your protection as I keep coming back to that simple prayer: Lord, protect me!

THAT FLAME IN YOUR HEART? TURN IT INTO A BLOWTORCH!

And one of the ways You seek to protect me is to help me see what a fool's errand it is for me to pursue those things which promote others' opinions of me. You go so far as to say their opinions of me are irrelevant! That is a huge challenge to my nature and everything I have worked for and done, especially as a professional. But also in my personal life, in every dimension of my life.

It is all about appearances after all, isn't it? I am a people-pleaser kind of guy. That is what motivates much of my energy and activity. Your wisdom is unassailable here, as others are as fickle as I am and their opinion of me can change in a flash.

And for what purpose do I even bother with this pursuit? So they will like me and affirm me? For someone who has spent so much time and effort on trying to be liked, the goal of indifference to others' opinions is only attainable if You do it in me, Jesus.

Yours is the only opinion that matters because Yours is the only opinion that is consistent and will last through eternity.

I can see, too, that this guidance is a very great protection, because the pursuit of human approval is so dangerous to the soul. It is this pursuit that leads to compromise and certain death. It should be blatantly obvious to me and to any Christian because the Bible is full of examples both of great prophets who ignored human approval and kings and governors who were brought down in their submission to human approval. Pilate and Herod come to mind quickly.

How do I start on this journey so foreign to me? To avoid working at promoting others' opinions of me? This is a place of learning, of going somewhere I have never been before. A new way of living my day-to-day life.

It almost seems that I need to poke others' opinions of me in the eye, in a sense! Like when I wrote that negative review on the web of the nun's book that was promoting homosexuality, masturbation, divorce, and all sorts of disorders. I was shocked at the viciousness of the attacks toward me. It disturbed me to receive such vitriol.

DAY 20 NO GAINING HEAVEN WITHOUT THIS NEW LANGUAGE

I am not one to seek out conflict, but rather avoid it. My growth in holiness, however, means that conflict is certain. It is my growth in the Heavenly virtues that will give me the courage and fortitude I need to face the conflict that inevitably will come when I give voice to the Truth. Lord, only You know the complexities and details of what I need to do as You prepare me for Your continued service.

I am reflecting at the moment on the Love You express for me, and the fact that You are always seeking my "betterment and well-being." And You say You are making my interests Your interests. Really? Let me consider the implications of this for a moment.

This level of caring about me seems unbelievable. It is a degree of intimacy I did not formerly know, or believe. Otherwise, I would have lived much differently. This is a much more personal relationship, one that I had not considered before.

You make my interests Your interests? I always knew You were looking out for me, but I thought it was in a general sense, perhaps like a shepherd for his flock, but not so individually intimate that You would have concern for my unique concerns, my personal interests.

This brings a degree of freedom and relief to me as I ponder the implications of this intimacy! It means I can get very personal about what is going on with me, and You not only listen but have an active interest. I do not need, then, to hold back, but can take all my concerns to You. You are no silent god on a high mountain or lofty structure or in the heavens, but a very personal God who is in intimate relationship with His creation.

And not just You! No, all those in Heaven are working with the people here on earth who are pursuing holiness and Your service. The Church Triumphant is actively working with the Church Militant, pleased at our efforts and intent and guarding our progress.

Do I even know who my Heavenly friends are? Obviously, I cannot know all or even most of them, but many I can know because they are held out to me as examples in their sainthood. Some I have already developed a relationship with. I want to get to know more of them and

THAT FLAME IN YOUR HEART? TURN IT INTO A BLOWTORCH!

develop my relationship so that I can constantly be in a loving conversation with them. Theirs is really the only appreciation I need to seek besides Yours because their appreciation is eternal.

So now I feel that I am part of a greater cohort, a multitude working together, with the advantage that they can see better what I face than I can. I pray for the grace to turn my attention to Heaven often to implore guidance and protection.

Then the sure knowledge that all that happens - crosses, joys, and even my sins that You reveal to me - is for the growth of my soul. I can rest confident that Your loving hand is on my shoulder at all times, no matter what is happening in my life. And all those virtues that I find so elusive are being formed in me ever so surely, like muscle from exercise.

> *Hope means hoping when things are hopeless, or it is no virtue at all.*
>
> *And faith means believing the incredible, or it is no virtue at all.*
>
> - G.K. Chesterton

It seems I can manage to keep that perspective – until I become ill. I have had no patience with illness in the past; I have not tolerated it well when it came to me. For several years I have battled this illness that strikes me down periodically, and it seems to me that my forward progress stalls as I am unable to work or pray and become derailed.

And now I am exhausted most of the time from battling two illnesses at the same time and the pain that keeps me up at night. On top of that to have the two infections that left me drained for many months this year has nearly crushed me.

I know that my job interviews during my illnesses were miserable failures in part because of all the compounded illnesses. Lord, it challenges my peace and serenity and confidence in Your loving care for me.

But despite my suffering I remain hopeful in Your promise to work energetically in my soul and in all those who suffer physical illnesses. I pray to grow in virtue so that when I am more ill in the future, as I

DAY 20 NO GAINING HEAVEN WITHOUT THIS NEW LANGUAGE

inevitably will be, I might accept it willingly and grow in holiness as You desire.

This then, again, is Heaven's language I need to learn, Heaven's virtues, which I seek to desire in my soul:

Love	Patience	Trust	Fortitude	Kindness
Compassion	Humility	Presence to Your Presence		Peace
Joy	Purity	Obedience		

Lord, help me to desire them!

THE POINT: Jesus wants the ultimate best outcome for your life – to join Him in Heaven. He is intervening in the world in a totally new way, in this case, giving you detailed guidance on the virtues necessary to attain Heaven. (As you answer the questions, address your dialogue to Him personally and directly.)

1. When you and I look back on your life from the vantage point of one minute after your death, how do you think you will describe it?
2. Did you have the ultimate best outcome of Heaven as your focus while you lived?
3. At what point did it become the focus?
4. What happened and why? In what way did you see My hand in your life?
5. For each of the virtues, how are you planning, working, and sacrificing to achieve them?
6. Do you believe that you are destined for great holiness if you remain united to Me?
7. Look within carefully: how much time and energy do you spend doing things that will cause others to have a good opinion of you?

THAT FLAME IN YOUR HEART? TURN IT INTO A BLOWTORCH!

8. Do you think the opinion of others is important to Me? Then why do you care about it so much?
9. I can see you striving for those virtues. How much that pleases me! Let's talk about each one! How can I help you as you look at each one?
10. What else have you learned about your relationship with Me?

Taking Resolute Action: Jesus, this is one thing I need to change in my life, to take action on: (write it down). Please grant me the strength and grace to do it now.

Day 21

Oh! Straight Talk from Jesus: Sexual Purity

(September 2, 2003 III)

The lack of purity – impurity – of mind and heart and being surrounds me in the very air of the culture I am forced to live in by my very existence. My attempts to grow in purity are made difficult by this environment, but still I am called to it, and I know You, Jesus, will give me the grace. My travel into New York City each week and teaching there surrounds me with it. It is very up-close and personal – in your face as it were. I am assaulted by it with no way of withdrawing from it.

I am saddened by it, really, because behind the lack of modesty I see such an emptiness and hollowness. A desire to be appealing and desirable, I suppose. And, I think, they are mostly unaware of what they are doing and their offense against You, Jesus.

For my part, I am resolute: I cannot tolerate any impurity in any form in me or my family. Nurture modesty in private and in public. I need to be bold in my defense of modesty. If the speech of others around me is not pure, I must not tolerate it, but correct it or walk away.

THAT FLAME IN YOUR HEART? TURN IT INTO A BLOWTORCH!

Impurity has so contaminated the very environment that it has poisoned everything I have taken into myself. It is a carcinogen that has caused a cancer to grow in every fiber of my being. My only hope is to purge my being of me and let You, Christ, become more and more in me as I become less and less in me. You, through Your Love, will burn out the cancerous growth as You heal me and restore my innocence to the original state You created.

> *Your original intent was that man live in complete harmony with You and all of creation, in peace and joy and fullness of knowledge and understanding. All that mankind desires from his depth was contained in Your original intent.*

It is the beauty of Your original intent that You desire to reveal to the world in a new way as You use the words of these Volumes. Your desire is not just for man to avoid certain actions. Rather, You want to draw man's heart from the emptiness of self-gratification displayed by impurity to that which he was created for in the first place.

Your original intent was that man live in complete harmony with You and all of creation, in peace and joy and fullness of knowledge and understanding. All that mankind desires from his depth was contained in Your original intent. Your call to purity is just the removal of impurity that has as its focus self-gratification, so that man can refocus on the beauty contained in Your original intent at the beginning of creation.

> *Your call to purity is just the removal of impurity that has as its focus self-gratification, so that man can refocus on the beauty contained in Your original intent at the beginning of creation.*

What must that have been, my Lord? Before You even knitted together the fabric of creation, You knew it. From the "womb" You called it forth in majestic beauty. What awesome intent You must have had for mankind, to have created for him the entirety of the universe!

The contemplation of it, even the slightest part of it, overwhelms my limited mind and heart at this moment as I pause

DAY 21 OH! STRAIGHT TALK FROM JESUS: SEXUAL PURITY

to consider it. As beauty attracts me and I stop to look over the beauty of Your creation, I cannot help but be attracted to it, drawn to it, and captured by it.

From there to consider the incomprehensible extent of the beauty of Your original intent for mankind and all of creation leaves me breathless and even overloads my emotions and heart! Considering that, how could I be drawn to anything of lesser attractiveness, particularly something fleeting, empty, and hollow?

You came to restore mankind, to heal in Your great mercy and give us back that which was lost, our relationship with You. And open the way to Heaven where Your original intent will be fully revealed, and we can enjoy all that You had meant for us in the first place.

The necessary gate through which we must pass in order to be open to see with clarity is the gate of purity. Without that, we are unable to see as our focus is on the wrong thing; the vision is clouded and we are condemned to wander through the maze of life.

No heart can be divided and be drawn to You solely as it was created to be. The true beauty of Your original intent can only be contemplated in the manner it was intended by You: with a purity of heart and mind. Then, unpolluted, the soul is drawn to You, to the beauty of Your original intent and the beauty of what You are doing now to restore the world as You engage it more actively than ever.

Breathtaking! Magnificent! Overwhelming! Awesome! Mighty God! Come! Restore us!

I am held riveted by the contemplation. It is hard to even move on, so much do I want to stay in this moment of ecstasy. It fills my mind and heart with wonder! What must it be to see with Heavenly vision?

Purity of mind and heart and soul is requisite to that contemplation. The pollution of impurity makes it impossible.

But how do I start off with a "clean slate" my Lord? I have tried asking for Your forgiveness and tried to forget my past offenses. It did not work. I was quickly overcome again by my memories and behaviors. It did not last.

THAT FLAME IN YOUR HEART? TURN IT INTO A BLOWTORCH!

The true beauty of Your original intent can only be contemplated in the manner it was intended by You:
with a purity of heart and mind.

The only way I have found is to turn again and again to Your sacraments which have continued to sustain me. And the precursor to purity of heart, mind, and soul is the acknowledgement of my sins, asking for forgiveness and receiving absolution in the great gift of Confession.

I am assured by the power invested in the priest and by Your words: "…and whose sins you shall forgive they are forgiven…" that my sins are truly wiped away. My soul for that moment is as pure and clean as when I was baptized.

Ah, what joy I feel each time I go to Confession! No lingering doubts or recriminations are possible. Neither my mind nor my emotions hold any sway over that conviction. No torment. There cannot be, otherwise I would be guilty of not believing You.

Jesus, I trust You more than I trust myself because I know that I am just a weak human being. I trust that my sins are forgiven and my soul wiped clean by the sacrament of Confession like nothing else can possibly do. Jesus I do believe! Christ, through Your Church You have wiped my soul clean. Purity is mine for the moment and grace from the sacrament is there to help me maintain it.

Now I can go to Mass and receive You in the Eucharist with a completely pure and clean soul, a thing of blazing beauty because it is Your beautiful creation! You made it so! What joy to receive You in that way!

A soul of blazing beauty receiving its Creator of blazing beauty! Experience draws me to repeat it! Then more grace comes to me to sustain me in my walk. And clearer vision to see Your Presence in Your creation around me.

Who would not want that jewel, that shimmering light, that pure simple joy in their life? Only those who have no awareness of what lies underneath the veil of dullness brought on by sin.

DAY 21 OH! STRAIGHT TALK FROM JESUS: SEXUAL PURITY

For now I am blessed to have a confessor readily available and daily Mass as often as I want and can make it. You have provided so well for me, my Lord, and I am truly grateful for these gifts. I can receive the sacraments as often as I choose, which was not always the case in my life. I am saddened that so many do not have the opportunity I have, and many who do, will not avail themselves. Truly, Father, forgive the latter ones for they do not know what they are doing or missing.

Purity of soul is expressed in purity of speech. My speech reveals my heart – and where is my heart? You know the tree by its fruits. One can almost look into the very soul of another by what comes from his or her mouth. The depth of the heart is revealed in the words uttered by the person. It is how we are known by others.

How am I known by others, Lord? What do they hear from my lips? Only You know all the dimensions of my heart and who I truly am. I will never get that from another person because they are incapable of knowing me completely, no matter who they are in my life. So, how am I known by the quality and content of my speech?

Jesus, You excite my heart and my being, and my speech reflects that. You are my Joy! I have come a long way, Lord, as this was not always the case. I blush to even think of it. Now my mind and heart are filled with You. You and the mission have become my preoccupation even as I work, take care of my children, and live my station in life. It is not that I have attained the goal of perfectly reflecting You and Heaven in my speech, for old habits die hard. But I am ever vigilant with Your grace.

Why do I tolerate so much of the impurity that surrounds me? Isn't it because at some level it feels good? The impurity of speech, video, music, the arts, etc., appeals to my sensuality and makes me feel good for the moment. It attracts me and draws me in. Or is it because I have become so accustomed to seeing and hearing it that I have become complacent?

And too, I am fearful of speaking up. I still want people to like me and appreciate me. I am fearful of being unpopular. I was unpopular as a child and it hurt. I don't want more of that.

THAT FLAME IN YOUR HEART? TURN IT INTO A BLOWTORCH!

Then, at some point in the past, I also knew that speaking up could have a negative effect on me professionally, even threatening my income. I was too fearful in those instances of speaking up because I did not want the disapproval of peers and superiors. I wanted desperately to get along, be part of the crowd, and enjoy their approval.

What terrible immaturity! How could I? Look at what I have wrought by my immaturity and cowardice! Lord, forgive me! As I look at it, I do not condemn myself or hold myself in contempt as I might have in the past. I see my failings for what they were in truth and rejoice that You have brought me out of that, to maturity and courage. I rest in Your forgiveness and Love. I am confident of Your Love for me, so I can boldly proclaim outrage in Your Name and as I do it, the grace to grow will come to me.

I know the attacks of Satan here in the area of impure thoughts very well, and I am aware that the more I strive for purity, the more he will attack me with temptations of impurity.

Memories. So often something will trigger a memory, and as I remember, my mind wanders into an area it should not go. It is a natural occurrence and forces an act of the will on my part to refocus my attention. I have often thought how wonderful it would have been if I had pursued You, Lord, with purity of mind and heart from my earliest days. Then I would not have been burdened and even tormented by these memories that cause my thoughts to wander into impurity.

Would that I had known what a millstone around my neck they would be that I must carry the rest of my days. It has made my striving for holiness unnecessarily more difficult than it should have been. Partly because of that, I have always been hyper vigilant with my children, trying to keep them as innocent in this environment as possible.

From this perspective, having struggled with this terribly, I have come to the conclusion that allowing children to be exposed to any kind of impurity is a terrible form of child abuse. It plants memories and feelings in the depths of their souls, and they have no ability to rid themselves of these things. It makes any later attempt at growth in holiness much more difficult.

DAY 21 OH! STRAIGHT TALK FROM JESUS: SEXUAL PURITY

This is my struggle and only You, my God, have the ability to help me overcome these obstacles. It is totally outside my capabilities as a human being. I can assert my will, but only You have the grace to allow me to carry through.

When I consider this battle and what You are asking, Lord, I must know the vulnerabilities of my frail humanity. In detail. Thanks be to God, when tempted or attacked, I am turning ever more quickly to You for protection. What joy! Jesus, You are my only defense for my purity.

I have gone along with this culture of impurity too easily and for too long. I have even accepted my own failings and denied my offenses, not wanting to face the truth. Jesus, help me to be very attentive to You in this area. Thanks be to God for Your generosity to me in this! I cannot even look back to my past as I become overwhelmed with grief at my offenses toward You, offenses which threaten to washed me away from You like a great tidal wave.

Thanks be to You, Jesus, for Your mercy knows no bounds! I can give You, dearest Jesus, the burdens and sins of my soul for You have purchased my freedom with Your Blood!

It is no hopeless cause, climbing this mountain of holiness. I have You drawing me there more and more, and as I climb, I feel the pull toward You become stronger and stronger. Toward Heaven. Toward the contemplation of the beauty of Your original intent. Toward the meditation of the mercy of the Father in Your sacrifice on the Cross. All pull me, tug at me, draw me, attract me. It is as it should be. It should not be other than this. "When I am lifted up, I will draw all mankind to Me." And so You are, my Lord! And so You are.

> *Virtue is not the absence of vices or the avoidance of moral dangers;*
>
> *virtue is a vivid and separate thing ...*
>
> *Chastity [therefore] does not mean abstention from sexual wrong;*
>
> *it means something flaming, like Joan of Arc.*
>
> - G.K. Chesterton

THAT FLAME IN YOUR HEART? TURN IT INTO A BLOWTORCH!

One last thought, my Jesus. When I read the words that You so much appreciate my obedience and service that every effort will be rewarded, I felt grateful. But when I read that, when I finally come before You and my sins are presented to You, You will turn Your head away from them, I cried with joy and gratitude from the bottom of my heart!

Each time I reread this, Lord, it causes me to cry in gratitude. Thank You, my dear Jesus, for your mercy knows no bounds! Lord, You know all my sins and You know how poor are my attempts to serve You and obey You. And still You would do this, You would treat me this well? Surely Your mercy knows no bounds! "Rest in peace" has a new dimension of meaning for me!

Sing praises, my soul! Sing His praises!

THE POINT: At least one of the saints, it is said, was told by Jesus that more people go to hell for sins of sexual impurity than all the rest combined. Here Jesus tells us that purity is exceedingly rare in the world! And that He holds you accountable for your actions no matter what the environment is that you live in – there are no excuses for impurity. These messages are very challenging because of our tolerance of impurity and our own habitual impurity. (As you answer the questions, address your dialogue to Him personally and directly.)

1. In what ways are you habitually impure in dress, speech, thought, and in what you do for entertainment?
2. What are your weaknesses in each of those areas?
3. What needs to change in each of those areas? What do you need to avoid?
4. Are you sensitive to the triggers which prompt temptations for you?
5. How do you handle temptations?
6. Do you call out to Me in your temptations? Why not?

DAY 21 OH! STRAIGHT TALK FROM JESUS: SEXUAL PURITY

7. Do you stand up against impurity in all its forms that are so offensive to Me and defend purity and modesty?
8. What else have you learned about your relationship with Me?

Taking Resolute Action: Jesus, this is one thing I need to change in my life, to take action on: (write it down). Please grant me the strength and grace to do it now.

Day 22

A New Twist: Two Obligations of Love of Neighbor

(September 3, 2003)

Jesus, as I read this section devoted to love of neighbor, I am struck by the fact that You divide it into two clearly distinct topics. The first, and I note the order, is the value You place on each soul whom You specifically place here on earth. And valuing them means You intend that each of them be adequately fed – by those of us who have enough to eat. The second is love of neighbor through forgiveness, compassion, and mercy toward everyone who has been a part of my life in any way.

Humanly, I think it is easier to express love of neighbor in the first way than the second. All people of good will can see suffering and be moved to alleviate it. But the second form of poverty, destitution, and hunger is harder to see and address as it calls me to examine myself much more carefully. Both kinds of people are starving for want of love from me.

THAT FLAME IN YOUR HEART? TURN IT INTO A BLOWTORCH!

Jesus, I know that each and every soul you create is placed here with deliberate intent, no matter what the circumstances, and is loved and valued by You. How can I begin to appreciate and know their value to You if I do not know my own value to You? Do I know how precious I really am to You, my Jesus, and how valuable I am to You? If I did fully, I would be constantly ecstatic. Therefore, my conclusion is that I do not fully appreciate how much You value each person, starting with me. Why is that?

> *Next to the Blessed Sacrament itself, your neighbor is the holiest object presented to your senses.*
>
> - C.S. Lewis

I need look no further than the condition of my own soul to begin to understand. I learned my value as a person from my parents initially and later from those around me. As good as they might have been, all were flawed human beings, incapable of perfectly reflecting You.

And so it is with me. My perception of my value to You is based on both how I felt I was valued by others and how I feel I value others. The latter comes into sharp focus as I become more and more aware of who You are and my own sinful condition. Because of that, I have rejected love: first, the love of others in my hurt and desire to protect myself, and second, Your Love as an extension of that.

"Love thy neighbor as thyself" is a big disconnect. No love of self, no love of neighbor. Little love of self, little love of neighbor. Oh, it is easy enough to be perceived by others as generous, loving, and giving, but the true test is in these two areas You are addressing.

Love of self. I have been an expert at self-hate from my earliest days. The abuse I suffered by others I blamed on myself. Often I contemplated and planned suicide. I hid my anger and depression in extraversion and being a comic. Many times I watched as I saw my body lying on the ground and myself kicking it unmercifully in anger and hatred for being who I was.

DAY 22 A NEW TWIST: TWO OBLIGATIONS OF LOVE OF NEIGHBOR

Many times I have hated myself vehemently. Enough to want to kill the person who is me. Lord, You know the full expression of my struggle could fill volumes as I pour it out to You. It breaks my heart to think of it now, I am so filled with remorse and sorrow at my pathetic state back then. How it must have hurt You, my Jesus. I am so sorry for my offense, tears well up within me.

But out of Your great Love, You intervened in my life! You taught me to accept Your Mercy and Your Love. It has come at times in great leaps and profound events, and at other times, it has come slowly with great struggle on my part to let go and understand.

Never have You abandoned my side, my Jesus! You have held me close though I have turned from You many times in the struggle, and I think You held me even closer in those times, perhaps because I had let go of You. It is "easier" for You when we are both holding on to each other and I am not fighting You, I am sure!

Out of the depths of the dark pit You have drawn me into the Light, the Light of Your Love! As I grow in the sure knowledge of Your Love, my love for all the souls of Your creation grows. That love is growing in me, by Your grace, into a passion for others, a love that is burning within that seeks to express itself in some way to each soul that You bring to my awareness, whether in person, communication, or in thought.

> *As I grow in the sure knowledge of Your Love, my love for all the souls of Your creation grows.*

Knowing how much You love me, if I have any humility at all, I realize how precious and valuable all of my brothers and sisters are, and love them as You do. Not only the ones who are low in worldly opinion but those on high as well who are so easy to disdain.

As You discuss hunger and starvation, Lord, it stings. Years later, I can still see You in the face of that poor woman and her little child huddled on the ground as I walked by in a hurry to keep up with the other business people I was with. And the old couple in the grocery store who

THAT FLAME IN YOUR HEART? TURN IT INTO A BLOWTORCH!

wanted only part of the package of bread rolls because it was all they had money for. The memories haunt me. It hurts to think of their suffering.

You bring a situation to my attention because You want me to DO something. You say I have a role in this. Jesus, may the seeing or hearing of hunger of another bring me up short when it comes to my attention. At the least, I need to fast regularly, to offer my little cross for the hungry, to know a little of their suffering and contribute as best I can.

Jesus, please show me what more I can do to help those who hunger. Here are the things I think You are asking of me at a minimum: pray, contribute, fast, beg for them, make their plight known, serve them.

This age is one of great selfishness and great waste. I am appalled at the degree of waste I see all around me, even in good people who are Your followers for the most part. It is the age of consumption and throw away, heedless of the Lazarus's who lie at our doors.

It is not just the food which alone is enough to condemn this age, but the consumption of all material things. I can see it in myself. Jesus, please reveal my disorder in this to me more and more each day. Give me the grace to correct this gross disorder which disregards the desperate needs of others for the satiation of my wants and pleasures.

The second part of love of neighbor – forgiveness for those who have offended or hurt me – is more under my control, at least as far as being able to do my part. It is also, I think, much harder for me. It means I need to carefully look within in a completely truthful way, to ask You to shine a light in the darkness and illuminate for me what You see there.

Lord, in my frail humanity, I know I have buried a lot for a variety of unimportant reasons. What is critical to my spiritual growth and development is that

> *It is the age of consumption and throw away, heedless of the Lazarus's who lie at our doors. It is not just the food which alone is enough to condemn this age, but the consumption of all material things. I can see it in myself.*

DAY 22 A NEW TWIST: TWO OBLIGATIONS OF LOVE OF NEIGHBOR

I can harbor nothing. No resentment, bitterness, anger, hurt, or offense can linger in the depths of my heart. All needs to be exposed like a cancer that is X-rayed and then, by Your grace, surgically removed.

How could it be otherwise? It is certain that I cannot enter the gates of Heaven with any of that harbored in my soul. None of it. Not a tiny remnant. There is only one Will in Heaven and that is Your Will alone. And Your Will is the innocence of purity of heart, mind, and soul that harbors nothing which is against Your Will.

When I think about those whom I dislike or those who have caused me hurt or pain, there are so many. What does that say about the poor state of my soul? And there are persons I know and those I do not know personally whom I just encountered along the way. Jesus, help me to search my mind, heart, and soul for any bitterness or judgment toward another. Shine Your compassionate light in my soul and illuminate every corner of it! Hide nothing from me that You need me to address in Your good timing.

As you have poured mercy, love, compassion, and forgiveness on me, Lord, help me to pour it out on all in my life, past, present, and future. Help me to be aware of Your Presence in each soul. As I encounter souls in my day, I pray for the grace to carry out Heaven's task for them, whether it be just a look in the eye and a smile acknowledging their soul, or something more specific. Jesus, what a delightful toil this part of Heaven's work is! It brings me joy!

And even though I believe I am acting with a pure heart and my actions are pure as I seek to serve You alone, I realize that my humanity is so broken from sin that my heart and actions are <u>not</u> totally pure. I can deceive myself. Some degree of self finds its way into my best intentions. Thanks be to God for Your patience, mercy, and Love for me!

I will seek a pure mind, heart, and spirit in poverty, realizing I have no power to achieve such beautiful riches. I shall beg You, my God, for Your generosity to provide them for me! I know You will make me rich in this way if I persist in asking! How great is that?! I can have what I want

THAT FLAME IN YOUR HEART? TURN IT INTO A BLOWTORCH!

knowing You desire to give it to me. And then I will do my best to serve You with every fiber of my being, every moment of my day!

Serve Him with gladness, oh my soul!

THE POINT: Jesus pointedly tells you that you have two obligations with regard to love of neighbor: first, you have a role in feeding the hungry, and second, you have an obligation to forgive everyone in your life no matter what has happened to you. (As you answer the questions, address your dialogue to Him personally and directly.)

1. With regard to the first, do you know what I am asking of you to feed the hungry? Have you asked Me?
2. What specifically is the role you think I want for you in this area?
3. Have you ever considered "begging for the poor" by promoting a particular cause or charity that serves the poor?
4. Are you wasteful of food? Would the starving want what you throw out?
5. Can't you order less, fix less, or use leftovers? Tell Me your plans.
6. What is the root of your carelessness about food? Is it thoughtlessness, habit, pride, arrogance ("I only deserve the best"), or something else?
7. What do you think My attitude is, Who suffered hunger in My family's poverty, toward what you do with food?
8. With regard to forgiveness, as you think about everyone in your life, who is the person you most need to forgive?
9. Why do you need to forgive him or her? What makes it hard? Have you asked Me for help?
10. Can you do that for everyone who needs your forgiveness, just as I do for you?

DAY 22 A NEW TWIST: TWO OBLIGATIONS OF LOVE OF NEIGHBOR

11. Sometimes the people closest to you need forgiveness for a thousand offenses. Can you offer them forgiveness?
12. What holds you back, My child?
13. I see your generosity and your charity toward others and it delights Me to no end! Can you celebrate what you have done and build on that with My guidance?
14. What else have you learned about your relationship with Me?

Taking Resolute Action: Jesus, this is one thing I need to change in my life, to take action on: (write it down). Please grant me the strength and grace to do it now.

Day 23

A Life Not Examined is a Life Not Truly Lived

(September 3, 2003 II)

"You can tell a tree by its fruits" (Mt. 7:20). The fruits of my life are seen in my actions. Purity of actions spring from purity of intentions which are the fruits of purity of heart, mind, and spirit. Jesus, when I look back at many of the choices of my life that ended in pain and suffering for me or for others, I must admit that many times my motives were not pure. No, I had underneath the choice a desire to gain some advantage for myself.

How many times in those instances I was a fake: my outward actions looked good to observers, but underneath, I had an intent quite different and often it was to my advantage. Somewhere along the way, the fruits of my dishonest intent became clear and revealed themselves in consequences that were negative for either me or someone else.

It is hard enough to have a positive outcome of actions when my intent is good. It is hopeless when my intent can only be called evil because it contains an element of selfishness. This is never more clearly demonstrated than in my own family.

THAT FLAME IN YOUR HEART? TURN IT INTO A BLOWTORCH!

> *The reality is that I cannot harbor anything within me that is for self. Only in poverty of spirit and humility will I be focused on serving You alone.*

The reality is that I cannot harbor anything within me that is for self. Only in poverty of spirit and humility will I be focused on serving You alone. Jesus, help me to focus on Your Will and what You are asking of me, and be detached from the results which are Yours, since I do not know what results You wanted from my cooperation with Your will.

That is a big transition for me, Lord. You know my nature: I determine everything I do based on the outcome I want. I am a driven person, a "Type A" personality, and so I want what I want when I want it, and nothing else will satisfy me. Even the "holy" things I undertake.

I must seek Your Will first and foremost in everything, before I form the intent and act upon it. I must learn to let go of the results because they are Your business.

Whoa! I need a miracle of grace to transform this nature, which has hardened over so many years. I am not a young person any more, but my heart is young and pliable and formable by its intense love for You!

May You have Your way with me, and may I be open to a complete revolution in my soul. "May it be done unto me according to Thy Will." Mary, I look to you to intercede on my behalf, that God may grant this holy request. I trust because in the words of Gabriel, "…nothing is impossible for God."

I see that this requires some changes in my lifestyle as I am a very high-energy person. I like to have a lot going on; it is hectic at times, but invigorating mostly. High octane living. It results in a great deal of unnecessary stress many times, though. In my independence and hurried lifestyle, my tendency is to make decisions on my own. Yet, I can look back on my life and see the futility of those actions.

Why do I persist in such futile and even destructive behavior, my Jesus? Such a sinful nature! So I see the necessity of moving through life in a calm, peaceful, deliberate, and reflective manner.

DAY 23 A LIFE NOT EXAMINED IS A LIFE NOT TRULY LIVED

You want me to be able to "walk in gladness with a light and happy spirit." And why do You want that for me? You have said it. First, You want me to be joyful and happy for my own sake, because You love me and want my good. And secondly, because if I am to serve Your Kingdom, I can only attract people to You and the Good News if I have a joyful disposition.

I want to cooperate fully with You in moving in this direction, so that my life can quickly be filled with this joy, just as You want it to be. To get there, I need to discern the circumstances of my living here and now, each and every action of mine, in particular my habits.

...a life not examined is a life not truly lived. Jesus, help me to truly live! Help me to examine my life!

Somewhere I read a paraphrase of Socrates, "A life unexamined is a life not worth living." Perhaps it might be better stated, that a life not examined is a life not truly lived. Jesus, help me to truly live! Help me to examine my life! Jesus, help me to be open to the Spirit of Discernment! Come, Lord Jesus!

Lord, my heart has only wanted to do what I felt and thought You were asking of me in the biggest decisions of my life – but they were mostly made with a focus on the earthly outcome. I am excited by the prospect of remaking my decision process to focus only on the Heavenly outcome! Jesus, grant me the grace! Lord, help my sole focus to be on the Heavenly path You desire for me.

Let us begin now, not in the future; break into my life now, dearest Jesus. Today I will begin making each of my decisions focusing on the Heavenly outcome. Tomorrow I will begin anew again. And the day after that...

Knowing that You, Jesus, have chosen my crosses for my humility and growth in holiness gives me delight, even as I am tired and exhausted. In caring for my son last night, I was so tired that I could hardly function at all. I could feel the frustration rising in me and sensed the shortness wanting to exert itself with him. I had to fight an intense battle within to

THAT FLAME IN YOUR HEART? TURN IT INTO A BLOWTORCH!

remain loving, though I know I fell short in that, as I could not muster up the happy face I know he needed right then.

As I reflect on it, I think that I learned a valuable lesson. I was preoccupied by my own interests, including the news of the day on TV, which had been momentous. I can see now Your wisdom is exactly what I need, my Jesus. Focus the intent of my actions on the Heavenly outcome, which in this case was to serve You by serving my son.

Knowing that You, Jesus, have chosen my crosses for my humility and growth in holiness gives me delight, even as I am tired and exhausted.

Had I done that, I know the grace to be more loving and tolerant and supportive of him, with all his deficits and needs, would have come much easier. The outcome of the evening would have been much different. Selfishness on my part raised its ugly head once again. It was a huge interior struggle to make sure he went to bed happy in the end and was not left with me being short.

I think, my Lord, that as pure as I want my intentions and actions to be, to focus on Heavenly outcomes, my nature is so very flawed that it seems self-interest permeates everything I do. Self-interest is like a monstrous octopus: when I cut off one tentacle of selfishness, ten more grow in its place and wrap around me, suffocating my attempts to defeat it.

As soon as I think I did something with a pure motive, I am shocked by the revelation of a part of me that was looking for something from it. Will this ever cease? Thank You for Your reassurances that it is effort that counts and not outcomes, otherwise I would despair for sure. Instead, I am heartened and strengthened to keep trying, and I am more wary of my flawed nature, which will always have its interests first.

So I operate by the Spirit, looking to You for the motives You want me to have in all my actions. Those motives I can trust, even if I am unable to give them full expression.

I can see how lovingly You designed my crosses, in particular this one, to be exactly what my soul needs to be perfected. Nothing else

DAY 23 A LIFE NOT EXAMINED IS A LIFE NOT TRULY LIVED

could fit so well. It gets to the core of my being, my weakness, and where I need to develop quickly and efficiently. I am filled with joy to know that You care enough to fashion each cross for me so that I can share intimately in Your work and Heaven's goals.

I pray for the grace to fully accept each cross You give me, and the grace, too, to desire more out of love for You. And also, I will continue to take You at Your word and beg You to relieve the crosses that seem to be crushing me.

Perhaps, Lord, what I also need to learn is that in those instances in which they are not lifted from me, I need to work harder at understanding Your perspective. Your intent is for me to be open to having the weight lifted from me though the cross remains, by being open to a revolution in my thinking. By being open to Your grace and to the Spirit.

In You alone, Lord, I find my solace, comfort, strength, and joy! I can go nowhere else to pour out my heart! No one can do anything about my crosses but You! In You I confide my pain and sorrows, not in anger, railing against my God, but in poverty, begging for Your help and mercy in dealing with them. And to be given the grace of Heavenly perspective – how You and Heaven see my crosses and suffering and the state of my soul in dealing with them.

I pray for the grace to be given "the eyes of Heaven" that I might see and hear as You see and hear – that I might respond with Your Heart. Yes, dear Jesus, I will except this gift in the totality You give it. It has already begun to change me as my crosses and suffering have become occasions of joy at times.

> *On the last day,*
>
> *when the general examination takes place,*
>
> *there will be no question at all on the text of Aristotle,*
>
> *the aphorisms of Hippocrates,*
>
> *or the paragraphs of Justinian.*
>
> *Charity will be the whole syllabus.*
>
> *- St. Robert Bellarmine*

THAT FLAME IN YOUR HEART? TURN IT INTO A BLOWTORCH!

Jesus, my answer is "yes" with every fiber of my being! The whole focus of my life and heart is Heaven, where I will be soon. I realize too, Lord, that my yes in this moment will be challenged by the weakness of my nature, by temptation and suffering. Jesus, help me to be firm and constant in my commitment. I delight in talking to You in every moment as I live my day!

Come, Holy Spirit! Fill the hearts of Your faithful and enkindle in them the fire of Your Love! Amen!

THE POINT: Jesus wants very much for you to see your own life and the whole world from His perspective, with His vision. To do that, however, requires that we have Heaven's intent in all our thoughts and behaviors. Our intentions and actions must be pure and not motivated by self-interest, as much as humanly possible. (As you answer the questions, address your dialogue to Him personally and directly.)

1. My child, be honest and forthright with Me: how much of your intentions are motivated by self-interest, what is in it for you, or what you can gain?
2. Can you discern the purity of your motives?
3. Isn't there a thread of self-interest, an impure motive as it were, in the best of your intentions and actions? Is there more than you would like to admit to Me?
4. Can you examine your motives and decisions with Me now and talk to Me about it?
5. What would it mean in your life if all your intentions and actions had My intent in them? Describe it to Me.
6. Are you making progress in seeing with the eyes of Heaven, in seeing with My perspective?
7. How does that affect your heart, your motivations, and intentions?

DAY 23 A LIFE NOT EXAMINED IS A LIFE NOT TRULY LIVED

8. Can you sense My joy at your progress? How does that make you feel?
9. What else have you learned about your relationship with Me?

Taking Resolute Action: Jesus, this is one thing I need to change in my life, to take action on: (write it down). Please grant me the strength and grace to do it now.

Day 24

The Secrets to Your True Success Revealed

(September 3, 2003 III)

Lord, as I sit here in Your Presence this morning and measure the state of my being, I am filled with emptiness and pain. They pierce my heart like a spear! As beautiful as Your creation is, as I look out on it in these early morning hours, with all the natural beauty of the setting, I still feel an emptiness and longing.

It is not that I am not grateful for all that You have given me. You know that my gratitude for where I am is boundless. No, the emptiness I feel and the pain I am in cannot be satisfied by anything that I can humanly appreciate. Winning the lottery would not satisfy me; when I was making more money than I knew what to do with, I had the same emptiness.

You know the emptiness because You created it in me, just as You have for every soul You have created and will create. This is an emptiness that only You can fill with the joy of Your Presence. The emptiness, the

THAT FLAME IN YOUR HEART? TURN IT INTO A BLOWTORCH!

> *We tend to set up success in Christian work as our purpose,*
>
> *but our purpose should be to display the glory of God in human life,*
>
> *to live a life "hidden with Christ in God" in our everyday human conditions.*
>
> - Oswald Chambers

longing You created, is meant to cause me to search, to seek You out and not rest until I find You.

It is not that all the prayers that I said this morning, contemplating Your Word in the liturgy of the day, was useless. Certainly I find You every time I open the Word of Scripture. But on some days, the state of my humanity gets in the way of "being" with You, though in faith I know I am with You.

Such was the start of this day. But prayer is efficacious. I know that only through prayer can I keep my heart open and waiting for You, "as the watchman waits for daybreak" (Psalm 130:6). The benefit, the result of my prayer, is Your doing, not mine.

I know, however, that I must keep a guard over my interior, including my emotional dispositions where the evil one can so easily enter and play. In suffering, it is easy for me to fall into all kinds of emotional traps that preoccupy my heart and hinder my ability to keep it open to You.

The joy I long for, and have tasted from Heaven's graces, is blocked by bitterness and distress to the degree I harbor them. I pray that You, my Jesus, would heal every trace of bitterness in my soul – known and unknown to me – that I might be filled with joy and the ability to love as You love!

Ah, to love without barriers, without bounds and restrictions, to love as You love! In that way, my soul takes flight and soars to the heights of Heaven! The joys of Heaven touch my inmost being and I am lifted up! Lord, I am not worthy. Only say the word and I shall be healed! Run, do not walk! Fill the longing of my heart.

There is no failure in a relationship with You, no matter how it looks externally, because I know that You only will my good and want an

DAY 24 THE SECRETS TO YOUR TRUE SUCCESS REVEALED

intimate relationship with me. Let me drop all those defenses I have put up as a result of my pain from human interactions. I have transferred those to our relationship and they have not served me well – only blocked my responses to Your many advances to help me.

Ah, to love without barriers,
without bounds and restrictions, to love as You love!
In that way, my soul takes flight
and soars to the heights of Heaven!
The joys of Heaven touch my inmost being and I am lifted up!

I will forget the past failures of trying to give myself to You and the fear of failing again so that I can give myself completely. Otherwise, I would look back on past efforts and failures with cynicism or humiliation which are not from You.

I do not know the reasons even now for those failures, if they were failures, but I can see that, had I achieved success, that in itself would have been the problem. I cannot achieve success in relationship with You. I can only persist and give You the results.

Perhaps the failures were successes from Heaven's viewpoint. Pride and selfishness lurk ever beside me, crouched, waiting for the slightest opening to pounce and take root even in the holiest of intentions.

Looking back on past failures with human eyes and values can be a trap of Satan, not just my weakness. It is the same with the "failure" of You, Jesus, at the Crucifixion. Your sacrifice from the human point of view certainly looked like a disastrous end, a dismal failure to all who witnessed or heard about it. The more I am in unity with You, the more I see with Your eyes the truth and reality of my own life.

Lord, I have tried <u>so</u> hard to put Your Will first in my life as I make decisions, but when I look back on my life from my perspective I see total and complete failure in every aspect of my life. It seems I am a failure worth nothing to anyone on earth.

The overwhelming amount of my interactions here on earth have been rejections, even more so in these last few years. I often feel like a

THAT FLAME IN YOUR HEART? TURN IT INTO A BLOWTORCH!

leper as I seek to make a living and live my station in life. Or like a prisoner, I cannot live my life freely or be myself, but must conform to the needs and expectations of the "cell" I occupy in my circumstances.

So it is with wonder that I dare to grow in unity with You and dare to accept Your invitation to re-examine my life from Your perspective. You constantly amaze me, my dear Jesus!

Each day I wake to begin anew, to start fresh with You. Then both my excitement and longing for You grows, both joy and heartache!

Lift high the banners of love!

(Christian song)

What beauty there is in a relationship with You! What a joy it is to consider that my heartache for You will grow from a little, poor, occasional experience to a dominant force occupying my every moment and thought until we meet in Heaven! Jesus, help my longing for You to grow! May I be totally consumed by it!

Come, Lord Jesus, come! Fill the hearts of Your faithful!

THE POINT: The desire for success in our lives has been planted there by God; therefore, it is not surprising that we all want it. In our sinful condition, we strive for human success: we distort a divine desire. The success God intends is Heavenly success, which may or may not bring human success, depending on His Will for us. And Heavenly success is God's doing if our desire is to do His Will. (As you answer the questions, address your dialogue to Him personally and directly.)

1. What is the focus of your desire for success?
2. I guarantee success if you abandon and surrender yourself into My Love. How do you take this guarantee?
3. What sort of successes do you want in your life?

DAY 24 THE SECRETS TO YOUR TRUE SUCCESS REVEALED

4. Can you write down the top ten successes you desire? How do they serve My Kingdom?
5. Can you let go of your past failures or do you still condemn yourself for them?
6. How do you feel about being a success in My eyes?
7. Is the longing for My Presence growing in your heart? Can you feel it?
8. Can you encourage it? Can you shout "Yes!" within yourself?
9. What else have you learned about your relationship with Me?

Taking Resolute Action: Jesus, this is one thing I need to change in my life, to take action on: (write it down). Please grant me the strength and grace to do it now.

Day 25

Cleanse the Soul, Heal the Heart, Feel the Joy!

(September 4, 2003 I)

As I contemplate Your creation of the world and the creation of mankind in the Garden of Eden, I think about the beauty of Your original intent. Man's heart was created to love You and to live in peace with all of creation. Such a beautiful, delicate flower was man's heart and soul! Of indescribable complex and beautiful dimensions that only You could fathom it as its Creator.

The human heart was not made for violence or anger or lust or suffering or any affliction. What a travesty it is that any of these should afflict the heart of anyone You have so lovingly created!

Oh my God, would that we could see with Your eyes the effect of every slight word or action on a person's heart that arises from the sinful nature of man! Would that we could see the fractured creation that has resulted from original sin! Ah, but we would not be able to fathom even

THAT FLAME IN YOUR HEART? TURN IT INTO A BLOWTORCH!

a tiny part of the devastation on even one soul, lest we die overwhelmed by the grief You experience.

Of this I am convinced, that You mean for the heart and soul of every person You create, from conception through childhood into maturity, to be protected and nourished as a delicate, beautiful flower so that it might radiate the goodness of its Creator.

The contemplation causes some anguish in me – would that I had been instructed by You in this when I got married and started a family. I tried my best, but I did not know or appreciate Your intent in this.

> *Of this I am convinced, that You mean for the heart and soul of every person You create, from conception through childhood into maturity, to be protected and nourished as a delicate, beautiful flower so that it might radiate the goodness of its Creator.*

Jesus, my soul needs to be cleansed so badly that it seems the task is impossible. In truth, it is impossible for anyone but You. I have been away from You so many times in my life that the pull even now is very strong. Jesus, I know what You are asking: to go back and look at events in my life, events that I do not want to re-examine because they're either forgotten or too painful to look at again or even remember, or even events that I felt did not affect me as I was "justified."

Each has left a "mark" and, in some cases, deep wounds on my heart that have impaired my ability to love as You love. Jesus, I do want to look at those events with You, and I'm excited to do so, to enter a new dimension of my life with a new freedom to love with such great capacity as You want for me!

But I also know that I will need your grace to recall the events, and I will need courage to re-examine them when my humanity recoils from fear or pain. Your Love is so strong, Lord, that it propels me beyond my doubts and fears and fills my heart with unspeakable joy! May I receive Your Love with boundless capacity and give Your Love freely to all whom I encounter as You desire me to! Lord, grant me the grace!

DAY 25 CLEANSE THE SOUL, HEAL THE HEART, FEEL THE JOY!

What has stopped me from that in the past? What stops me today? Why am I closed off from that which I desire and which gives me joy? Why am I closed off and not open to it to the degree You desire for me? Why am I limited in my love? Certainly pride has caused me not to want to reveal myself to another, but also loneliness – no one seemed to care.

Lord, when You have me look at my life filled with so much sadness, grief, sorrow, and disappointment in this new way, I can for the first time acknowledge the bitterness that I was unaware of, really. And see my heart completely enclosed and entrapped in it. And see the unintended hardness that was there, some of which remains even now I suspect, though I cannot readily identify it.

What hopeful insight! This is a remarkable revelation! How often I have turned away from love in my loneliness, bitterness, anger, or despair. Now I see how I have turned from the only thing that keeps me alive – love – for without it I exist but do not live. And without Your Love I do not even exist!

As much as I desired greater spiritual growth, it was beyond my reach without the capacity to love as You love and want me to love. There is no spiritual growth without love. Love that only comes from You, because You are Love, and all genuine love has only You as its source. Intellectual knowledge alone is not spiritual growth; it can only be the source of pride unless it is completely dominated by and subservient to love.

Lord, I do want You to cleanse my heart! Oh God, come to my assistance! Lord, make haste to help me! Do the impossible in me and fulfill your promise and my desire to cleanse my heart and change me! May I love as You created me to love!

Lord, the disappointments in my life are many and profound. My life seems like such a wreck; I am overwhelmed with failure in every area of my life. And it is readily visible to everyone around me; it cannot be hidden. My peers look at me as though I were a leper. I cannot even go to a reunion and show my face.

THAT FLAME IN YOUR HEART? TURN IT INTO A BLOWTORCH!

What account could I give for my life to those who have accomplished so much? What use has my life been, of what value? Have I lived all these years to see my life as wasted, the best years of my life uselessly spent?

The accuser haunts me with those questions constantly, waiting to fling them in my face, to appeal to my pride and cause me again to enclose myself in bitterness, cutting myself off from Your Love. Each time pride rises up in me ever so slightly, the evil one pushes those thoughts in front of me. And then I feel the despair rise up in me and my emotions fight to take over my disposition. From there the distance to depression is very short, a quick slide down a familiar path.

No! Your Love draws me quickly from the precipice of despair!

My heart, Lord, remains steadfastly fixed on You, and I will not be distracted by bitterness or anxiety over my condition. My growth in holiness and the time and way You want to do it, I place in Your hands. I long for holiness with all my heart but trust in Your Holy Will.

In a way it occurs to me, Lord, that holiness on my part is justice toward the rest of Your creation. What does it matter to the rest of Your creation what I suffer or what interior battle I am fighting? It is irrelevant. In justice, Your creation deserves only one thing from me: love.

How could I presume to have any other reaction or interaction with the rest of Your creation? What gives me the license to abuse it in any way? Whether human, animal, or inanimate object, each and every part of creation belongs to You, King and Creator of the universe.

You who are Love Itself created all of creation, each tiny part of it, out of love. And I presume to use and abuse it? Shall the creature abuse what the Creator has made? The servant abuse the treasures of the King? Only arrogance or stupidity arising from sin could blind me to such a

Thus, it makes no difference to ... anyone else in my life what is going on within me, what the sufferings or battles are.
That is irrelevant.
They deserve only one thing: love....
That is the meaning of true charity.

DAY 25 CLEANSE THE SOUL, HEAL THE HEART, FEEL THE JOY!

degree! What retribution should I, as such an abuser, expect from the One who knows my every offense?

Your retribution is Love? And an expressed desire to draw me into intimate love? Where is Your anger toward me? Why do You so readily forget my offenses?

I can only cry at this very moment as I am overwhelmed with both sorrow at my offenses and gratitude for Your boundless Love! The tears pour out of me just now, as my heart is torn in sorrow and feels Your Love! I am in anguish! You draw my heart and fill it to the point of bursting! Hot tears fill my eyes as I sob. Jesus, my Jesus, forgive me! I have offended You and so many people! Accept my simple and weak contrition. Forgive me, Lord, for I did not understand what I was doing!

My disposition toward Your creation – all of it – can only be one of love and respect for You have provided it for my good. Thus, it makes no difference to my children or anyone else in my life what is going on within me, what the sufferings or battles are. That is irrelevant.

They deserve only one thing: love. I must be a reflection of the love You have for them so that they can grow in love and peace and the security of knowing the love of God. That is the meaning of true charity.

So too it is with co-workers, employees, neighbors, and everyone else I encounter, and all the creatures and objects of the world. It is the reflection of You as Man on earth that I can take as my model. Though You suffered and were rejected by many, You loved anyway and healed those whose hearts were open. That is love. That is suffering for love of the other.

How different this is from our culture of pop psychology. It is, in fact, counter-cultural. We wear our emotions on our sleeves, allowing our emotions to dictate our actions, are told not to "stuff it" and understand nothing of true love that suffers even something so slight as to withhold an angry emotion for love of another.

All of culture is fixated on doing what feels good here and now, on self-gratification in every form. How familiar I am with it, having bought into all of that! How pathetic we have become in our sin and weakness.

THAT FLAME IN YOUR HEART? TURN IT INTO A BLOWTORCH!

Were it not for Your Love and grace to draw me out of this pit of mire, I would be the worst of the lot, as I know my nature of itself is attracted so strongly to this culture. It pulls mightily at me now. I am fully capable in the weakness of my humanity of giving in to it.

At times, there is a type of helplessness that sweeps over me, urging me to give up and give in – Satan spurring my emotions. He knows my weaknesses and vulnerabilities better than I do.

> *May it be done unto me according to Your Will.*
>
> (Luke 1:38)

Thank You, my Jesus, for my free will that allows me to turn toward You and choose. Choose Your love over my weaknesses and temptations. Freedom of choice! Freedom to live as I choose! Freedom to choose love over self-gratification! To choose good over evil.

Lord, as I look back over my life as You have asked me to, I see so much hurt that it is overwhelming. From the abuses I received as a young child who deserved only love to the present time and the rejections I suffer even now, I have had many crosses. Yet, it is my freewill choice whether to allow the bitterness to rise up within me or to offer each hurt to You out of love.

Jesus, I cannot choose bitterness or resentment or blame or anger or revenge, because those destroy love. They cannot occupy any space in a heart You are healing and filling with love. There is no room for them in this heart of mine. I choose to turn my back on them, not in denial, but in full recognition of what happened and what I am doing now to preserve love within me.

I choose to love the people who have hurt me. I do not regret the hurts of my past. They have allowed me to join my suffering with Yours. Even at this point, I join my suffering of being in this place of poverty of spirit, so very painfully aware of my inadequacies in serving You in this mission.

What great joy fills my mind, heart, and spirit as I contemplate Your promise to restore my heart to its original loving state, to the way You created and intended it to be!

DAY 25 CLEANSE THE SOUL, HEAL THE HEART, FEEL THE JOY!

How could I, therefore, object to the time and the way You choose to do this? No, I do not begrudge the circumstances You have created to draw me to the work You have destined for me. I am the servant and You the Master, the King I have sworn to serve. I will put my trust in You. Simply. Completely.

You know the formation my being requires if I am to serve as You want me to. Whatever time and in whatever way You choose to form me, I accept with complete trust.

Just as the suffering of Ranger School in the military formed me and gave me wisdom and knowledge that could not have been gained otherwise without risk of almost certain death in actual combat, so this time of formation I understand is Your way of preparation for spiritual battle.

I was not wiser than the Ranger sergeants who trained me, nor am I wiser than the Creator who forms me.

May I be spared the suffering that is without benefit to me, and may I always embrace the suffering that You send for my formation!

Oh God, come to my assistance! Oh Lord, make haste to help me!
Glory to You, Father, Son, and Holy Spirit!

> *Be not dispirited; be not afraid; keep a good heart; be bold; draw not back; you will be carried through... O children of a heavenly Father, be not afraid!*
>
> - John Henry Cardinal Newman

THE POINT: Our hearts, designed for tender love, have been afflicted by hurts and disappointments. This has left marks on our soul and blocked our ability to love freely as Jesus wants us to do. (As you answer the questions, address your dialogue to Him personally and directly.)

1. Do you have the strength, the courage, and the trust to re-examine your life with Me?

THAT FLAME IN YOUR HEART? TURN IT INTO A BLOWTORCH!

2. Can you let Me take you by the hand and explore the deep recesses of your heart where past hurts lie hidden?
3. Will you let Me heal you and remove the debris and damage from your soul?
4. Can you learn to love unconditionally everyone I put in your life? Can you get excited about that? Desire that?
5. Is the Fire of My Love growing in you? Can you feel it, sense it?
6. What else have you learned about your relationship with Me?

<u>A bold statement:</u> if you have read this far in the book and reflected on the content and questions, I, Jesus, your King, certainly have had an effect in your soul. It could not be otherwise if you are having an open and honest dialogue with Me. Can you describe it in detail?

Taking Resolute Action: Jesus, this is one thing I need to change in my life, to take action on: (write it down). Please grant me the strength and grace to do it now.

Day 26

You, a Close, Dependable Friend of Jesus?! Yes!

(September 4, 2003 II)

Lord, You delight my heart with Your invitation to become a friend to You! But a dependable friend I have not been and I am not – my humanity is so fickle. You would not extend an invitation, however, that I am incapable of accepting and committing to.

My complete trust in You, therefore, tells me: accept His invitation! Say yes, my soul, and He will supply all that is necessary to be all that He invites me to be!

My history is one of inconsistency, showing up to pray only during the hard times, the times of suffering when I needed You, and then when things were going well, drifting away.

And even in those times when I was in need and praying daily, I found that I often drifted away from You for short periods, sometimes even within the period of 24 hours! I get through a struggle and begin

THAT FLAME IN YOUR HEART? TURN IT INTO A BLOWTORCH!

to feel good again and, in the face of temptation, give in to it and turn from You. My nature is unbelievably weak and fickle.

My appetites for human consolation and pleasure are bigger than I am! Alone I am defenseless. You are my defense, my Jesus. Come, stand at the door of my heart, oh my Defender!

Being a dependable friend to You means that I must remain constant even through all the issues that I struggle with, even the most trivial ones. Yesterday, as I struggled with so many temptations in the quiet of the day, for the first time, I took the temptation to You. I started talking to you about the temptation and why it appealed to me and how I felt about the way it appealed to me.

Alone I am defenseless. You are my defense, my Jesus. Come, stand at the door of my heart, oh my Defender!

Yes, I have prayed my whole life for Your help when tempted. But I have not discussed a temptation with You! Are You disgusted with how I felt about it and why it appealed to me? And with the way I wanted to give in just this once so I could feel better, if only momentarily?

Ah, to give in to anger or lust or laziness or selfishness or pride just momentarily would satisfy me for this moment and then I could return to You. Confession is for later but for now, this temptation. It is the defective thought process of a drug addict.

What freedom it is to bring the details of all of it into a dialogue of the heart with You! Of course, You are not disgusted with a friend who comes to You to talk about the intimate details of what I am experiencing!

Whom else could I confide such intimacies to? Who else knows the details of my heart and soul better than You do? And who else can give me the strength and wisdom to resist such defective thinking? Who else can cast out Satan and his minions with all their deceitful temptations? Only You, my Friend! Only You!

I pray that You do a very great work in me and increase my fidelity, as my heart longs to be constantly in Your Presence! To behold You continuously! I am learning to turn toward You with every small concern

DAY 26 YOU, A CLOSE, DEPENDABLE FRIEND OF JESUS?! YES!

every moment of my day. My peace and joy within grow as I learn to walk with You every hour of every day.

What freedom it is to bring the details of all of [my temptations] into a dialogue of the heart with You!
Of course, You are not disgusted with a friend who comes to You to talk about the intimate details of what I am experiencing!

My nature is so undisciplined that I revolt at routine and prefer my ways of seeking pleasure and comfort over anything else. Lord, I need Your grace to help me rule over my unruly nature!

As much joy as I experience at being in Your Presence, it would seem that I would be completely faithful in prayer. There is a very big difference, I find, between the routine of prayer and being in Your Presence, heart to Heart, person to Person.

You know, Lord, that for as long as I can remember, more than 30 years, with very few exceptions, I have devoted time to reading Your Word in the liturgy of the day and meditating on it every morning no matter where I have been on the face of the globe. But so often, I did not bring my person to the time of prayer, but rather, just showed up for a variety of reasons.

I know the difference between an act of my humanity and an act I engage in with my heart where I bring my person. It is the same as when I make a meal for the boys and myself. I can just do it mechanically, or I can be there with them out of love. I suppose like preparing a meal, I could even pray with resentment over the time and effort I put into it.

The prayer of my person to Your Person, my heart to Your Heart, is an active and alive dialogue, an act that pierces my heart and soul. To be faithful in that prayer is my heart's desire! Whether it is a place of joy or sorrow, of consolation or desolation, peace or suffering is Your business, but mine is to be there with my whole person, my whole heart, in active dialogue.

THAT FLAME IN YOUR HEART? TURN IT INTO A BLOWTORCH!

Even as I do that, however, I am shocked and disappointed at my unruly nature and my slavery to sin. The battle rages within me. In my will, I do want to be faithful to You. My own heart desires to turn to You a thousand times each day! To be in constant communication with You in each moment of the day while I am conscious and even when I am at rest in my subconscious.

I am keenly aware that my feelings, my nature, are fickle. I separate my feelings from my faith and live my life in the knowledge of what my faith and reason tell me You desire.

You did not call your Apostles once they were good enough to be in Your Presence. No, you called them while they were still very much in their sin. Each of them had to deal with their habits of sin, their weaknesses and temptations, even as they served You.

You entered the house of Matthew and dined with him and all his tax collector friends, who all were caught in the sins enabled by their ill-gotten wealth. He became a saint and wrote a Gospel as You lifted him out of his sinful condition. So it is with each person whom you call – which is every single soul You have created.

"Come out of Your sin into holiness, for I have great work for you to do" is Your call to me and to every soul.

No, I do not feel holy today, only tired, but I am devoted out of love to this relationship. And yet my feelings so often get in my way, so it becomes a struggle to stay in Your Presence and service. But I know too the joy and awe of watching Your grace at work in my soul as I am drawn beyond my weak nature.

> *If we let Christ into our lives, we lose nothing, nothing, absolutely nothing of what makes life free, beautiful, and great.*
>
> *No! Only in this friendship are the doors of life opened wide.*
>
> *Only in this friendship is the great potential of human existence truly revealed.*
>
> \- Pope Benedict XVI

DAY 26 YOU, A CLOSE, DEPENDABLE FRIEND OF JESUS?! YES!

How I feel is irrelevant to our relationship and my ability to bring myself into prayer in Your Presence because, just as You say, I know You would not turn away from me because I do not feel holy.

No, you are a God of Love, always. I only have to look back a very short distance to see how You have worked in my life, no matter what my struggles were.

I rejoice at Your victory over my nature. My heart leaps for joy and my spirit is lifted high, even as my humanity is exhausted and in pain.

So once again I contemplate the invitation. Your invitation to be a close friend is both delightful and shocking. Close friend? Who, me? The Saints were close friends and so were the Apostles. I am a nobody, certainly not a saint! In fact, I am a terrible sinner. In saying that I am careful not to doubt, but rather I completely trust You and know that You will do what You promise. I just see that You have a lot of work to do in my soul.

And I am delighted! Amen!

THE POINT: Jesus wants a very close dependable friend in you. Do you desire the same? The starting point of that friendship, He points out, is to begin with prayer, otherwise there is no quality communication and you cannot know what is in His Heart. If you do not pray daily, He wants that fixed immediately. (As you answer the questions, address your dialogue to Him personally and directly.)

1. Do you come into My Presence and pray every day without fail? Why not?
2. Can you set a goal to set aside at least one hour a day for prayer and dialogue with Me?
3. How much time do you devote every day to developing a close, personal relationship with Me?

THAT FLAME IN YOUR HEART? TURN IT INTO A BLOWTORCH!

4. What takes higher priority in your life than your time with Me?
5. Do I deserve less than your best?
6. And if you begin the day in prayer, do you return to Me throughout the day?
7. Do you understand how happy it makes Me every time you speak to Me, glance toward Me interiorly, petition Me, and just chat with Me? Do you realize it makes My Heart jump for joy?
8. How do you think I will respond to you if you develop a habit of prayer?
9. As a team, you and I have great work to accomplish as I work through your "Yes" and your human capabilities. Do you sense Me working with you, alongside you?
10. I am fanning the flame of love in your heart! Can you feel its heat?
11. What else have you learned about your relationship with Me?

Taking Resolute Action: Jesus, this is one thing I need to change in my life, to take action on: (write it down). Please grant me the strength and grace to do it now.

Day 27

You Have Specific Souls You Are to Save!

(September 4, 2003 III)

I was just reflecting on the fact that in all our dialogues, no matter what my state of mind and heart is, You are fully and completely present to me. You are completely attentive to me! Not distracted like I am. Fully present. And to each of the 7 billion other souls on earth now if they chose. And to all who ever lived on earth! And to everyone who will ever live in the future! To them all, You are fully and completely present. Not distracted or preoccupied. Stunning! It overloads my mind to contemplate it!

And in that same way, You died for my sins, and those of others. Fully and completely for each person. What must it be to behold You in Heaven and fully comprehend who You are and the glory of Your immeasurable generosity to Your creation! Let me pause to consider that.

As You put each soul
in my life,
You have a purpose for
that encounter.
That purpose is clear in
the larger sense:
the revelation of You,
Jesus Christ,
is always the purpose of
every encounter.

THAT FLAME IN YOUR HEART? TURN IT INTO A BLOWTORCH!

So it needs to be with the souls You put in my life – to be present to them as fully as I can humanly be, that I might attract them to You, with the peace and joy I have in my life. No matter what is going on in my life. In fact, the witness is that I have faith in You and live that life, particularly when I am suffering or when there is chaos and uncertainty!

As You put each soul in my life, You have a purpose for that encounter. That purpose is clear in the larger sense: the revelation of You, Jesus Christ, is always the purpose of every encounter. Though Your Name may not be mentioned specifically, You are revealed in the love that is communicated in each and every encounter.

Whatever else You intend for each encounter, I need to be open to Your counsel. Lord, help me to be attentive to You as I pick up the phone, send an email or text, or meet each person throughout my day. Just as You sent the prophets to Israel, though they were just common vine dressers, shepherds, and field workers, so You send Your disciples, Your followers today, to convert those who have turned away and to encourage those who are already working in your vineyard.

And so you send me, a nobody, a common man who can claim no worldly or spiritual success, to those you put into my life. I can only go as a very lowly messenger of the King, for certainly there are much better and more notable and holy messengers.

Mine is but one of your many messenger roles, nothing of any particular note any more than the next person in the pew beside me. My freedom to say "yes" to Your request lies in the fact that nothing depends on me when it comes to results; that is all Your business.

Mine is just to be the messenger and give You the results and the credit for any good that is done. It is not even for me to see any results, lest it feed my insatiable appetite for pride.

Just as You sent many people to me when I had turned away, so You send me as one of many to others to draw them to

Maintain a spirit of peace

and you will save a thousand souls.

- St. Seraphim of Sarov

DAY 27 YOU HAVE SPECIFIC SOULS YOU ARE TO SAVE!

You. Lord, I know that each person has free will, just as I did, to accept Your messages of love and mercy. In my profession in sales, I have been rejected many times, but still, it hurts when someone rejects the message I try to deliver from You.

I know all kinds of rejection in the normal course of living, but the rejection of Your Love that saved me from the depths of the pit really hurts because I love them and I love You. I cannot even fathom how much it must hurt You if it affects me like that.

I know You say that I must be at peace, and I know that the message I deliver for You will not change everyone, but still it hurts. I go on, though, trusting in Your Mercy and that I am just one of many messengers for each soul You put in my life.

All I can do is listen to Your wisdom concerning how You want me to relate to each person You put in my path, do Your bidding in that instance, and then continue on in my mission. It is not my wisdom that I can count on because I do not know the heart of the person. Only You know that, so how I relate to them has to be Your way, not mine.

What I experience more and more these days with each person, no matter who they are or for what purpose we are engaged, is an over-riding sense of love for them, to the point that it dominates my consciousness at times, particularly when we are face to face.

I want to say to the other person, "…and let's talk about what God's Will is in this. What does Jesus want in this matter?" The only way I can convey to another soul that the only answer to everything is You is if I live that myself and it has become part of my very nature. I cannot give what I do not have.

I can remember so well the years of late-night discussions with my daughter at the kitchen table as she was doing homework and I was reading my business journals. I sat there waiting for her to talk. So often, as she discussed issues at school or in her life, I found that I had little that was meaningful to contribute except in the end to bring the discussion around to You and the maturity of her decisions made based on faith.

THAT FLAME IN YOUR HEART? TURN IT INTO A BLOWTORCH!

You know, Lord, that You have been and are the only answer for everything in my life. That knowledge is in every fiber of my being and I live it because I know nothing else. At the end of every discussion, every problem, issue, or situation, there is only You. How could it be otherwise since You are the Creator of every atom in existence? How blind and limited my humanity is! How infinitely good and patient You are! You protect me in every way, even from my own foolishness!

My heart is delighted and reassured to know that I have such a powerful and determined Defender of my frail soul. I have been so wounded by leaving myself exposed. And how do I leave myself exposed? By not staying in constant dialogue with You throughout my day. I have learned that lesson very painfully just within the past few days.

I had an encounter with someone in a meeting that brought up a lot of old, very painful conflicts around a very good cause: fighting for what was best for my sons. Still, I got caught up in it, and the anger and resentments came to the surface. I left the meeting caught up in the anger and then as I saw it in myself, I began to despair about the kind of person I am.

Where did that go? Into pushing You away and hearing the voice within me saying I could not write or witness to God because I was not holy, not a good witness, just a delusional fool chasing another illusion. And then, as if on cue, I had a phone call with a peer who reminded me about another of my poor decisions that has caused me great financial difficulty.

I found myself withdrawing into myself and away from You. I did not want to look at Your images around the house or converse with You, as I succumbed to my despondency. From there, the distance was short to finding compensations and escapes that made me feel better at least for the moment. My sins resulted from not turning to You.

My culpability is my own, as I was fully conscious of the slippery slope I was on. I just did not want to turn from it because the interior pain was so great and I wanted to salve it my way immediately. It is a very

DAY 27 YOU HAVE SPECIFIC SOULS YOU ARE TO SAVE!

easy and well-worn path for me. You are the only answer to my life's situations; I am unable to defend or rescue myself from my weak humanity.

It is curious how emotions works. Even now, as I recall that past incident and relive it, a mighty force rises up in me to draw me back into those sins and compensations. Here I am in dialogue with You and yet that force draws me so powerfully that I am surprised at its strength. If You were not standing at the doorway of my heart at this very moment as my Defender, I would be sucked back into it, so powerful is the appeal to my nature. How subtle is Satan! How weak is my nature!

If You were not standing at the doorway of my heart at this very moment as my Defender, I would be sucked back into it, so powerful is the appeal to my nature.

But now I seek to hide myself within Your wounds that You can defend me and protect me, even as I allow You to work in the world through me. In every situation, You know my soul and the souls of those around me! In Your Presence I can be attuned to what You want of me.

If I own my will, then I own each and every word, action, and thought. How I desire that each action and word and thought be guided by Your Holy Will as I reflect on the futility of all that I have done outside Your Will! And compare that to all that I have done in union with You!

I saw a miracle yesterday, worked by Your Hand, by being in union with you. I had to deal with someone who has in the past lied to me and cheated me, even stolen from me, and now I suspect from clues I am picking up, is working on something that will have a negative outcome for me. Still, that person was in great need at the moment; even I could see that through the resentment that had arisen in me.

I remember as I was in my office, working on a pressing project, Your prompting and the quick dialogue I had with You. Just a simple, "Lord, help me to love and respond with joy

Onward Christian soldier!

As to war!

(Christian song)

THAT FLAME IN YOUR HEART? TURN IT INTO A BLOWTORCH!

to the person's need." And then I walked out of the office and went to offer help. By the time I got to the person, I was laughing about the fix he or she was in, and he or she joined in the humor of it. Many hours and hundreds of dollars out of my pocket later, the issue was solved and the person left happy. Lord, that situation was beyond impossible for me, but I felt Your kind graces wash over me and the miracle of a change of heart within me was nearly instantaneous. You are the God of the impossible! Thank You for Your mercy and kindness!

You say, "the answers are all with Me." This is not theoretical or theological for me – it has become my lived reality. I cannot imagine how I could live without Your Presence in my life. You are my constant companion, even when I turn from You momentarily. I am learning to turn to You, with every situation in my life, for Your insight and wisdom, no matter how trivial the situation seems at the moment. Even in my business planning in my profession, I constantly turn to You as I pray for the wisdom I need to help a particular client.

The answers are truly all with You. How could I have turned away so many times except in foolishness? What a terribly lonely path I have walked at times.

As I look at the world more and more through Your eyes and see the futility of the struggles and conflicts of those who are away from You, I am moved with compassion because I see a reflection of me. I cannot judge even the "worst" because I have been there, even to the point of attacking You in my ignorance and arrogance. What a sinful man I am! Lord, forgive my offenses, as grave and as many as they have been.

It is that ignorance and arrogance and the sin that was the result that led me to live in fear – fear of getting too close to You, of Your Will for my life, and of what the future held. You know I spent time on this because I was trying to anticipate what would happen next.

This is still a huge battle for me because there is so much chaos and uncertainty in every dimension of my current life situation. Even my health is problematic and uncertain. And then, on top of that, there is what You are asking of me now, asking me to go forward. It seems that I

DAY 27 YOU HAVE SPECIFIC SOULS YOU ARE TO SAVE!

am on an entirely new path that I have never traveled before. Everything is unknown. Nothing is certain or settled.

Fear? It only arises in me when my love fails. Here I am trying to anticipate a future that only You know, but thinking about it causes so much anxiety and fear that at times I am unable to sleep or relax or even work. Until I find myself coming into Your Presence and contemplating Your Love.

Nothing illustrates the extent of Your Love more than the Cross. The thought of spending eternity contemplating Your Passion is a great joy because it is in Your passion that the depth of Your Love is revealed, and that Love transforms me! Even as I begin that contemplation now and carry it on into eternity!

I am a servant of the Lord.
For nothing is impossible with God.
Let it be done to me according to Your Will!

(paraphrased Luke 1:38)

Ah, that thought just caught me – a small explosion of delight went off in my heart! My love and contemplation of You is a single journey, begun here on earth, that carries me through the doorway of death into the eternal joy of Heaven! I am caught up in the meditation and joy fills me! What a beautiful path You have created for Your children! It causes me not to escape into a fantasy, but rather to engage all of life more fully as I am filled with confidence about Your growing Presence in my life!

Therefore, I remain in Your Presence because there is nowhere else to go. You have drawn me like a powerful magnet, fixing me in Your Presence! All other places are empty and without meaning. I know because I have wandered away, only to be drawn back to You.

When I consider my life, it is easy to look at it with so much regret. So often, Lord, I have wasted the opportunities You have given me because I was so focused on myself. But I do not regret and do not look back in that way, and I do not give in to self-pity! Rather, I rejoice at where Your mercy has brought me now.

THAT FLAME IN YOUR HEART? TURN IT INTO A BLOWTORCH!

Thank You, my Lord, for Your mercy, which reassures me that all mistakes are forgotten for those who serve You! I have no time to waste with those regrets! I am drawn more each day to ask You to show me new opportunities, and I rejoice in each of those possibilities to serve You! I have my work You have assigned to me that needs to be done.

On with it! Let it be done to me according to Your Will!

I am excited and joyful! I am captured by the thought that, as You see straight into my humanity, You know every fiber of my being – heart, mind, will, strengths, weaknesses, sin – all of it, and still You love me! Your Love is beyond all measure and understanding!

Lord, You are my sight and courage. You give me the strength to know Your Will and carry it out each day. And the reward for doing so is so sweet; Your Love is so powerful that it draws me ever more quickly forward!

Again!! On with it! Let it be done to me according to Your Will!

THE POINT: Jesus is fully present to you at every moment of your life, always working to defend and protect you, drawing you closer to Him that you might do the great work He has destined for you! He wants you to be filled with excitement and joy! (As you answer the questions, address your dialogue to Him personally and directly.)

1. Are you excited by the prospects of drawing closer to Me, dear child?
2. Does the fact that I have specific work designed for you, unique to who you are and your capabilities, excite your mind and heart?
3. Does that motivate you to seek with more determination both what work within you needs to be done as well as what I want in your relationships?
4. What is the work within you that needs to be done?

DAY 27 YOU HAVE SPECIFIC SOULS YOU ARE TO SAVE!

5. I, Jesus, the King, call to you, My servant! And you answer, "Yes, Lord!" How does that make you feel?
6. Can you pray with more intensity to hear My Will every day? In every relationship?
7. You are meant to draw encouragement and strength and wisdom from fellow co-workers in the renewal. Who are those in your life? How can you support them better? And how can you let them support you better?
8. Do you see why I want that for you?
9. What else have you learned about your relationship with Me?

Taking Resolute Action: Jesus, this is one thing I need to change in my life, to take action on: (write it down). Please grant me the strength and grace to do it now.

Day 28

The Ways You Need to Prepare for His Return. Now!

(September 5, 2003)

Be prepared! That is Your word to Your children. And it is delivered with urgency.

In these final hours before You return, and darkness claims its final victories, it is critical that we know the purpose for which You created each of us.

In all things, Lord, Your timing is perfect. It cannot be otherwise. You are God. You are perfect. Can the imperfect question the perfection of the perfect God? Perhaps. But the imperfect can only accept with humility the ways of the Perfect.

Your perfect Will created me at this particular time in history to serve Your Kingdom in a particular way, chosen by You. Therefore, my quest is to know Your heart and mind with regard to Your

In all things, Lord, Your timing is perfect. It cannot be otherwise. You are God. You are Perfect.

desires for me, because it is perfect for who You created me to be. It is not my way that is perfect, it is Yours.

As you draw me forward into further service of Your Kingdom, You prepare me for the next mission. I can easily look back and see Your strong and guiding hand in preparing me for the next phase of my life.

Having been a soldier, I know to submit to the wisdom of those training me for battle. They have been there. They have been in battle, have the scars, seen their friends killed, and have come back to train the inexperienced and hone the advanced skills of those who will go back on another mission. The training never ends because the enemy becomes continually wiser and more sophisticated.

To rely on the skills and tactics that worked yesterday is to invite disaster.

Therefore, I can only trust Your wisdom in preparing me for tomorrow as I focus on what You ask of me today.

It is readily apparent to me that, had I continued on the course I was on and not gone through the trials and suffering of the ordeal of these last few years, I would not be writing any of this, nor understand this particular mission. Your designs have prepared me in ways I could never have conceived. Like Ranger School, the sufferings have been worth the preparation.

But then, too, how often I find that, had I listened and followed your promptings, I would have been better prepared for later situations. Instead, I did not listen or respond because I was too self-absorbed. I am not the most docile of trainees, nor the most enlightened regarding the big picture, which is Your Will.

Perhaps that is why I feel so at home with everyone around me. The big leagues, the pros, are beyond my grasp. I apologize as I know the consequences are so serious, but I almost had to laugh as I thought about You trying to coach such an unruly bunch as we humans are. Like a pathetic junior varsity team more interested in the flights of fancy at that age than the training and preparation for the game. Or a bunch of

DAY 28 THE WAYS YOU NEED TO PREPARE FOR HIS RETURN. NOW!

green soldiers more interested in partying after hours than the training that will save them as they are sent into harm's way.

Do You ever get frustrated and just want to throw up Your hands? Why am I laughing? Certainly, there are images that easily spring to mind. Like the little kids on the soccer field who have no idea what is going on really, wildly running around just to kick the ball. Luckily there are a few more mature and wiser kids on the team that guide it to an outcome.

Jesus, forgive me for all my foolish ways and send Your Spirit to strengthen me. Your plan, Your Will, is the original purpose of my creation by You. Lord, help me to discover, embrace, and carry out that purpose!

By waiting and by calm you shall be saved,

in quiet and in trust your strength lies.

- Isaiah 30:15

Your call for us to be influential caught me off-guard. I do not think I have ever heard it expressed that way. To be influential for You, drawing others to You, is my calling! Be influential! To grow in holiness and in the process draw others to You. Not in the world's way of being influential, though for some that may be a requirement of the assignment, but to be quiet, peaceful, joyful, and loving to all in all situations. In this way, I can draw all Your children to You.

So there is much work to be done, first within my own soul and then in the world, in the time and place You have designated. Just as any soldier must develop himself within the training he is going through before he can serve his country on any mission, so I must look within at the qualities that need improvement.

I am drawn, enticed, by Your promise to have work for me to do constantly in my soul! I marvel as I see what You are accomplishing in my soul and the transformation of my exterior that allows me to accomplish Your work in the world. One flows from the other of necessity.

You warn of the dangers of contentment with whatever I did yesterday, as it is easy to slide back into the world. I know very well that path, as

THAT FLAME IN YOUR HEART? TURN IT INTO A BLOWTORCH!

I have gone that way many times. It is a very short distance from contentment to complacency and from complacency to mediocrity and from mediocrity to disaster. It is true in the world and even truer spiritually.

What great temptation there is to look back at my former life and the fleeting pleasures of sin, so often triggered by emotions and memories! How subtle the deceit. It is a temptation because it can cause me to withdraw from You and give up the hope of growing in holiness. But wisdom is there as well, if I look with Your eyes, with You present as I do so.

Now I have learned. With each fall, each sin, I have learned to stop and consider the trigger that led me to that place. Where did it come from, what was going on in my head or heart? I seek wisdom to see and know the "near occasions of sin," as it were.

What has become readily apparent to me, and why You keep warning me never to leave You, is that as long as I am in constant dialogue with You throughout my day, as long as I remain in Your Presence, I am protected.

I recall with great clarity that day in Chicago when You said to me, "Stay with me!" I can still hear the sound and tone of Your voice, deep, clear, full of love, and pleading with kindness.

The meaning grows more clear as I grow closer to You. I have not stayed with You in the past. I am trying with every fiber of my being, with all my humanity, to "stay with You" now, without reservation, giving over everything to You. Nothing is more important to me. Nothing. To stay with You every waking moment of my day, and to rest in You every moment of my sleep!

> *I am trying with every fiber of my being, with all my humanity, to "stay with You" now, without reservation, giving over everything to You.*

If it sounds like an obsession, it is. Nothing is more important to me. An urgency fills me as I have wasted too much time already!

That is my focus ... until I leave Your Presence and am drawn back into my worldly concerns. But then the fire of Your Love is so much

DAY 28 THE WAYS YOU NEED TO PREPARE FOR HIS RETURN. NOW!

stronger that it propels me forward again. Your Presence in me causes me such joy that I cannot leave You!

I am delighted at Your offer to dialogue with me throughout my day. To take every concern, every need, every decision I have to You. I appreciate Your wise counsel in everything, even the smallest of my concerns.

You are truly my best Friend! Each time I turn to You and graces are sent to me, my very being is transformed in small, imperceptible ways but surely.

I grow ever more absorbed by your constant Presence in me. And if I am constantly in Your Presence, then I can only be at peace, fearing nothing, without anxiety, serving the Kingdom first and foremost as Your interests are my interests, my Love, my best Friend!

My Savior. My God. My King. Thy Kingdom come! Thy Will be done on earth as it is in Heaven!

THE POINT: Jesus wants you prepared as He readies His return! (As you answer the questions, address your dialogue to Him personally and directly.)

1. Are you ready? Do you know what preparations you need to make within your soul?
2. Do you know what I want of you that you might become a saint?
3. I want you to be influential on earth by your calm, peaceful, holy, and joyful nature as you stand confidently in My Presence. Can you see the vision of that kind of holiness which draws people to Me?
4. What does that specifically look like for who you are and where I have placed you?
5. You holy? Yes! You a saint? Yes! I mean it! How do you respond?

THAT FLAME IN YOUR HEART? TURN IT INTO A BLOWTORCH!

6. The flame becomes a blowtorch within you, My child! It burns brightly! How does it feel now, child? What is it accomplishing in you?
7. What else have you learned about your relationship with Me?

Taking Resolute Action: Jesus, this is one thing I need to change in my life, to take action on: (write it down). Please grant me the strength and grace to do it now.

Day 29

Protecting You from Your Own Weaknesses

(September 5, 2003 II)

Blessed Mother, I know well the protection of your maternal heart and how you have drawn me there. So often I have had recourse to you as only a mother can provide! I fly to the comfort and solace of your womanly heart, your Immaculate Heart, that offers a place of nurturing life.

I marvel at the miraculous ways in which you have provided the means for me to make pilgrimages I could not possibly have made on my own. Those pilgrimages provided me with what I needed to resume my service to the Kingdom just at the point when I felt I had consumed all my strength and had nothing else to give.

I am tired, exhausted, and worn out at times from carrying out the duties and responsibilities Heaven has given me, from the struggle with my weak nature, but I am full of joy to the point of bursting because I labor in all of it for the Kingdom! I have never known greater joy, even as I am being crushed by life.

THAT FLAME IN YOUR HEART? TURN IT INTO A BLOWTORCH!

I know my frailty and weaknesses and that I can fall from the service of Jesus and the Kingdom so easily. Mary, I'm in such need of your help to overcome the bad habits of my weak nature that lead me to distraction and sin. I need so much grace to discipline my nature.

So often I have consecrated myself to your Immaculate Heart, knowing full well that as often as I reaffirm it, I renew my confidence in your protection.

Never was it known that anyone who fled to your protection was left unaided! "Hail Mary, full of grace! The Lord is with you!" (Luke 1:28)

It takes my breath away when I read, "Heaven and earth are joined as never before." Ah, to be joined with Heaven as never before, what joy and consolation! With every fiber of my being, I choose to seek Jesus completely and solely.

May nothing else occupy my mind, heart, and soul!

We are not the sum of our weaknesses and failures,

we are the sum of the Father's love for us

and our real capacity to become the image of His Son Jesus.

- Pope John Paul II

THE POINT: The Blessed Mother knows your strengths and weaknesses intimately and desires to help you reach Heaven. She will always lead you to the path Jesus has designed uniquely for you. (As you answer the questions, address your dialogue to Him personally and directly.)

1. Do you know the joy of a relationship with My Mother?
2. Can you take your weaknesses and fears to her so she can help you with them?
3. She tells you to live with joy. Do you?

DAY 29 PROTECTING YOU FROM YOUR OWN WEAKNESSES

4. Do you know the joy borne out of confidence in your relationship with Me as she leads you to Me?
5. Are you diligent in observing the Marian feast days, whether a formal Holy Day of Obligation or not, as a way to honor My Mother, Mary, and develop your relationship with her?
6. What else have you learned about your relationship with Me?

Taking Resolute Action: Jesus, this is one thing I need to change in my life, to take action on: (write it down). Please grant me the strength and grace to do it now.

Day 30

Your Ongoing Conversion. You're Not Done Yet!

(September 5, 2003 III)

Mary, I thank you for your loving care as you remind me to persevere in my own conversion. I do not need to look far to see the evidence of that need. I need Heaven's graces to continue my conversion each day because I am so easily distracted and turned away.

Your warning about spiritual pride is very pointed for me in particular. It seems to me that pride is constantly lurking to draw me in and I am such an easy prey to it. I, who have nothing in my life that I can legitimately boast about, am always looking for anything I can to make me feel better about myself. I can fall so easily into spiritual pride – it is such a short distance from joy!

When I see what God is accomplishing in and through me, I am filled with joy, but from there it is only a very short distance – a small claim that I had anything to do with the victory – that leads to pride and my fall. Then I am humbled, even humiliated, by my sin. And then when

THAT FLAME IN YOUR HEART? TURN IT INTO A BLOWTORCH!

I call out for His mercy, how quickly I am received back like a prodigal son!

Spiritual pride is such a trap for me. It is so easy for me to think I have anything to do with becoming holy. It is 100%, not 99%, God's gift. He needs only my "yes." I want to be a saint to more fully serve the Kingdom and experience Heaven's graces.

Mary, you tell me to have no fear, but I struggle with that because, while I fear little outside me, I am fearful of my weaknesses and attraction to sin. I am a sensual person who is very much attracted to the world and all it offers. The discipline and asceticism of the Saints is not yet a grace that I possess or can say I actively aspire to, though I know I shall be drawn there in God's time. No, I am but a very common man with only my "yes" and my free will to offer Him, which I give in the totality of my being, without reservation of any kind. Without any higher priority.

Did a Magdalene, a Paul, a Constantine, an Augustine become mountains of ice after their conversion?

Quite the contrary.

We should never have had these prodigies of conversion and marvelous holiness

if they had not changed the flames of human passion into

volcanoes of immense love of God.

- St. Frances Cabrini

Still, I am the kind of man who finds God in the mud, the blood, and the beer. The struggle of every common man and woman is one that I know well. Mine has not been a life of commendable virtue. Rather, I have sunk to very low places. Only by your protection which I am vividly aware of, have I been preserved from remaining there. Even in the suffering that was inflicted on me from outside myself, I can see how my soul was protected by your loving maternal heart.

But even now, I know how easily I fall into sin and offend you and Heaven. Mother, help me to stay in a constant state of prayer every waking moment, that I might stay open to grace and your protection and direction. Then I shall surely know no fear!

DAY 30 YOUR ONGOING CONVERSION. YOU'RE NOT DONE YET!

As these complex and troubling times deteriorate and the level of chaos and violence increases in the world, I continue to advise my clients in the art of the "fast pivot." That is, finding ways to celebrate the diversity of people and their interests and various roles to draw them together as one team, focused ever more intently on the strategy.

And then when circumstances change, and new direction is needed quickly, they can act as a single organism. Heads and hearts in the same place for the greater good, ignoring the impact on themselves.

So it is with the Kingdom of Heaven and the mission of Jesus, the Returning King. I pray for the grace to be open. Open heart. Open mind. Ready.

Fast pivot at the prompting, to take on a new task, to take a new direction. Quickly respond. Looking to Heaven for guidance. Without reservation, to be guided by the Queen of Heaven as she directs me along the path of her Son, the King.

Blessed are you among women! And blessed is the fruit of your womb, Jesus! Holy Mary, Mother of God, pray for us sinners now and at the hour of our death!

Amen! Amen! Amen!

May the flame in my heart become a blowtorch for my constant conversion!

THE POINT: Our Lady desires to protect you and help lead you as a soldier in the Army of Light. (As you answer the questions, address your dialogue to Jesus personally and directly.)

THAT FLAME IN YOUR HEART? TURN IT INTO A BLOWTORCH!

1. Do you know her Motherly love and protection? Have you asked her for protection?
2. Do you know your need for continued conversion?
3. Have you consecrated yourself to her under one of her titles?
4. Do you know the experience of her Motherly guidance?
5. How can you improve your relationship with her?
6. What else have you learned about your relationship with Me?

Taking Resolute Action: Jesus, this is one thing I need to change in my life, to take action on: (write it down). Please grant me the strength and grace to do it now.

Reflections on the Process of the Dialogue of the Heart

Lord, it has taken me more than five years to write these reflections, this dialogue with Your Heart. It should not and could not have taken less. No, the time was necessary as You wanted to walk through all the pain, suffering, and chaos of those years with Your words of the Volumes to sustain me. I could not have foreseen the beauty of Your plan! (Is 48:10)

Here I am, professional strategist, but clearly my strategies and plans are nothing in comparison. They are like a small puff of smoke, blowing away in the wind. Nothing in comparison to even the smallest plan of the Creator! How magnificent are Your ways!

What will happen to this work, my Lord? I have felt compelled to write, even urgent to complete it this last year. I have felt driven to put great effort into it these last few months as though there were a deadline looming. Urgency has arisen in me to get it done. For what reason? Only You know. I do not need to know the answer to my questions. The servant does not need to know why the King makes preparations or asks for a task to be accomplished at a certain time.

This I do know: the writing and rereading of these reflections has had a very powerful effect on me. My heart, mind, and soul have been changed, even transformed. Jack Canfield, the author of the *Chicken Soup for the Soul* series, said that, "Writing a book changes an author." So writing my reflections has changed me.

Should even one other soul ever read any of these words and, as a result, turn ever so slightly toward You, it would just be an unexpected benefit. That alone, one soul turned, would make the whole effort worth it, regardless of its effect on me.

The work is finished. Into Your Hands I commend my soul and this work, this dialogue of my heart with Your Heart.

Completed this day, Easter Sunday!

Assessment:

The 30 Days of Dialogue

You have finished the 30 Days of Dialogue with Jesus. Take an hour of quiet time to reflect on where you were when you started and where you are now.

1. What will you say to Jesus about what you have learned? Tell Him now:
2. What do you want to thank Jesus for that He has revealed to you? Tell Him now:
3. What are the commitments you need to make to help reignite the fire of spiritual renewal in others? Tell Him now:
4. Finally, what decisions have you made, or still need to make, for the future He is calling you to? Tell Him now:

Epilogue:

Foundations of an Interior Prayer Life

I have been asked many times about the practice of prayer and how to pray to nurture the interior life. In terms of a prayer life, it is the gateway to a dialogue of the heart.

First and foremost, there is nothing more important for you to do in your life than pray. It is more important than eating or sleeping or even breathing. Only prayer will allow you to develop a relationship with Jesus. Good intentions or knowledge from reading about Him will not suffice. Only prayer will reveal what is in His Heart for you. Prayer alone will allow a relationship to develop and grow. Consistent prayer. Every day. Without fail. No matter what. Quiet prayer. Alone with Him. Centering prayer. Meditative prayer. Prayer of the heart. Listening prayer.

Developing an interior prayer life is critical to the life of every Christian. And it is not difficult. There is nothing here that any ordinary Christian cannot do. It is quite simple or I could not do it. The interior prayer life and a dialogue of the heart with Jesus is meant for every one of God's children. It is meant for every soul on earth without exception.

I remember being told about centering, meditative prayer thirty years ago by the late Fr. Francis Marino, one of the founders of the Anawim Community. Five minutes of centering prayer was my goal. Ten years later, in Medjugorje, the seers were advocating three hours of prayer a day! At that point, my morning prayer was normally an hour, but three seemed out of the question.

Today, that is what I strive to do, though I am inconsistent as I try to balance work and the duties of being a single father. If I count, as they advocated, morning prayer, Mass, a Rosary, prayer while I am commuting (not the best quality time for it, but better than the radio), and nighttime prayer, then perhaps I am getting there. As a matter of fact, when I exercise, I tend to "run the Rosary" – I am not aware of how far I run, only how many Rosaries I run! Head down and focused, I can get totally lost in the interior dialogue during my running Rosaries. Try it! Again, not the best way to say a Rosary, but if you are exercising, why not pray at the same time?

One other point Fr. Marino taught me: have a particular place, a chair, a reading spot in your home, that is reserved only for prayer and spiritual reading, if possible. I do have it. It is a ratty old easy chair with a foot stool that is out of date and ugly. It should have been thrown out twenty years ago, but it is comfortable and it's my place. I am there every morning no matter what. I typically spend 1-2 hours there, but have spent as much as 8 hours.

A friend, Laura, once told me that when her kids were young and she was always tired from babies interrupting her sleep (she has 6 children) that she was lucky to get in 10 minutes of prayer a day. (Actually, I think she got in 20 hours of prayer! Mother Teresa would say that, in serving her needy children, she was offering God the best prayer, the finest incense in the temple of the home.) Anyway, she said she felt guilty about that for a long time. And you know what? As soon as she let go of the guilt, her formal prayer time increased! (One needs both kinds of prayer to be a real Christian, according to Mother Teresa and the Gospels.)

So to me, the foundation of an interior prayer life starts with centering or meditative prayer. There are lots of good resources to guide you. And the subject of the start of my meditative prayer is the daily Liturgy, the scripture readings for the day, the Heart of Mother Church as she forms us. How often I have discovered that the grace which I needed for that day was contained within the Scripture readings for Mass that day.

A great resource for Scriptural reflection is *The Anawim Way: Pondering the Word* published by the Anawim Community. www.anawim.com Besides the readings, it contains a very simple, straightforward meditation and questions for reflection. It is a great resource for the everyday Catholic (or any Christian for that matter). More widely known is *The Magnificat*. Though it does not have the questions for reflection, it does have good articles. www.magnificat.com And of course, the readings for the day can be easily found on the internet.

The second part of my prayer is centered on the materials from Direction for Our Times as mentioned in the Introduction. www.directionforourtimes.org Without fail, I read the monthly message that Jesus has sent to Anne, which they distribute by email or you can get in book form. I read it every day, over and over again, for the entire month, for a reason. Like anything we learn, repetition makes it stick. Re-reading the message of Jesus every day makes it sink into my subconscious until it becomes a part of the fabric of my being without me having to think about it. Very often, a sentence that I read previously without particular notice will leap off the page and hold me, sometimes for a very long period. And of course there are the Volumes as well as all the other materials from DFOT (as it is called), which I use for meditation.

I recommend reading other things Anne has published. The "Heaven Speaks" booklets precisely address many of the conditions humanity finds itself in. The books by Anne on Heaven, purgatory, and holiness are worthy of meditation.

There are, of course, many other great resources for one's prayer life, but these are foundational for me. I could not stop without mentioning the Liturgy of the Hours or Divine Office, which has traditionally been the prayer of the clergy throughout the world. It is now widely used by the laity. Published by the Catholic Book Publishing Corp., the set with user guide is readily available from many sources.

And finally, the ultimate support for the interior prayer life is daily Mass as well as Adoration. Taking within yourself His Real Presence has no equal. Being in His Real Presence in the tabernacle has no equal place on earth. Making the effort to avail yourself as often as possible brings huge dividends which only He can and has promised to supply.

The interior liturgical life for me has been supported by Sunday Mass at my parish, but also frequent daily Mass at the Shrine of the World Apostolate of Fatima, which is very close to my house. There the liturgy and the homilies are true to the teachings of the Pope and the Magisterium of the Church. Finding a parish that is true is critical, even as I acknowledge that any validly performed Mass contains all the graces and benefits available in any Mass.

Still, finding clergy and a homilist grounded in the truth of the Church's teachings is absolutely requisite to knowing the Way, the Truth, and the Life, which is Jesus. No compromises of today's pop psychology, which has so permeated parts of the Church, can or should be tolerated. I have been in parishes where pleasantries and very humanistic homilies and ministries were the norm. They are dangerous to the spiritual life. I am sorry, I cannot soften the truth. "Feel goods" will join the wide and easy path to hell, as Scripture says. The way to Heaven is narrow.

<u>This is a very high-stakes game: Eternal life</u>. I want a preacher who will make me uncomfortable in my pew. I know my nature, and it is weak and prone to veering off-course with pleasant sounding ideas. I need and desire constant course corrections. Being offended by piercing truth is good for my soul and an antidote to my normal, prideful, lazy self.

I cannot end without this last comment. Frequent Confession, no matter what one thinks of the practice, no matter how long it has been, no matter how "bad" the confessor is, done in the humility of obedience and with faith, will have absolutely remarkable effects. See Days 13 and 21. (It is true that not all priests have the charisma of being a "good" confessor. That does not take away from the effectiveness of the sacrament received in faith. Go anyway. Finding a good confessor or spiritual director is very helpful, though, if you can.) Confession will clear away the debris of sin and open the soul to the healing graces of the Savior like nothing else can. John Paul II said that those who frequently go to Communion should frequently go to Confession. Good guidance. Receive Him in a state of grace. Or not, at your eternal peril.

These, then, I think are the foundations of an interior prayer life as I have come to know them. There are many more, but this is a start.

Are you ready for a new beginning?

Come, Holy Spirit!
Fill the hearts of Your faithful!
Enkindle in them the Fire of Your Love!
Send forth Your Spirit!
And they shall be created!
And You shall renew the face of the earth with Your Love!

(adapted from the Catholic prayer Come Holy Spirit)

Notes on Catholic Theology from a Layman's Perspective

There are a number of terms used in this book that are unique to the Catholic faith that I have been asked about. What follows is an explanation of some of these terms from my personal perspective. These explanations are not theological, nor are they an attempt to defend them in any way. They are just tenants of the faith as I interpret them and which I obediently and enthusiastically believe as taught by the Church. You should investigate them for yourself from reliable sources.

1. Tabernacle: From the Old Testament, the tabernacle was where the Ark of the Covenant was kept and where God met Moses face to face, so there is a long tradition of God occupying the tabernacle. Because Catholics believe the consecrated Host is the Real Presence of Jesus (see next item), and the Hosts are kept in the tabernacle in the Church, Catholics believe that God Himself, in the Person of Jesus, resides in the tabernacle of the church.
2. Real Presence: Catholic teaching is that when the priest at Mass repeats the words of Jesus from the Last Supper when He said, "Take this and eat it, for this is my Body," at that moment, the host, while maintaining the appearance of bread actually becomes the Real Presence of Jesus. We take Him literally at His Word. And the same when He gave them the wine and said,

"Take this and drink of it, for this is my Blood." Elsewhere in the New Testament, He had said, "'Anyone who eats my Body and drinks my Blood, will not die, but will have eternal life.' After this, many of his disciples left him." It is the same today. Many who do not believe Him have left Him.

3. Confession: One of the 7 sacraments of the Church. A really beautiful and very misunderstood sacrament. Jesus said to the Apostles, "For whosoever sins you shall forgive, they shall be forgiven and whosoever sins you shall held bound, they shall be held bound." Confession for the Catholic, frequently received, monthly ideally, is an opportunity to live the virtue of humility, and the private one-on-one confession to a priest is an opportunity to face our offenses against God in truth, to repair the damage done, since no sin is private or without consequence for the Body of Christ, to make amends and reparation. It clears away the debris of sin, and opens us up to the grace of Heaven. An additional benefit I have found is that many priests are also very wise and good counselors in the spiritual life and can help us in our struggle to grow in holiness.

4. Holiness: We are all called to it, as that was the original state of creation before original sin. Baptism provides special graces, as it removes the stain of original sin from our souls, even as we must continue to suffer the effects of original sin in our human natures and the world. That points to another thing: all sin, all offenses against God, while forgiven in Confession, have consequences which we will have to suffer to some degree. An obvious example: murder. While God will forgive us if we confess it and repent, we will still have to face the consequences of jail or execution as well as all the emotional, psychological, relational, and human consequences. All sins have the same set of consequences to varying degrees.

5. Sin: an offense against God. The simplest is breaking the 10 Commandments, but goes well beyond that. How many ways are there to offend a person you love? How many ways are there to

offend the One who created you and loves you beyond your wildest imagination? As a person grows in holiness they become ever more sensitive to the ways they offend the One whom they love with increasing passion. In their growing appreciation of their offenses, their sins, the person growing in holiness becomes more desirous to make amends, to confess his sin, and obtain the forgiveness offered by Christ's representative.

6. Mystic or Private Revelation: The Catholic Church, in her wisdom down through the ages, has cautiously accepted some rare occurrences of God wishing to make Himself and His desires known plainly. The tradition has its roots in the Old Testament: God spoke to Abraham, Moses, Elijah, David, and on through the life of Jesus and the Apostles, although these were Public Revelations, recorded in Scripture, intended for all believers. There is no more Public Revelation; it ended with the death of the last Apostle, St. John. Since that time, however, as recorded in the history many saints, Jesus has appeared to certain people just as He did to the Apostles. He has also permitted appearances by Mary, and occasionally, a saint. Oftentimes, they speak in dialogues which take the form of "interior locutions," words spoken clearly and distinctly within the soul of a person. For every one judged worthy of belief by the Church, myriads of imposters have also been identified. The Church does not obligate her members to believe those that she judges worthy of belief, and only goes so far as to say that, if it helps people in the advancement of their faith and growth in holiness, they are permitted to use the revelation. Anne's writings have received the official imprimatur of the Church which means they contain no doctrinal error, thus giving assurance to the reader that they can be read if they are helpful to the faith. There is more good news regarding Direction For Our Times and its relation to the Church which will be forthcoming soon. You can follow it on the internet on their website. Please see the letters from the Bishops that follow.

Recommended Resources

1. Volumes 1-10 by Anne, Lay Apostle, Direction for Our Times
2. *Climbing the Mountain* by Anne, Lay Apostle, Direction for Our Times
3. *Lessons in Love* by Anne, Lay Apostle, Direction for Our Times
4. *Serving in Clarity* by Anne, Lay Apostle, Direction for Our Times
5. *The Mist of Mercy* by Anne, Lay Apostle, Direction for Our Times
6. *Whispers from the Cross* by Anne, Lay Apostle, Direction for Our Times
7. *Rediscovering Catholicism* by Matthew Kelly
8. *Surrender* by Fr. Larry Richards
9. *Making Peace: A Catholic Guide to Turning Conflict into Grace* by Ed Gaffney and Terri Sortor
10. Liturgy of the Hours, Catholic Book Publishing Company
11. *The Anawim Way,* by The Anawim Community
12. *Magnificat,* by Magnificat
13. *My Utmost for His Highest,* Oswald Chambers

Extract of Messages from Volume Two

The following are the messages extracted from Volume Two with permission from Anne and Direction for Our Times. They are provided as a convenience for your reference but I would recommend that you purchase the Volume for your use or obtain the free download from the website www.directionforourtimes.org

Messages excerpted from:

"VOLUME TWO"

Conversations with the

Eucharistic Heart of Jesus

Direction for Our Times
As given to "Anne," a lay apostle

Used with Permission from the Publisher:
Direction for Our Times
9000 West 81st Street
Justice, IL 60458
708-496-9300
www.directionforourtimes.org

Direction for Our Times is a 501(c)(3) tax-exempt organization.
Copy of painting of *Jesus Christ the Returning King*
by Janusz Antosz, reproduced with permission.

MESSAGES FROM VOLUME TWO

Direction for Our Times wishes to manifest its complete obedience and submission of mind and heart to the final and definitive judgment of the Magisterium of the Catholic Church and the local Ordinary regarding the supernatural character of the messages received by Anne, a lay apostle.

In this spirit, the messages of Anne, a lay apostle, have been submitted to her bishop, Most Reverend Leo O'Reilly, Bishop of Kilmore, Ireland, and to the Vatican Congregation for the Doctrine of the Faith for formal examination. In the meantime Bishop O'Reilly has given permission for their publication.

Introduction

Dear Reader,

I am a wife, mother of six, and a Secular Franciscan.

At the age of twenty, I was divorced for serious reasons and with pastoral support in this decision. In my mid-twenties I was a single parent, working and bringing up a daughter. As a daily Mass communicant, I saw my faith as sustaining and had begun a journey toward unity with Jesus, through the Secular Franciscan Order or Third Order.

My sister travelled to Medjugorje and came home on fire with the Holy Spirit. After hearing of her beautiful pilgrimage, I experienced an even more profound conversion. During the following year I experienced various levels of deepened prayer, including a dream of the Blessed Mother, where she asked me if I would work for Christ. During the dream she showed me that this special spiritual work would mean I would be separated from others in the world. She actually showed me my extended family and how I would be separated from them. I told her that I did not care. I would do anything asked of me.

Shortly after, I became sick with endometriosis. I have been sick ever since, with one thing or another. My sicknesses are always the types that mystify doctors in the beginning. This is part of the cross and I mention it because so many suffer in this way. I was told by my doctor that I would never conceive children. As a single parent, this did not concern me as I assumed it was God's will. Soon after, I met a wonderful man. My ffirst marriage had been annulled and we married and conceived five children.

Spiritually speaking, I had many experiences that included what I now know to be interior locutions. These moments were beautiful and the words still stand out firmly in my heart, but I did not get excited because I was busy offering up illnesses and exhaustion. I took it as a matter of course that Jesus had to work hard to sustain me as He had given me a lot to handle. In looking back, I see that He was preparing me to do His work. My preparation period was long, difficult and not very exciting. From the outside, I think people thought, "Man, that woman has bad luck." From the inside, I saw that while my sufferings were painful and long lasting, my little family was growing in love, in size and in wisdom, in the sense that my husband and I certainly understood what was important and what was not important. Our continued crosses did that for us.

Various circumstances compelled my husband and me to move with our children far from my loved ones. I offered this up and must say it is the most difficult thing I have had to contend with. Living in exile brings many beautiful opportunities to align with Christ's will; however, you have to continually remind yourself that you are doing that. Otherwise you just feel sad. After several years in exile, I finally got the inspiration to go to Medjugorje. It was actually a gift from my husband for my fortieth birthday. I had tried to go once before, but circumstances prevented the trip and I understood it was not God's will. Finally, though, it was time and my eldest daughter and I found ourselves in front of St. James church. It was her second trip to Medjugorje.

I did not expect or consider that I would experience anything out of the ordinary. My daughter, who loved it on her first trip, made many jokes about people looking for miracles. She affectionately calls Medjugorje a carnival for religious people. She also says it is the happiest place on earth. This young woman initially went there as a rebellious fourteen-year-old, who took the opportunity to travel abroad with her aunt. She returned calm and respectful, prompting my husband to say we would send all our teenagers on pilgrimage.

At any rate, we had a beautiful five days. I experienced a spiritual healing on the mountain. My daughter rested and prayed. A quiet but significant thing happened to me. During my Communions, I spoke with Jesus conversationally. I thought this was beautiful, but it had happened before on occasion so I was not stunned or overcome. I remember telling others that Communions in Medjugorje were powerful. I came home, deeply grateful to Our Lady for bringing us there.

The conversations continued all that winter. At some time in the six months that followed our trip, the conversations leaked into my life and came at odd times throughout the day. Jesus began to direct me with decision and I found it more and more difficult to refuse when He asked me to do this or that. I told no one.

During this time, I also began to experience direction from the Blessed Mother. Their voices are not hard to distinguish. I do not hear them in an auditory way, but in my soul or mind. By this time I knew that something remarkable was occurring and Jesus was telling me that He had special work for me, over and above my primary vocation as wife and mother. He told me to write the messages down and that He would arrange to have them published and disseminated. Looking back, it took Him a long time to get me comfortable enough where I was willing to trust Him. I trust His voice now and will continue to do my best to serve Him, given my constant struggle with weaknesses, faults, and the pull of the world.

Please pray for me as I continue to try to serve Jesus. Please answer "yes" to Him because He so badly needs us and He is so kind. He will take you right into His heart if you let Him. I am praying for you and am so grateful to God that He has given you these words. Anyone who knows Him must fall in love with Him, such is His goodness. If you have been struggling, this is your answer. He is coming to you in a special way through these words and the graces that flow through them.

THAT FLAME IN YOUR HEART? TURN IT INTO A BLOWTORCH!

Please do not fall into the trap of thinking that He cannot possibly mean for you to reach high levels of holiness. As I say somewhere in my writings, the greatest sign of the times is Jesus having to make do with the likes of me as His secretary. I consider myself the B-team, dear friends. Join me and together we will do our little bit for Him.

Message received from Jesus immediately following my writing of the above biographical information:

You see, My child, that you and I have been together for a long time. I was working quietly in your life for years before you began this work. Anne, how I love you. You can look back through your life and see so many "yes" answers to Me. Does that not please you and make you glad? You began to say "yes" to Me long before you experienced extraordinary graces. If you had not, My dearest, I could never have given you the graces or assigned this mission to you. Do you see how important it was that you got up every day, in your ordinary life, and said "yes" to your God, despite difficulty, temptation, and hardship? You could not see the big plan as I saw it. You had to rely on your faith. Anne, I tell you today, it is still that way. You cannot see My plan, which is bigger than your human mind can accept. Please continue to rely on your faith as it brings Me such glory. Look at how much I have been able to do with you, simply because you made a quiet and humble decision for Me. Make another quiet and humble decision on this day and every day, saying, "I will serve God." Last night you served Me by bringing comfort to a soul in pain. You decided against yourself and for Me, through your service to him. There was gladness in heaven, Anne. You are Mine. I am yours. Stay with Me, My child. Stay with Me.

Prayers to God, The Eternal Father

Dear God in Heaven, I pledge my allegiance to You. I give You my life, my work, and my heart. In turn, give me the grace of obeying Your every direction to the fullest possible extent. Amen.

God my Father, help me to understand. Amen.

MESSAGES FROM VOLUME TWO

August 17, 2003
Jesus

My children, I am speaking to you from the depth of My Eucharistic heart. My dearest little souls of this world, you must come back to Me. I want your love now, as never before, and I want to protect you as never before. Because Our time is not like your time, I can communicate with you in a timeless manner. This is what I wish to tell you. I am going to share My deepest secrets with you. I am going to remove the veil from the tabernacle as never before. I want you to know Me. I want you to know Me in My miraculous form of the consecrated host. I am the Bread of Life. Yes. And I am your Jesus, also. I was a humble Man, who walked your paths of difficulty, want, and hardship. Many treated Me badly, so I understand the pain of hurt. We had little money, so I understand the pain of hunger. I was different, so I understand the pain of isolation. Little ones, I am with you. I want to teach you things that souls of past times did not learn until they came to heaven. I am doing this because I am raising up a tidal wave of Christians to wash over the shore of badness that has taken control of this world, so lovingly created by My Father. This process will cleanse your world, making it safe once again for God's children. I am going to bring you knowledge, wisdom, and love. I am going to introduce you to the divine to make your hearts burn like furnaces of divine love. You will be given the opportunity to work with Me. Children, come with Me now. Walk this walk of the divine with Me, your Savior. Together, we call out to others to join us. In this way, we rise up against evil and reclaim goodness for the world, for its people, and for God in heaven. I am omnipotent. By cooperating with Me and working with Me, you share in My power. You will learn to love in a way you have never known before. I am revealing Myself in a new way, such as I have never done. Come, let us together pay homage and pledge obedience to God the Father. It is He who decrees this work. Thank Him often and deeply for these graces, for with these graces, you will help Me to save the world.

THAT FLAME IN YOUR HEART? TURN IT INTO A BLOWTORCH!

August 18, 2003
Jesus

I want to show My children the great devotion I have for them. I reside in tabernacles all over the world. I do this because I desire My children to have a living Christ in their midst. Such holiness is available to souls who visit and venerate Me in the Eucharist. I am the cure for every ill. I am the calm for every storm. I am the comfort for every sorrow. Because I intend to lead My children in a more enhanced way, I am going to show you the Life that is enclosed in each tabernacle. My dear ones, if you but knew the value of each and every visit that is made to Me here, there would be crowds all through every day and every night. It is this crowd of souls I invite now. Dear children of this world, I, your Jesus, am not limited by the laws of nature. I can do anything. My powers are unimaginable to souls who have not seen the heavenly vision. In other words, to souls who remain on earth. Much is said in your world about power. This one has this power and that one has another power. Children are being deluged with images of occult or magical powers. I want this to cease. There is an obsession with powers that are NOT heavenly powers. My children, even some of My children of light, say these are good things, or at least harmless. I tell you now, in all of My Godly Majesty, that if a power is not from Me, it is evil. Search every day for these impostors and remove them from your life. You do not see the damage being done, but I, your Savior, assure you that this opens a door to your soul that you do not want opened. Your children must be protected from entertainment or games that feature "powers."

I wish to guide you in this specific manner. I wish to warn and correct you. I wish to teach you. Most of all, I wish to love you. Have you ever loved someone passionately, but been rejected? Was your love ever tossed casually back at you? If this has ever happened to you, then you understand how I feel. I am rejected by the majority of humanity. I gave My very life for this humanity, so that their sins would be overlooked and forgotten. Humanity, poor foolish humanity, flings this gift back at My feet, as if to say, "Your gift is worthless. It has no value anymore." Dearest children, this is ignorance in some cases. Many of these children do not understand that the gift they toss aside is their eternity, their salvation.

They do not understand this in many cases because they are not being told. I will rectify this situation shortly when I reveal Myself to your world, leaving no room for doubt that Jesus Christ lives and that Jesus Christ saves. At that time, souls will know Me and will be free to make a choice based on knowledge. My little one, how consoled I will be by the souls who make the choice in advance of that day, based on faith. I am sending My Spirit into the world now. The Spirit, the third person of the Trinity, is resting upon every soul who welcomes Him. My words must be spread and when these words reach a soul who is housing the Spirit, that soul will light up in a spectacular manner. Truly, the light of each of these souls will reach heaven, where the triumphant ones will rejoice to see another soldier returning to the cause. Be alert, dear ones, to My every whim. Practice responding in obedience to My requests. You will walk in peace, I promise you that today. Adore Me in the Eucharist as I teach you about love.

August 19, 2003
Jesus

I wish to speak to you today about love. I am all love. All love is Me. My children of this world must learn about love again, because, for many, the essence of love has been so distorted, they do not recognize it as valuable or seek to obtain it. Love is quiet and steady, My children. Love can be relied upon. Love does not diminish in the face of temptation. There are many kinds of love upon earth and all genuine love has its place. I want My children to examine the genuine opportunities for love in their lives. Certainly a family is a primary source of love. But many families have failed in love and their members drift away in bitterness. Children, the obligation to love someone does not mean you will not be hurt. On the contrary, often, and I must say usually, this obligation to love insures that you will be hurt and it carries with it another obligation and that is the obligation to forgive. If you would like to see an example of someone who

THAT FLAME IN YOUR HEART? TURN IT INTO A BLOWTORCH!

has been hurt, look at Me. You did not deserve to be hurt, little one. I understand and I see everything. I also did not deserve to be hurt. I tell you now, dearest ones, that you have hurt Me many times. Your neglect alone wounds Me terribly. But I love you. I understand you are not perfect. I look upon you and truly, I forgive you. Please accept My forgiveness and let Us begin Our walk together anew. Please, dear wounded child, take My forgiveness into your heart and let it make a home there. If a guest is welcome, a guest causes little trouble to his host because a guest who feels truly welcome will make himself at home and not cause his host any trouble. A welcome guest sees to his own needs and seeks to help his host. Isn't that true, dear one? I am your Guest. I am a Guest in your soul. Make Me welcome and I will heal, nourish, and recover your soul. Your heart will beat only with love. I will cleanse the bitterness and permanently remove the hurt. I will leave such a surplus of forgiveness that you will have plenty to lavish upon those who have hurt you. Dear children of this one true God, seek out people who have hurt you, especially in your family, and offer your forgiveness. You don't need to look for it. Ask Me where it is, dear child, and indeed, I will hand forgiveness to you. If you do this, you will heal. You may say, "Jesus, it is too hard. I cannot do this as I have been hurt too badly." My child, again I counsel you to practice. Say these words of forgiveness in your head. Then say them aloud. Become used to the sound of them. With My graces, it will not only be possible, it will be easy. Trust Me, who loves you with a genuine love and seeks your peace. I want no barrier of bitterness between Us. I want to heal you. I want to heal families. Do not be afraid. If someone rejects your forgiveness, that is his loss. You will heal, and you will be rewarded. It matters not to Me what a recipient does with a gift you have given. I look only at the fact that you have given when I examine your life. So welcome Me as your Guest, My beloved one. I will put so much love and forgiveness in your heart that you will not be able to give it away fast enough. I am your God. Believe in Me.

MESSAGES FROM VOLUME TWO

August 20, 2003
Jesus

Today I speak to you about unity. There is great disunity in the world. This disunity has permeated most modern life, but I speak in a particular way of disunity within the family. I intend to return a sense of unity to every family that will allow Me to do so. My children, when there is family unity, the members experience a steady flow of love. My peace, always available, draws the family through the inevitable times of difficulty and members of such families possess a calm and steady bearing. Prayer will bring unity to a family in a swift manner. If a family makes a decision to make family prayer a priority, I can bestow many graces to that home. Families devoted to Our mother already understand this connection between prayer and family unity. I want this for all families. Make a firm decision on when your family will pray together. If something interferes with this time, do not take that as a sign that your prayer commitment was a mistake. Simply reschedule to a more suitable time. I, your Jesus, am watching. I understand all. If you tell Me that your family never has enough time together to pray, I help you to find that time. It is possible you are all too busy and should eliminate certain activities. My children of this busy world must understand the very significant difference between entertainment and duty. An obligation to meet with friends is not as important as an obligation to family prayer, and it is possible that your priorities require examination. Do not fear this examination because I will help you. Together, we will examine your life and see where we can schedule time for you to draw your family together in prayer. Believe Me when I tell you that you will be abundantly blessed in this decision. I will put unity in your family.

Unity is also important for the purpose of identity. Children, in particular, must understand that they are expected to view life and respond to life differently because they are Christians. This begins in your home. My youngest children of this world do not understand their inheritance.

THAT FLAME IN YOUR HEART? TURN IT INTO A BLOWTORCH!

With many of My adult children, it is more serious. They have rejected their inheritance. So our goal is two-fold. We must educate Our youth and call out in love to Our adults. Look at your brothers and sisters in the world. Many are experiencing disunity in their families and walk in bitterness. They do not appeal to Me for help. They simply accept that this is how people behave. I assure you, My children, Christians do not behave this way. I intend to bring families together. From this secure love source, children will learn responsibility to others and to God. I intend for this to be the norm again. Will you help Me? Let us agree today that each family will respond to this message by praying together. Start small, if you must, with one Our Father. Then advance gradually. I would like families to pray the Holy Rosary. Let that be your goal. Devotion to My mother will advance a family to Me very quickly. Devotion to My mother will heal many deep wounds. My mother is united with Me in this work and brings many, many souls back to Me. Pray now, as a family, and rejoice as I restore unity to your home.

August 21, 2003
Jesus

Today I wish to direct attention, once again, to the hectic pace of this modern world. Children, come and sit with Me in the Sacrament of the Eucharist. I am in every tabernacle throughout the world. Think of one now, and picture Me there. Do I have a television? A radio? Of course not. Yet I am truly there. "What does He do?" you might ask. I tell you, My child, I am not bored. I think about you. I worry if you are far away. I suffer if you have chosen worldly paths and you are endangering your soul. I am sad each day if there is no hope of a visit from you. I ask My Father to have mercy on you. I direct My angels to watch over you in the hope that someday you will return to Me. My child, how often during your day do you think of Me? You are thinking of Me now, as you read these words. So while your mind is resting upon Me, let Me tell you that I love you. I want only your happiness. I can help you in everything. I can solve your problems and heal your wounds. My child, come and sit before the Eucharist in any tabernacle.

MESSAGES FROM VOLUME TWO

My graces and blessings will flow out to you. I want you to sit and soak in the silence. You may close your eyes there and I will fill your precious head with a stream of heavenly thoughts. I have so much to share with you. I have seen every injury you have experienced. I longed to comfort you. Let Me comfort you now.

Again I entreat you to eliminate as much noise from your life as possible. Noise is not conducive to holiness and while you might have to tolerate noise in the world, you can diminish noise in your home and in your car. In silence comes peace, little ones. You will find Me in silence. I am waiting for you and I have never once turned My gaze away from you. You must know that I forgive you for everything. I want only your love.

Souls find this concept difficult because your modern world has scoffed so often at selfless love that souls are suspicious. 'Why does Jesus love me? I am not very lovable,' they think. Indeed, many souls in this world do not like even themselves. So they find it hard to imagine that anyone, particularly the God of All, could desire their well-being and love them completely. I tell you, dear child, that the truth cannot be denied. I am the Truth. And I love you beyond anything you can imagine. My only wish is to bring you back to Me, where I might protect you. Do not be afraid. You will not be punished for your misdeeds. Come back to Me now and I will pardon your sins. We will proceed together as though these sins had never been committed. Sins leave a certain residue on a soul. Come to Me now, My beloved child, and with a heavenly breath, I will blow away the residue of sin so your soul proceeds in joy and newness.* I am your God. I love you. That will never change.

---

* See Volume Three, August 9, 2003 regarding the Sacrament of Reconciliation.

THAT FLAME IN YOUR HEART? TURN IT INTO A BLOWTORCH!

August 22, 2003
Jesus

The love in My heart gushes forth upon your world. In an unparalleled manner, I lavish graces on souls. My children, My love is such that I can no longer contain it. I see so many in need of Me, and truly, they shall have Me. Bring My words to those who suffer. My words will be the balm you will use to nurse souls back to wellness. Like heavenly nurses, you will apply My words to every wound and you will see miraculous results. My children, I am working through you. I am using you as healing instruments. Your world is sick and suffers from a disease far worse than any disease of the body. The very soul of your world struggles to find the source of healing it requires. And I am here. I intend to heal your world. I want you to be joyful representatives of your Eucharistic Jesus. The Eucharistic Jesus calls out to His children in firmness. I call you each by name and I say to you, "It is time to return to Me." Come to Me, waiting in the tabernacle, and I will reveal Myself to you in such a way that you will have no doubts. You will be glad in your heart and peaceful in your soul. Rest near the Eucharistic heart of your Savior and you will be granted everything you need. Faith is a gift, My dear one. I wish to give this gift to you. But you must turn to Me so that I may. My heart beats only with love for you. I can promise you that I will not reproach you. I will help you understand that only joy and light is suitable for a child of God. You will return to Us one day. Let Us make that the most joyful day of your life. Come to Me, My child, and I will show you how. You say, "Jesus, I forget how to pray." My child, does a small one forget how to cry when he is hurt? Of course not. Come before Me and cry out your pain, your hurt, and your fear. We need not do it all in one day, but take the first step to Me by coming in front of Me. Put yourself in My Eucharistic presence and I will do the rest. The work will come from Me. I will move you back swiftly to that place that has been reserved for only you in My Sacred Heart. You see, My child, if you have been away from Me, that place has been empty. I, your Jesus, have felt the emptiness terribly as I waited for your return. My heart aches waiting for you, so do not let Me suffer another moment. Do you begin to understand? I love you totally. You were meant to be with Me. Do not let anything hinder your return. I am your God, the God of All. The world wants to trick you out of your inheritance, but I hold it for you. It is safe with Me, My child, so return to Me now, that I may begin to heal you.

August 25, 2003
Jesus
Our work continues. I remain a prisoner in this tabernacle. I wait for every soul who is absent from Me. My children must understand that I am drawing souls to Myself. I can no longer stand by and watch so many souls lost for eternity. In days past, there would be a small number of souls who chose to remain parted from Me for eternity. This caused Me suffering, it is true. In these times, though, My presence in the world and dominion over this world is treated so casually that many souls choosing darkness are led to believe this is almost a meaningless decision. They do not understand the impact. Indeed, some of My children are casual about their eternity because they believe they will have several attempts at life in this world. I tell you today, children, this is a Godless notion created and perpetuated by the evil one who would like to downplay the importance of what you do with this time. There is only one life allotted to each soul. There can be no question about that. Do not believe that you will come back to earth again for another chance. It is this life you are living that will determine your eternity. So, My children, now that We all understand the importance of this day, and this series of days allotted to you, let Us make a decision on how you will spend the remainder of your time. I would like you to help Me. I know exactly how many days are left before you appear before Me in the next life. I have special work that needs to be done. Indeed, I have special work for each one of these days remaining to you. If you will say "yes" to Me, I can rest more easily, knowing those tasks will be completed and souls, the certain number attached to your work, will be saved. Additionally, I will have the joy, the happiness of knowing that My immeasurable love for you is returned. My child, come to Me and do My work. You will find no greater joy on this earth. Ask My true followers. They know the ecstasy of feeling My

smile in their soul. I want that for you. Let Me assure you that, in most cases, My work for you involves you remaining in your current role. I simply want you to be at peace. I want you to know you are loved. I want to be with you as you struggle and I want to keep you safe. You will experience your days differently when you unite them to Me. What formerly caused distress for you will be barely a ripple against the great peace I am offering. I can take even the smallest, humblest acts of love and obedience and use them to rescue a soul. So instead of merely surviving your time here, you will be using your days, already and always finite, to rescue souls who are living without Me and, in some cases, living against Me. We must have hope for every soul, My dear one. Rest in My tremendous grace during this time as I continue to reveal My great secrets to you.

August 26, 2003
Jesus

Children, I want to speak with you about obedience. I, as your God, am obedient to you. I protect you when I am asked. I render assistance when I am prevailed upon. I created a beautiful world for you to learn about love so you might earn your heaven. I, your God, am doing My part. I am asking you now to do your part. I speak only from concern, My children. Your world, distorted as it is, seeks to confuse you and make you think that obedience is a negative thing that weakens you. I assure you, My child, I am all-powerful. I am Jesus Christ and if you look at My time in your world, you will see that I was obedient to all whose obedience had call upon Me. I was obedient to God. I was obedient to the laws of that time set forth by the governing rulers. I was obedient to the religious authorities. I was also obedient to My parents. If you study My life you will see a life of holy obedience and meekness. And yet, a man with more power never walked the face of your earth. There is great strength in obedience, and I want to show that to you. Come to Me in the Sacrament of the Eucharist and I will teach you about obedience, revealing its beauty and the strength that lies with this misunderstood virtue. What am I asking of you, you might wonder. I am asking you to obey your Church, first of all. My Church has suffered in this time. Many children have taken this passion time of the Church as a license to be disobedient. Children, this must cease. You are called on to be obedient to your Church and in this way you are obedient to Me. I do not seek your destruction, My child. I seek your salvation. That is why I have given you this Church with all of its wisdom. Many souls say that the world has changed and because of this, the Church must change. Well, I assure you today, I have not changed. Heaven has not changed. You will discover this first-hand one day. The changes have occurred in your world and I am coming to you today through this prophet to tell you that the changes are destroying mankind. Change is not always bad, of course, but your world has deteriorated to an Age of Disobedience and too many souls are being lost. I am intervening in a significant way now to reset the course and direction for you. Heed My words this day. I come to you in love, My children. I bring you unlimited graces. Do not be afraid to change your life, even though it means admitting you have made mistakes. A wise man does not fear mistakes because he knows they are inevitable. Indeed, it is through these mistakes and through the study of past mistakes that we learn for the future. And it is the future I am concerned about. I want your future to be glorious. I want only good things for you. I have the graces necessary to insure that you succeed spiritually. You need not fear that you are not holy enough to follow Me. My child, I know all. I call you because your destiny lies with Me. I am your God and I call you by name into My heavenly service. Do not disappoint Me. Begin by the smallest acts of obedience to your Church and I will lead you to the heights of holiness for which I created you. Fear nothing. Sit with Me in silence and I promise to direct you. You need only come to Me and the changes will begin. How you will welcome these changes. Your world does not offer peace. Peace comes only from Me. Make haste to return to Me for My graces are waiting.

THAT FLAME IN YOUR HEART? TURN IT INTO A BLOWTORCH!

August 27, 2003
Jesus

Today I wish to speak to My children about heaven. Heaven is real, dear ones. It is a place and I am there. Most of your deceased family members are here along with all of the saints and many others whom you have not met. There is great fellowship in heaven, particularly among souls who served Me in similar ways. You will feel no pain or fatigue here, but, at times, you will rest in ideas and concepts so that you can learn them. You see, My children, your learning continues and the quenching of the thirst for knowledge is a part of heaven because everyone is able to learn about any topic that sparks their curiosity. You can then build on that and graduate to even deeper levels of knowledge and knowing. This does not feel like school. It is joy and wonder. It is innocence and love. It is coming into the mystery of your universe in such a way that you then help to direct the universe. My children, because of your limited understanding, which is necessary while you remain on earth, I cannot tell you everything. But I wanted to share this glimpse of heaven with you and I will continue to part the curtains, as it were, so that you understand where you are going. It is good to know your destination so that you know how to prepare. I, your Jesus, am helping you prepare. If you listen to Me and prepare well, you will be ready for heaven when it is time to come here. In this way, the day of your earthly death will be the best day of your life. Believe Me, My children, when I tell you that all of Us here in heaven await your coming. <u>We are linked to you</u>. My children on earth like to think that holiness is someone else's call. If you are listening to Me now, you understand that holiness is your call. If your destination is heaven, and of course it should be, then you must begin your preparation now. You would hardly travel to a foreign country without learning at least something about what you will want and need there. So take heed when I tell you that you will want to practice the virtues while you remain on earth. Try to view it as learning to speak the heavenly language before your arrival here.

I want to tell you, My children, that the saints, everyone here, clamors to assist you now. You are living in dark times and many of you have fallen into a spiritual sleep. I am preparing to make a loud noise, in a manner of *speaking, to awaken your world. Better for you, My child, that you open your eyes gently now and begin to serve from love and obedience, as opposed to fear. If you follow Me now, you will nearly eradicate fear from your life. I felt stabs of human fear for fleeting moments, as in the Garden and when I was condemned to death. But My faith and knowledge assured Me that man could hurt My body, but My soul remained intact, belonging to God and this heavenly world. It will be the same for you, children. You will fear nothing. Additionally, if you follow Me, you will receive extraordinary graces to deal with anything that frightens you. I will manage any fears you have, both now and in the future, and this is another solemn promise I make to you. Also, I give you permission to be like small children, often saying to their parents, "You promised!"*

August 28, 2003
Jesus

My children, I am with you. You have heard Me say that many times before. Perhaps I have said it so often that you do not really hear it. Today, I want you to both hear these words and understand them. I am with you. Does that mean I watch you from heaven, hoping all goes well with you? Does it mean I gaze out over My whole world, seeing only the large events? No. I am with you. I am with YOU, My child. That means I see the world from your eyes. I walk your walks and I experience what you experience. I am there when you are hurt. I feel the sting of human unkindness when you experience it. I feel the weakness and pain in your body when you are sick. My compassionate gaze, so filled with love and understanding, rests upon you every minute of every day. I forgive you any sins even before these sins are committed. But you must admit to your sins and ask forgiveness. My child, do not think you have been abandoned. I say with divine solemnity, I am with you.

So, begin to focus on the fact that every minute of every day, your Jesus is present. Talk to Me, dear child. I have so much to tell you. I have the answers for your difficulties. I have explanations for things you do not understand. I have love for people that you do not feel. So if you focus on the reality of My presence, you will begin to rely on Me. My child, then the transition

THAT FLAME IN YOUR HEART? TURN IT INTO A BLOWTORCH!

can begin. Once you begin to rely on Me, your life will get easier and less stressful. You will walk away from even the most difficult situations and leave them behind, instead of carrying that worry with you into the next area of your life. You will find this to be so liberating that quite quickly it will become your habit. And then, child, it will be Me working through you. And when that goal is reached, there is no limit to what you can do. Again I say to you today, you must practice for something to become a habit. So today, concentrate on My continual presence. Ask Me what I would like you to do. Ask Me what words I would like you to use. Then listen to My answer. My Spirit will speak to you and you will hear the words, resting upon your soul. In this way, We can communicate all day long. Have faith. I give you faith today, as you take these first steps to unity with Me. There is no situation where you should leave Me. Even in the most difficult of circumstances, call upon Me. Even in sinful conditions, or should I say especially in sinful conditions, cry out to Me. I am there anyway, My child. You cannot hide your sin by ignoring Me and hoping I have gone away. So speak to Me. Say, "Lord, help me." You will not be disappointed. I will help you. I bring you these words today so that you may understand that I am with you. I will never leave you. I await your notice and stand by, ready to assure you that you are cherished by Me and that I did not put you on earth to do work that was too hard for you. If your life is too hard, My little soul, it is because you are trying to accomplish it alone. You need Me. And I am here for you. So let us waste no more time. Jesus, your Jesus, is asking for your attention. Once I have your attention, We can proceed. You will never regret having returned to Me. Do not hesitate. Come and sit before Me in the tabernacle and We will begin.

August 28, 2003
Jesus

I want to draw souls into My Sacred Heart. This is the place of safety for you, My dear ones. It is here, in the security of My love, that you can rest and begin to see your world with clarity. Just as I told you that I see your world through your eyes, because I am always with you, I want you to see all through My eyes. In this way, gradually, you and I become one. When you look at a situation that troubles you, I want you to think, 'What would My Jesus say about this?' If you are unsure, simply ask Me. I will tell you. In the same way, when you look at a situation that causes you joy, ask Me if I also feel joy. We can then exult together. And there is much to be joyful about, My little one. I am joyful, for example, about you. I see your struggles and do you know why seeing your struggles makes Me joyful? Because you are trying to be good. We, in heaven, observe this struggle for improvement and We send you all manner of little rewards and assistances. We are with you in your struggles, more than you can imagine. My heart beats with such tenderness for you when you struggle. My child, you must not take this struggling as a sign that you are failing, but rather as a sign that you are succeeding. There is little struggle in badness, you see. There is a quiet, ominous acceptance or acquiescence. So do not be afraid. As long as you have the desire to serve Me, I will meet you there, at that initial desire, and I will bring with Me everything you need to succeed. My child, I will make it easy for you. It is not in My nature to confuse, so you must believe that confusion does not come from Me. Fear, anxiety, restlessness do not come from Me. Bitterness, hatred, deceit do not come from Me. Does that mean you will never experience these things? No. It is part of your earthly cross that you will encounter these things. What I am telling you is that you must bring these things to Me. I will then take them from you and you will be free of them. You may encounter these things again, perhaps within the hour. Come back to Me, in your heart, where I remain, and I will take them from you again. You see, My little dear one, your struggles are Mine now. I am stronger, wiser, more able for these things and I want to remove any negative thoughts from you. I seek to heal you and renew you. I can do this if you will let Me. I do not make this promise for now, this moment. I make this a lifetime pledge to you. When you experience a difficulty with your emotions, you bring it right to Me. And that's where it will end. I do not want My children troubled by obsessions. And because you belong to Me, and seek to serve Me, this is a right I bestow upon you. You may think of it as an advance on your eternal inheritance. I intend to give you a portion of the peace We enjoy in heaven. This is My gift to you and is a special concession for the difficult times you are living. Bring your troubles to Me, little soul of My heart. I, your God, wish to bring you relief.

August 28, 2003
Jesus

On this day I cry out to all families. How My Sacred Heart mourns the loss of so many families. My dear ones, We must work together now to strengthen the Sacrament of Marriage. It is on this sacrament that I base the family. There have always been cases where a family is without one parent. This can sometimes be My will, as when a parent dies. I have My reasons for allowing this to happen. But in most cases, My will involves a man and a woman, united in Holy Matrimony, bringing up children. My dear ones, I have so many reasons for structuring your lives this way that We could speak of nothing else for days. Let Me begin Our discussion of families by saying this. I have not changed My will in this matter. Your world would have you believe that both parents are not necessary. Children, this is not the case. A father brings to the family formation that a mother cannot and a mother brings things to a family that do not come from a father. I understand all. As God, I do not require explanations. There are so many cases today where one parent is forced to accept all responsibility. In some cases, this is My will and I do this because I have decided that one parent is damaging to the children. You are responsible for the moral and physical safety of your children and if your children are in an environment where they are unsafe, you have My permission to remove them, either by leaving an abusive parent, or removing a child from a place where that child's innocence is being destroyed. I am with you and give you every guidance in this very serious matter. I want your children protected, and I will help you to do this.

There are also cases, though, where a parent simply refuses his or her responsibility. These souls want to be children themselves and seek an extension to their childhood. Dear ones, your childhood is a time of formation. When it is over, you must understand that I expect you to put childish things behind you and spend your time doing My will. If I have gifted you with children, I expect you to parent them with all love, patience, and responsibility. This is your holy duty and your duty comes first. It is in this way, by the completion of your duty, that you obtain heaven. I want the family supported. I want each one of My souls to focus on their family and always put family interests first. Be attentive to your earthly spouse. Consider your marriage as the primary consideration for every decision you make. I have given you your spouse so that you can lead each other to heaven and help each other obtain a higher degree of holiness than you could have obtained without the participation in this sacramental union. So always view your marriage as a holy covenant, in which I participate. If you do this, My children, I will have no more concerns about families, because your children will be honored and loved, as I intended them to be.

August 29, 2003
Jesus

The love I feel bursts out from My Eucharistic heart. I cannot contain it. For such a time now, I have watched My children falter and err. I have seen them behave in such a way that they bring great pain and damage to their souls. Because they do not turn to Me, I cannot heal them and counsel them as I long to do. Thus they stumble on through their lives, repeating the same patterns and falling deeper into sin. Because of their pain, they inflict pain on others. Children, if I am describing you, I tell you now, it is time to stop. I am calling a halt to your destructive behavior, and I am giving you a unique opportunity. Come back to Me now, My little lost soul, and I will lift all punishment due you. Repent and throw yourself into My arms. I will forgive you immediately. I have already done so. But in order to heal and to be comfortable in heaven, you must repent and seek My forgiveness. You must come to Me to seek My forgiveness. You must come and get it from Me. I am here, in the tabernacle. Come to Me here and I will forgive all sin. I will make you as pure as if you had never sinned. My children, all in heaven are awed at the scope of this promise. I want you to consider that this is an opportunity you should take advantage of. You will not have forever to do this. You do not have eternity

THAT FLAME IN YOUR HEART? TURN IT INTO A BLOWTORCH!

on this earth. You have made mistakes and left the path to heaven. I implore you to return to Me now, before it is too late for you. You must understand that your soul can be lost. If you linger too long in mortal sin, My child, you will take to it as a child takes to a bad habit. The time to return is now. I come to you in these words because My love can no longer remain unrequited. It longs to comfort and console, and you, My child, are in need of comfort and consolation. If you let Me tell you of My love for you, you will begin to understand how irreplaceable you are to Me. Your gifts, strengths, and skills were given to you so that you could further My Kingdom on earth, as an obedient and loving child looks after the interests of his father. But, for some time now, you have not done that. You have looked after your own interests, either through the slavery of addiction or through the quest for worldly goods and sensual experiences. My child, I know you feel this is your business and perhaps you feel you hurt only yourself. I tell you now that you are My child, I love you, and I take it very personally when you hurt yourself. I am telling you now to stop. Stop any behavior that is separating you from Me. Are you unsure what those behaviors are? Come to Me, here in the tabernacle, and I will tell you exactly which behaviors I refer to. You know already, as you read these words. You must not trade these behaviors for your eternal life, My child. You must not. That is the second part of the reason why I compel you to return to Me. The third reason you must change your behavior is because I need you. I am your God, the God of All, and truly I say to you, I need you. There are souls in your world that only you can save. You must be working for Me to save them, because I have to tell you how and you have to be listening. So please, little souls of My heart, come to Me now, because the first part of the reason compelling your return is that I love you and separation from you is making My heart ache with loneliness.

August 29, 2003
Jesus

I wish to speak to My children about their speech. My children, does your speech accurately reflect who you wish to become? I want you to desire holiness. And I want your speech to be the conversation of a holy soul.

MESSAGES FROM VOLUME TWO

My child, I know that you struggle and often do not feel holy. We allow this to protect your humility. But I want you to speak as though you have achieved the level of holiness I desire for you. "Jesus, what do you mean?" I hear you ask. I am with you, and you are with Me. Your speech must display or illustrate Our unity. Do not think that you have gained this unity but must keep it hidden. My child, that would threaten part of Our goal for you, which is that others look at you and see Me. Others must also listen to you and hear Me. As a holy exercise, and in that same spirit of practice We have adopted, I want you to listen to what you say. Listen to your voice. And understand that I am also listening with you. Pay attention to your words, of course, but also to your tone and the inflections you use. Are your words, tone, and inflections meant to convey love? Do they accurately represent God, whom you carry within yourself? You will find, I am certain, that at times you will see that your speech does not reflect Me. Do not be upset by this, little learning soul. That is why We are checking. We are leaving no stone unturned to secure your beautiful reward in heaven. So when you identify something in your speech that you feel I would not approve of, ask Me how to say that thing differently. My child, you have been reading My words and hearing them in your heart. I wanted this for you because I wanted you to know Me. After all, I am your Savior. It is fitting that you be intimately acquainted with Me. So now that you have listened to Me, I want you to speak to others as I speak to you. Let Us review. I speak the truth. Always. Children, do not tell lies. To lie is to sin and remember that sin requires repentance. I speak with great kindness. I am gentle, but I do not withhold the truth, My child, because I fear your anger. If you are called upon to correct someone, do so. Counsel a friend or loved one in moral matters if you feel they are mistaken. Ask Me if I want this from you and I will tell you. Often I prompt a soul to correct a loved one. I understand that this calls for courage but I will see that you do not lack courage if you are following My will. Speak with great love and gentleness and speak the truth. Often, hearing the truth will anger a soul. Remain calm and loving in the face of this anger and know that people were and are often angry with Me.

THAT FLAME IN YOUR HEART? TURN IT INTO A BLOWTORCH!

Children, do not spread unpleasantness about others, either factual or not. Say nothing unless you speak to protect another. Usually you should remain quiet about the sins of your sisters and brothers, as you have enough of your own to be busy about. Speak of kindnesses, sacrifices, and loving acts that brought you joy. Focus on the many, many good qualities of others. Remember that if a soul is not united to Me, that soul feels a gaping emptiness, a loneliness, and a sadness. Dearest children who are close to My heart, have compassion and mercy as I have had compassion and mercy for you.

I am your God. For every kindness you show to others, you will receive a personal kindness from Me. Guard your speech well, little one. Let your speech bring only Me to others. I will help you. Together we will be certain that your speech profits heaven.

August 29, 2003
Jesus

My children, would you like to know how to please Me? Would you like to know what consoles Me and comforts Me in the face of widespread disobedience and hatred? Humility comforts Me. Humility consoles Me. Truly, the humility of My chosen souls softens My heart and deflects punishment from a cold world, undeserving of the mercy of its God. My children, the closer you come to Me, the more you recognize My goodness. Your intellect will automatically compare your holiness to My perfection and the result is humility. This is good. Do not fear the knowledge that you are imperfect and must improve. That is the journey, My child. When I walked your earth, people called Me "Teacher." I am still a Teacher and I am teaching you now. Like many teachers, I teach by showing you how to do a thing. My child, when you read scripture you will become familiar with how I lived. You must do this daily and through scripture you will learn about Me. Days will pass and your life will unfold before you and you will find yourself becoming Me. You will watch your heart be moved with pity for humanity, as Mine was moved. You will accept hurts with dignity and understanding, seeking no revenge. Yes, you will change. And change is what We seek together. You cannot stay the same and become holy. That would be impossible. The very call to holiness, and I know that you, My little soul, understand that it is to you I speak, demands change. You are in the process of becoming a saint and that is what I have predestined for you.

My child, you must not be jealous of the holiness of another. I have given each of My children different gifts, suited to the tasks I require from them. It would hardly do for Me to give you the spiritual gifts of your neighbor, and then expect you to complete tasks that require different gifts. My way is perfect. My plan is perfect. I am perfect. You want to be My friend, My little soul. I am the only way for you. Soon you will realize this but I want you to realize and accept this right now. Heed My words and take My hand and I will put you on the path I have laid out for you. It will feel right to you as it has been designed only for you by your God, who knows you with a perfect and complete knowledge. My will for you includes peace, and peace will settle upon you as you begin to follow Me. My child, I have many enemies and few friends. May I call you My friend? Will you stand by Me during these days of disobedience? Please, join your heart to My heart and join your will to My will. Together We can save souls. My gratitude flows out to you and you will never understand the power of a grateful God. Truly, I am a slave to My children who serve Me, despite difficulty and ridicule. If I were dragging My cross through your town, surrounded by angry mobs, would you watch from a safe distance? Or would you stand with Me, taking a share of the weight of that cross? My child, do not fear if you answered from weakness. If you come to Me and let Me change you, I can make of you the most loyal and courageous servant. I am with you as you struggle to detach from the world and join My loyal followers. I am putting you together so that you may draw strength from each other. Be at peace. I am God and I call My world back to Me.

THAT FLAME IN YOUR HEART? TURN IT INTO A BLOWTORCH!

September 1, 2003
Jesus

I am with My children. My presence is silent but constant. I am directing many of the seemingly unimportant events in your lives, so that My will can be accomplished. My children are practicing faith, and that pleases Me. But My protection is so great that My children could have an infinite amount of faith in Me and still more would be justified. My faithful ones, who are struggling to serve Me and be holy, please trust Me for I am with you. I have pledged My protection to you and I will not leave you vulnerable. Offer Me small little prayers when you are frightened or unsure and I will place My calming hands upon you, steadying and reassuring you. You will look back at this time of service to Me and you will be so grateful that you said "yes" to your God. My children, you will look upon so many souls sharing eternity with you who would be absent if not for your service. Can you imagine the joy you will share with these souls? So be brave and continue in My service, walking the path I have illuminated before you. It is there you will find your peace and your key to eternity.

For today, I want to warn you about a snare or a trap. My children often want to do big things for Me, and truly, big things are necessary and big things will be asked of you. But your holiness lies in the small, dear soul. It is in the small unseen tasks and duties that I whisper to your soul, that I mold a bit here, reform a bit there. You do not feel these changes because they are so subtle, but changes occur, My child, in the small things. So do not begrudge Me the mundane. Complete small, humble acts with love and patience so that I may do My work in your soul as quickly as possible. Yes, We are going to save many souls, and bring the world back to the light, but We are going to do that one soul at a time. Right now, I am starting with you. So give yourself to Me that I may change the world. Together, you and I must perfect your beautiful soul, insuring that it reaches its fullest potential, both here and in heaven. Do you trust Me, My child? Trust can be difficult, but this is one time when you can step out in complete trust and confidence because I will not let you fall. I am here, ready to save you. I have waited for this day, My child, for so long. My heart aches with love for you and watching you read these words creates an even stronger love in My heart. I will take care of you and you can close your eyes and rest in My heart. You have suffered because of the distance between Us. Often you did not know where the pain originated, but I assure you, the pain began when you turned away from Me. Our standards must be high now, as I desire your happiness. I want you to remain in My heart, where I place you today. I will help, My dear child. You are infinitely precious to Me and if you show Me the smallest desire, I can keep you firmly joined to Me, despite the winds that try to tear you away. Have every confidence that the smallest bit of faith will be rewarded in these days of difficulty. Heaven is united with earth in this mission of salvation for souls. All assistance is available to each soul who seeks to be saved. Be at peace, now, My little soul. I am holding you tightly.

September 1, 2003
Jesus

I want My children to be calm. Even in My service, My children tend to rush to and fro, as though this life were a race. My children, when you are hurrying, I cannot help you to listen. I may want to whisper something to your soul, an instruction, a bit of encouragement, or a word of love if you are being maligned. Often, though, you are moving so quickly that your heart and mind are already on the next task, leaving the current task incomplete or improperly executed. So, slow down, dear ones, that your Jesus might be truly united in your work and in your recreation. I do not like to hurry, and you carry Me with you. There are times, My child, when I wish to work through you to guide or console a soul in distress. If you are hurried, you will miss My cue and the soul will remain without necessary consolation and guidance. Children, this is the state of affairs all over your world at this time. Do you notice that loneliness and despair are everywhere? Children, you will not find loneliness and despair where I am. Indeed, even in the most wretched of circumstances, if I am present, you will see eyes that smile and offer kindness, and you will see great hope, even in the face of suffering and death. So what is missing in your world? I am missing. Few souls allow Me to work through them. When I am allowed, you will see hope begin to flourish again. Faces will be more at peace and joy will flow naturally from one soul to another. I will put such joy in your faces that you will be unable to conceal your unity with Me. Crosses will feel lighter and hold great meaning. Children, I have so much to offer you, both in these words and in My constant presence in your lives. So do not turn away, even for a day. Draw closer to Me, that We may proceed. What feels difficult to you, anticipating changes in your life, will come easily. That is another promise I make to you. Such will be Our union that you will consult Me on everything. Your life will reflect heaven. Souls will be drawn to you because of this and you will be equal to the representation of your God. Be joyful now because My plan has been set in motion and all creation awaits My coming. You will see changes in your world and you will understand and welcome these changes as a sign that your Jesus has heard the prayers of His children and is responding in love. Be calm, My child, in the face of all difficulties because I am steering the direction of the world now. I want My children practicing a quiet and thoughtful approach to every single day, and every hour in that day. Your thoughts, of course, should be turned to Me whenever possible. A small prayer, a sentence in your heart, is enough to ignite the faith and trust in your soul, which returns calmness to you. In this way, when upsetting events occur in your life, you will be comfortable confronting troubles in unity with Me, your Jesus. How different you will find life. How peaceful and joyful. I want the times when you are hurried to be rare. So much so, that you will note the rushed feeling and immediately seek to alert Me that you are not recollected. I will then restore your quietness so that you serve Me thoroughly.

September 1, 2003
Jesus

My child, with such gratitude I view your efforts. I am here, waiting in the tabernacle to thank you and encourage you. You are trying to serve Me in your life and it is not always easy to do this. Until a complete union or surrender occurs, you continue to wrestle with the pull of the world and *worldly attractions and distractions. This creates conflict in you because I am calling you in another direction. This conflict makes you feel discouraged, dear one, but you should not allow this feeling. There is not growth without some bit of discomfort. So, when you feel unsettled and you long for old habits, remember that you used those habits to console yourself in emptiness. I am now filling that emptiness for you so you do not need to rely on these things anymore. Worldly habits or addictions did not make you happy, My little soul. You felt unrest and bitterness without Me. Now, with Me, you are beginning to experience true peace, the peace which comes from heaven. This is a sign that your soul is directing the movement and action of your body, which is how man is intended to live. The body is under your dominion, or the dominion of your soul, and the soul, your precious and irreplaceable soul, is under My dominion. In this way, in this small corner, the world is as it should be. You belong to Me, My child, and I have defended you fiercely, despite your temporary indifference to Me. We will keep moving forward now with our movement toward unity. You may feel as though you are moving quite swiftly in these spiritual matters. Do not fear this haste as I am personally determining the speed at which I need you to ascend. In days past, perhaps your conversion would be more gentle and leisurely. I do not will that now and it is not what I require. I need My soldiers prepared quickly. Because I am God, and all created things bow to Me, I can do this with a soul like yours who seeks to assist Me and please Me.*

My child, never be afraid of holiness. When you doubt, look to your duty and remain calm until I desire to erase your doubts. You will carry small crosses of fear and doubt at times, but that is, again, more practice, and these little exercises are good for your soul. Make small acts of faith to Me and the doubts will lose their power to distract you from My service during your days. I am with you, My little souls, and We have discussed exactly what I mean when I say that. You are with Me and We move purposefully through your life together. Look for opportunities to serve Me in the people I place in your path. If you sense that I need you to assist a soul, let your spirit go quiet while I place the proper inspirations in your heart and mind. Then you may respond to the need in this soul for Me, and My word, My presence, will have been achieved. Dear little soul, so willing to serve Me, can you imagine your world if even a small number begin to live this way? Your world would change and that is what I am seeking to accomplish. Be at peace. Your God is pleased.

September 2, 2003
Jesus

I want My children to be at peace. You know this, children, as I often say this to you. Today, I am going to teach you how to keep peace in your hearts at all times. My children, when a parent rocks a child and sings a soft lullaby, the child knows peace, so much so, that the child often closes his little eyes and falls effortlessly into a peaceful sleep. My children, I am holding you in My arms. I am rocking you gently. Many times throughout your day, I want you to stop what you are doing for a brief moment and close your eyes. I will momentarily soothe your soul with that very same gentleness and, if only for a moment, you will know the sleep of peace. You will be fully aware in your senses, of course, but your soul will rest in complete union with Me and your entire being will be restored and balanced. My children, this is how I intend to keep you at peace. You must fear nothing, not even death. Why would death frighten a soul who is destined for eternity with Me? You are merely coming home, My child, and the brief moments of death are an almost instantaneous transit time. No, do not fear death. That will distract you from life and We want no distractions from the completion of your earthly duties.

My children, are you attempting to remain with Me throughout your day? Remember that you are practicing and trying to consider My presence and how I would speak. You are asking Me often what I would like you to do. This is the way, children. Do you see the changes I am making in your soul? Do you see the difference in how you view your brothers and sisters? You understand now that I am making these changes and that you can trust Me to keep My word. We are making progress, My child, and that pleases Me. This world will shift the smallest bit each time a soul moves closer to Me in trust. I want you to feel joy, My child. Your world is not at peace, but you must be. I am placing peace in your souls and the world is going to draw it from you, much the way an infant draws nourishment from her mother. That is why I am asking you to come to Me often in your day. As the world draws peace from you to quiet the terrible unrest, I will replace it in you. So do not worry or fret because the world takes your peace. It is for the world I give it, and I have an endless store with which to replenish you. Do you begin to see the depth of My plan? I need many souls to help Me and right now I do not have enough. So We must take My plea to the world so that all souls of good will may answer and assist Me. It is fair and just, My child, that each be given the opportunity to answer for themselves. I am asking and each soul must answer. In their soul, they know they are being asked to choose and they make the choice. I am God. I know all. I need souls. There is no hiding from Me. If a soul rejects Me now, it is finished. You cannot reject your God and claim heaven as your inheritance. Be at peace, My little one. Your God moves to right all wrongs.

September 2, 2003
Jesus

My children, these words are lessons in love. I seek to teach you that love is sacrifice. The two words, love and sacrifice, are nearly interchangeable from the heavenly perspective. If you love someone, you are willing to sacrifice for their wellbeing. In earthly terms, if you value or love a thing, you are willing to work, save, and plan to acquire that thing. If you place that same concept into heavenly terms, you can take a virtue, such as the virtue of obedience. If obedience is a valuable thing to you, a desired thing, you will work, sacrifice, and be patient until you can acquire this virtue. It is the very same with all of the heavenly virtues. I want you to value and put great emphasis on these heavenly virtues. I, your Jesus, am saying to you, truly, you will need to have these things to acquire heaven. You believe Me, and know that I speak only the truth. So you must begin to concentrate on the acquisition of these virtues. You must sacrifice to achieve these virtues. You are practicing and these virtues are becoming more second nature. You see them in your daily lives and your behaviors are changing.

THAT FLAME IN YOUR HEART? TURN IT INTO A BLOWTORCH!

We are working on patience. We are working on trust. We work on fortitude. You are becoming kinder and more compassionate. My children, all is going as it should be. I tell you that you are destined for great holiness and you will achieve this holiness if you remain united to Me. And you will do so because I will protect you.

Children, do not seek to further or advance the opinion others have of you. It is irrelevant. Please spend no time at all wondering or worrying about this. Worldly opinions change with the wind and a person could think well of you one day and slander you the next. You must not rely on these opinions for your peace because, as you have learned, you will be disappointed. Instead, rely on Me, who does not change. My opinion of you remains steady. I will always love you. I will always seek your betterment and well-being. I will always help you and consider your interests My own. So spend no time entertaining grief that the world does not appreciate you. You will be appreciated in heaven, and indeed this is already the case. Heaven is pleased with holy souls and seeks to assist them. Your heavenly friends will do more good for you than worldly friends who are not rooted in God. Be at peace, dear ones, as I will warn you when another seeks to harm you. I will protect you. Be assured that if you follow Me, all that occurs in your life will be for the advancement of your soul and the virtues I wish your soul to house. If you are ill, particularly, spend your days with Me and I can show you heights of holiness that will leave you breathless. I work with great energy in the soul of someone who suffers physically. Trust Me, please, with everything, for I am caring for you lovingly.

September 2, 2003
Jesus

Today We must talk about purity. My children, lack of purity is a very significant problem in your world. I search for purity and only find it in rare pockets. Because the tolerance for impurity is so profound, We are going to have to work very hard on this problem. Purity must be restored to every aspect of existence on earth. First, I speak of purity of dress. Do not dress in such a way as to indicate that you will behave sinfully. Dress as though you are a servant of Mine and seek My will. It is never My will to dress in clothes that lead others astray. Children, you know what I am referring to and I want this to stop. Modesty must be restored. Use these words often in your speech to remind people that purity and modesty are to be valued and applauded.

Next I speak of purity of speech. You must speak like a Christian, keeping your language worthy of your soul and the work I am doing in your soul. Language is often the method used by the enemy to spread the contagion of impurity. Use words that glorify Me. If you use My name to curse, My child, I will be personally offended and you will have to make amends to Me.

My children, I ask that you take offense to impurity in every form of entertainment. No longer should you sit idly while those who claim to be artists desecrate Me. Defend Me. I am your God. I want to hear your cry of outrage if I am maligned. If you, who know Me so well, do not defend Me, who will? Speak with immediacy when you are offended by forms of entertainment such as music, television, writings, or art. Do not let the enemy think he has overcome all Christian thought. I will reward you beyond your understanding for efforts against the scourge of impurity. Your youth are being poisoned this way and We must change this with decision now.

Impure thoughts can be more difficult because often you do not will these and they are a cross for you. If We change this type of dress, speech, and entertainment, though, you will see the volume of impure thoughts diminishing quickly. It is the constant reference to the impure that sparks these thoughts. Nevertheless, My little ones, push the impure thoughts from your head calmly. Distract yourself by looking away from objects of impurity. Ask for My help and I will assist you. Prayer and a consistent participation in the sacraments will arm you against these attacks on your purity.

I want you to understand that living in the world as it is will not be considered a valid excuse for either behaving impurely or leading others to impurity. I hold each soul accountable for actions committed knowingly. Parents, guide your children in these matters and set positive examples. Children, obey your parents in these matters and know that I am with you always. We will work on this together and together We will overcome impurity with a dedicated and purposeful outcry. I am with you and will show you exactly what I am asking for in this regard. My children, I want to thank you, now and always, for your obedience and service to Me. Your every effort will be preserved and rewarded. When your sins are presented to Me, I will turn My head away. That is what comes from your effort to serve Me. Be at peace now and do not let past sins of impurity disturb you. All is forgiven and My memory is short when it comes to My servants.

September 3, 2003
Jesus

I want to talk to souls about love of neighbor. My children, people are precious. Each and every person on this earth is of infinite value to Me and to My heavenly plan. But often the value is overlooked because of a worldly view of life. If I have placed a person on your earth, I intend that the person be adequately fed. You must proceed from that assumption. Dear little soul, so earnestly trying to serve Me, if you know of a soul who is not fed, perhaps I intended that you feed that person, and that is why I reveal that person's plight to you. Be thoughtfully considerate when you hear of a person or a group of people who are hungry. Then, ask Me what it is I am asking that you do in the matter. Perhaps I am merely looking for prayers. Perhaps I am making you aware of the great blessings that have been bestowed upon you. Or perhaps I am asking that you share in your wealth and support My workers who are attempting to feed these souls. Again, perhaps I am asking you to be one of those souls who ministers directly to unfortunates, who lack the barest necessities for human existence. You have a role. You must ask Me to reveal it to you so that souls on earth are not housed in bodies that cannot develop because they lack food. I see every need of every soul on earth. It is My intention that My children serve each other and in this way achieve holiness. Many are starving today in your world. My children, this is yet another symptom of the Age of Disobedience, a time in which more souls defy Me than serve me. I do not want people starving. Ask Me what you can do.

Children, I want you to think of the person you like least in this world. You have many reasons for disliking this person. You have been hurt, possibly, and it is difficult to forget that pain. Perhaps you fear that person would hurt you again if you were to attempt reconciliation. I am asking you, though, to love your neighbor. "Jesus," you ask, "what do you want from me?" I tell you, My child, that I fear for your spiritual development if you are harboring bitterness, whatever its source. Because bitterness often originates from another soul, I want you to examine any bitterness in your heart closely. If indeed you do, and you can identify this person who has caused you harm, I want you to spend this day praying for that individual. My child, ask Me to have mercy on this person. My just wrath is a terrible thing to behold and you would not like it to be directed at you. Therefore, you must also seek to spare others this destiny. Love of neighbor delights Me. Mercy and compassion given freely to others delights Me. Forgiveness? I need not even tell you about the happiness that comes to Me when I see souls offering forgiveness to each other. Understand, little souls, that I place people in your path with an intention and with a hope, a heavenly hope. Do not be quick to run from a soul, simply because he does not please you. Consider My will and be certain to ask Me if I have a heavenly task for you with regard to each person. It is in this way I will bring love to each soul, through love of neighbor.

September 3, 2003
Jesus

My children, often examine your intentions, seeking purity of your actions. I want you to act from your heart and when results are not what you hoped for, come back to Me and I will console you. Often in your life you will obey Me with a predetermined notion of what the outcome will be. My goal or desired outcome may be different than what you expect. Do not allow yourself to be disappointed when events in your life turn out differently than you thought they would. My will is being served if you are doing your best to obey Me. Concern yourself only with what I am asking of you. In this way you can walk in gladness, with a light and happy spirit, because you are serving your God and doing your part to bring about My Kingdom. My

THAT FLAME IN YOUR HEART? TURN IT INTO A BLOWTORCH!

child, how grateful I am to you. And what kinship is sent your way from your heavenly comrades. Be joyful.

Look to Me when you are faced with decisions. At times you will need to look closely at why you are choosing a course of action. I am warning you about this because I want you to begin to discern your own motives. In this way you can avoid acting from human weakness and seek only the divine or holy in your life. The enemy seeks to interfere with your decision to serve Me but We will not allow any more diversions from your heavenly path. We will together seek only heavenly motivations and your every task and project will further both My will and your soul. My yoke is easy and My burden is light. I allow crosses for your humility and improvement. If you feel a cross is too heavy, you may ask Me for relief. I will not be offended by this, My child. And unless it is necessary for you to retain that cross, I will remove either the cross itself, or the weight from it. We are united and We can discuss everything. Often you rail against your circumstances but do not come to Me to object. Of what use is complaining to others? They cannot lift your cross or even ease your burdens. Talk to Me and listen to others. In that way you will not fall into sins of the tongue, which do great damage in this world. I am here, waiting to listen to your every complaint. Every sorrow you suffer finds a warm, comfortable place in My heart and, truly, when you share sorrow with Me it is diminished. I want to give you eyes of heaven. I want you to see your life, this world, and its people, with these heavenly eyes so that you will begin to respond like Me, your Jesus, who loves you so dearly. My child, I am offering this new vision to you. Will you accept this wonderful gift from Me? Truly, you will be astonished at how this viewpoint will change your life. Most of what disturbed you in the past will simply fade away, out of your line of vision, because it will hold such little importance for you. Do you want this? I am so hopeful that you will say "yes." I want so badly to show you the world from My eyes. I can teach you such great things, My dear one. And if you share My vision, We can talk as freely as one soul. Be this for Me, please. Allow Me to dictate your perspective.

MESSAGES FROM VOLUME TWO

September 3, 2003
Jesus

I wish to tell My souls about the joys of heaven. My children, there is no bitterness in heaven. Bitterness and distress are not intended for you, even on earth. These are experienced by every soul at some time during their earthly time, but souls should not see bitterness and distress as the defining characteristics of their life. My child, if you feel you struggle often with these destructive patterns, you must spend time with Me. I am the Divine Healer. I can remove all hardness from your hearts so that you are liberated to love with no barrier. In that way, you become a more effective servant because you are open to receiving love, as well as giving love. My child, I do not wish to add to your grief. You will not pursue a relationship with Me and be disappointed. Run joyfully into this relationship with Me because you are guaranteed to succeed. I, the God of All, am making this guarantee to you. You fear failure, perhaps because in the past you have failed. Consider, My dearest, that you may be attributing failure to yourself where none exists. Put another way, once you begin to walk in unity with Me, your God who loves you, you will see success and failure more clearly. What may have appeared to be failure to you in your past, may look like success to you when viewed from My eyes. I am looking at effort, not result. The result of an effort is My affair and you must leave that to Me. So, in the name of reflection, look back now on your life. Think of these things that haunt you as failures. Did you try in these endeavors? Did you often do your best? When you saw a thing falling apart did you attempt to change your approach? Perhaps your failures were not failures at all. Perhaps you were seeking and not finding. Be at peace. You have found Me now and I will bring you every success, regardless of how the world views your endeavors. You are succeeding now, My beloved child, because you are sitting quietly while I minister to your soul and heal your wounds. Yes, We are a success. Together, we do not fail. Today is your beginning. Start freshly with Me right now and all possibilities open before you. Your heart begins to ache and this feels almost like pain, but a pain you would not

THAT FLAME IN YOUR HEART? TURN IT INTO A BLOWTORCH!

run away from. This is divine love, little soul. This is how it feels when you allow your God to love you. You feel a longing. Your heart looks around initially, because your heart cannot determine the object of its longing. This is the beginning of becoming a saint, My child. These first stirrings are a desire for unity with your God. This desire grows stronger and stronger and you can measure your holiness, if such a thing were necessary, by this aching. I tell you solemnly, with all of My Godly majesty, you will achieve fulfilment of this longing in heaven.

September 4, 2003
Jesus

I have come to cleanse souls. Much as a mother cleans her house, My child, I am cleaning and organizing your soul. If you have been away from Me, We must be busy. Events in your life, from your past, must be looked at now in a different way. This is an important task, and that is why I am spending time on it with you. Events can leave marks on your heart when you are not praying. Hence, My goal. To clean these marks and leave a heart that gives and receives love freely. When you pray, My child, I help you to sift through the experiences occurring in your life. Perhaps you have a disappointment today. Taken alone, without My assistance, you might feel down, sad and discouraged. If pride is a problem for you, and many suffer from pride, you might not share your sadness and disappointment with even another soul. It remains on your poor heart and, after a time, this turns to bitterness. Now, earthly life being what it is, and human beings being flawed, as they are in their search for perfection, you encounter yet another disappointment or betrayal. Pride asserts itself and again you do not adequately share your grief.

Another patch of disappointment turns to bitterness and covers another area of your poor little heart. My child, when this process continues, you have a heart enclosed in bitterness. A heart needs love, in the same way your lungs need oxygen. Your heart was designed this way, dearest, and if your heart is enclosed, the love is blocked off. How handicapped you are in the spiritual sense. How it grieves Me to see you so disturbed and unhappy. My little one, I am coming to clean every mark from your heart so that you will love freely, as I love. Do not think this is an impossible task. I am Jesus. I am God. I can cleanse your heart in no time at all if you are willing to let Me. I will restore order to your soul, I will adjust your thinking, and I will place the kind of love in your heart that is so genuine and abundant that this love reaches your eyes. All who see you will experience this love and know it is from Me. My child, My child, how grieved I am that those who should have loved you did not. I am sorry that anything hurtful has ever happened to you. But you must see that We benefit from suffering. Let Me show you how to make everything bad that has hurt you work to your benefit. Talk to Me. Pour it out to Me and I will grant you a peace, a forgiveness, and an order to all that has occurred in your life. I must tell you that when you have a disappointment in your life and you bring it to Me, I immediately help you to understand and recover. It could be that your recovery time is going to be a period of growth, during which you and I will grow closer and more dependent on each other. Would you begrudge Me that time, My child, if I needed it to make you into the kind of saint I need for certain work destined for you? Of course you would not because you are searching for My will. If you pray, I will not let you suffer unnecessarily. That is a pledge I make to you today. Please take that sentence to heart and hold it closely. If you pray to Me, I will not let you suffer unnecessarily. Ask Me for relief of your suffering, and if it is not benefiting you, I will remove it. Be at peace now and tell Me of everything that occurs in your life. Together We will ensure that no further blocks fall upon your tender heart.

September 4, 2003
Jesus

My children, I would like you to become dependable friends to Me. I want to rely on you. You are wondering what that means so I will tell you. It is true, I am walking with you. I am sharing your life and worries. Your business is My business and I help you with everything. No detail is too small for you to share with Me and seek assistance. You find Me there, always. You know

THAT FLAME IN YOUR HEART? TURN IT INTO A BLOWTORCH!

I never leave you. You are only being wise to have this confidence in Me, My child, because it is a confidence that rests on the rock of truth. I am that rock and I am that truth. In the same way, with every allowance made for both your frail humanity and your earthly duties, I want you to walk with Me. I would like to know that you will come to Me every day in prayer. We begin a journey together and then you disappear from Me. I remain with you, of course. I am your God and will not leave you. But We must finish the work We begin. Do not be haphazard about your time with Me. You are busy and I understand because it is often I who have given you your duties. But if you do not have time to pray to Me, there is something amiss in your life and I want it sorted out immediately. I need you. You are My friend and I need My friends to be faithful right now. So do not come and go anymore. Please, stay united to Me so that We can work together on the tasks left undone by others. My child, you must understand that when you come to Me in prayer, if only for a moment, I am consoled. My heart is comforted, which allows Me to give you untold graces, of course, but also, your prayer allows Me to soften My justice toward others who never seek Me. When you meet Me face to face, you will see clearly every happiness you have caused Me. I need you and so appreciate any fidelity offered to Me. If only for the sake of repayment you should come to Me often, as I reward each prayer, each glance, each petition even, beyond anything you might imagine. Please do not worry if you do not feel like you think you should feel. My child, how does a saint feel when that saint is laboring on earth? Very often, My saintly souls feel tired. They feel tired because they are laboring. But they also feel determined and these saintly souls come back to Me in prayer, even though they do not feel holy every moment. Do not let your feelings dictate your prayer time. Imagine a marriage where the two people only served each other in times of romantic love. I need not tell you that the marriage would be doomed. It is the very same with your relationship to Me. Serve Me always, regardless of how you feel. Do you imagine, My child, that you will come to Me in prayer and I will turn away? Will I say, "Go away, you do not feel holy enough to talk to Me"? Does a husband say, "Go away, my wife, you do not feel enough love for me"? How ridiculous. It is particularly in those times when you do not feel holy that I must listen to you and soothe and love you. We are to be close friends, which means We will be friends in times of spiritual joy. But, as close friends, Our friendship will become even more precious, more valuable, and more indispensable during times when you feel a spiritual dryness. Be at peace. I seek to explain everything to you now, leaving no questions and no hurtful marks on your heart.

September 4, 2003
Jesus

My children, I am not aggressive, unless one of My own is under attack and needs My protection. Normally, I am gentle and slow to anger. You will find Me a calm companion to your days. I see events clearly. I am able to read the intentions in the souls of others so I am the one to consult when you have difficulty. If you are needlessly upsetting yourself with a person, I will tell you. I am very patient with My children, particularly when they have turned away from Me. I will send many chosen souls to them in an attempt to get their attention. But I cannot will their response because they own their will. I would not give a gift to you and then take it away. If a soul rejects you, you must be at peace. Consult Me often when you are working with a soul. Pray for him. Love him. Show him by your example what it is to live the life of a follower. Are you calm? Are you peaceful? Those qualities are very attractive to a soul who is experiencing distress. You must convey to a struggling soul that the answer for everything is with Me. He may say that you don't understand that his problems are grave, complex, and unsolvable. He may cite reasons why he does not follow Me, always blaming others. The answers are all with Me. There is no reason to reject God. No excuse will gain pardon on judgment day. I have never shown a soul unkindness or cruelty. I deserve love, loyalty and respect. Understand My power and you will begin to understand My gentleness. Foolish souls equate gentleness with weakness. It is the truly strong who are wise enough to be gentle. So treat your brothers and sisters gently, particularly those who are not united to Me. They wound so easily. They do not have Me to console them when they are hurt. Can you imagine such loneliness? Would you like to return to a world that did not include Me

THAT FLAME IN YOUR HEART? TURN IT INTO A BLOWTORCH!

in any way? Do not even imagine such a thing because I have promised not to let you go. Truly, I will not. But be compassionate.

My child, have no fear about your future. Do not spend time imagining what will happen to you and what I will ask of you. This type of dreaming is not productive. Rather spend this time meditating on My passion. That type of exercise is productive and will allow Me to reveal Myself further to you. Our union will be deepened and you will gain much. You will have the joy of knowing that when others ran, you remained. I cannot convey to you the joy this will bring to you. Let Me say that throughout all eternity such knowledge will delight you. It is difficult for you to imagine eternity, but the closer you come to Me, the more real it becomes. Your exile from Us on earth is a testing time. Do not fail the test by wasting opportunities. Do not fail the test by spending your today feeling badly about yesterday. Did I not assure you that My memory is short? Your failings will be forgotten, child. Only do not turn away from Me now. I place great trust in you because I, your God and Savior, know you. I see straight into your humanity and know each capability. You are able to do great things, My little servant, but not without Me. You were formed and designed to work with Me. Without Me your work will remain undone because you will not be able to identify it, much less accomplish it. When this occurs, and I tell you I do not expect this from you, others must carry heavier loads and do your work as well as their own. It is for this reason that My true servants carry heavy burdens. But, My will is being accomplished and My time of renewal draws near. Have no fear. I am reclaiming My world.

September 5, 2003
Jesus

I want My children prepared. Today it is My wish to help My children understand the times in which they live. Children, you are close to My heart. You were put on earth for this time so that you could serve Me and assist Me in ushering in My Kingdom. The time of darkness takes its final souls as I prepare to return. The result is assured, as I often remind you. What is not assured is how many souls will choose light and how many souls will choose darkness. Be influential, My children. In your quiet, calm holiness, with eyes that reflect all of My kindness, be influential. Others must see more and more of My peaceful children, standing firmly in My presence. In this way, they will be attracted to Me. That is Our mission. My words here in these pages are intended to assist you in this process, the process of holiness. And holiness is a process of becoming, My dear ones. Will you ever say you are holy enough? Of course not. While you remain on earth, I will have divine work for you, both in your soul and in your world. Never content yourself that you have done a good job yesterday. To content yourself in spirituality is to begin the slide back into the world. Our standards are high but you are able and again, together, We succeed. I am with you daily, hourly, and through everything you experience. Please give glory to Our Father in heaven for His countless mercies during this time. He has been disobeyed in every area of humanity, and even now His concern is for His children. Dear ones, I have prepared you well. You are responding to My grace and becoming saints. How pleased I am with your progress, and also with the zeal with which you seek to share My words. I am calling and you are answering. I give you tasks and you complete these tasks. When this happens, all is at peace in your soul. Do not be afraid. Fear nothing. Did I not assure you of My power? Come to Me often and discuss every concern, every joy and every decision with Me. In this way you will be certain you serve Me and not the world. I wait for you often during the day to glance My way, and the moment you do, graces are sent down upon you. I will preserve you in My grace. I will open the path before you. I will count your enemies as My own and your interests will be Mine. We are united. Always proceed from that fact. You and I are one. Truly, you carry Me, your Jesus, your Savior, with you, My child. I leave you with that statement for now because you must live your whole life be that one fact. Be at peace, to serve My Kingdom.

September 5, 2003
Blessed Mother

Dearest children, nestled in my Immaculate Heart, you must live your lives joyfully. Jesus, my beloved Son, has given you everything you need to become true servants. In order to have peace on this earth, you must serve Him, who is all light, all goodness. I am His mother. I am also your mother. Call on me often, little children of this world. I have helped many souls reach heaven and I will help you. Confide your fears to me and I will console you. A motherly heart understands each weakness in her children and can help her children overcome habits that distract them from their union with God. Children, let me help you. Run to me when you fear you are not serving Jesus and I will lead you straight back to His holy path, the path He has marked especially for you. We are near you always, in everything. Truly, heaven and earth are joined as never before. Take full advantage of this. Heaven is happy, dearest children, because God is there. But you can be happy on earth also, because God is with you now. The more you seek Him, the more He will reveal Himself to you personally. All is well. We guard you and your loved ones without tiring, and you will see that your service to heaven brings you joy and more joy. Be with Jesus, children.

September 5, 2003
Blessed Mother

My children, I am anxious that you persevere in your conversions. There are many graces available to you so that you stay this course to holiness. Because I am a mother, your mother, I anticipate dangers that threaten my little ones. Beware of spiritual pride. Jesus intends to bring each of you to a high level of holiness in a relatively short time. At no time should you think this holiness comes from you. Your faith, your love of God, is God's gift to you so do not hold yourself above your brothers and sisters who are not responding as fully and hence not receiving the same level of grace. My little one, you might wonder what it is you are contributing if everything is coming from Jesus. You are contributing your free will. You are contributing your time on earth. You are giving Jesus your heart and saying "Yes, Jesus, I want to be a saint." Truly, little child of my heart, Jesus can do anything with a soul such as yours who has made a decision for heaven. Consider yourself now a soldier in the army of light. I anoint you as such and you work only for goodness. Prayer is your weapon and you are armed with the holiness acquired through your obedience. No evil can prevail against you. Such is the power you wield with Jesus as your leader. Fear nothing. We are with you. Be available to accept your direction through prayer so that as times change we can instruct you in everything. We are always available to you. I bless you now and entrust you to my Son, Jesus Christ. Serve Him faithfully and you will know heaven. How your loyalty will be rewarded. Truly, children, you will be overwhelmed with happiness. We have every answer, so bring every trouble to Us. I am with you and seek to help you as a mother helps her children through difficult times. When you need me, dear ones, I will be there, with additional guidance for your time.

Bishop's & Theologian's Letters

The letters on the following pages are meant to provide the reader of this book with the assurances that the original text by Anne, A Lay Apostle, and published by Direction for Our Times, used for my personal reflections, is theologically and spiritually sound and is subject to the authority of the Catholic Church.

It is with this confidence that I read and ponder the messages daily and have written my private reflections. As stated in the introduction, these reflections are my own, and have not been formally submitted to the Church, though I myself submit all that I am and do to the Church's authority and teachings.

The inclusion of these letters with permission from Direction for Our Times in no way is meant to reflect any endorsement from them of this text. As I have stated, this book is a compilation of my own prayerful reflections and does not have any formal approvals, only a reading and the blessing of my local Bishop. It is meant solely as a potential benefit to the reader to help ignite his or her spiritual life and dialogue with the Person of Jesus Christ. To that end, I have submitted it to my local bishop and his *censor librorum* who read the text and confirmed to me that it does, in fact, contain no doctrinal error. The bishop did give me his blessing:

"I read the text and marvel at your perseverance and discipline in the midst of such familial and professional challenges.

I turned the manuscript over to my censor for review. After a careful study of the text, the censor acknowledged that the manuscript contained no doctrinal errors.

….I would encourage you to continue on your spiritual journey with the Lord and inspire others by the witness of your deeply committed Christian life with my blessing."

This reassures me that I can provide this text to you with confidence that it can only lead you closer to the Person of Jesus Christ. My desire is that reader would be drawn closer to Christ and His Body the Church through this text.

DIOCESE OF KILMORE

Tel: 049 4331496
Fax: 049 4361796
Email: bishop@kilmorediocese.ie
Website: www.kilmorediocese.ie

Bishop's House
Cullies
Cavan
Co. Cavan

To Whom It May Concern:

Direction For Our Times (DFOT) is a religious movement founded by "Anne", a lay apostle from our diocese, who wishes to remain anonymous. The movement is in its infancy and does not as yet enjoy canonical status. I have asked a priest of the diocese, Fr.Connolly, to assist in the work of the movement and to ensure that in all its works and publications it remains firmly within the teaching and practice of the Catholic Church.

I have known "Anne", the founder of the movement, for several years. She is a Catholic in good standing in the diocese, a wife and mother of small children, and a woman of deep spirituality. From the beginning she has always been anxious that everything connected with the movement be subject to the authority of the Church. She has submitted all her writings to me and will not publish anything without my permission. She has submitted her writings to the Congregation of the Doctrine of the Faith and I have done so as well.

In so far as I am able to judge she is orthodox in her writings and teachings. Her spirituality and the spiritual path that she proposes to those who wish to accept it are in conformity with the teachings of the Church and of the great spiritual writers of the past and present.

Leo O'Reilly   Date _16 June '06_
+Leo O'Reilly
Bishop of Kilmore

Diocesan Seal

DIOCESE OF KILMORE

Tel: 049-4331496
Fax: 049-4361796
Email: bishop@kilmorediocese.ie
Website: www.kilmorediocese.ie

Bishop's House
Cullies
Cavan
Co. Cavan

2 September 2011

To Whom It May Concern:

I offer an update on the present status of Anne, a lay apostle and Direction for Our Times.

I initially granted permission for the distribution of the messages and written materials of Anne. This position remains unchanged. The writings and materials may continue to be distributed. As pointed out in my letter on the DFOT website, the permission to distribute the messages does not imply a final judgment on whether they are authentic private revelation. A final judgment on that question must await the outcome of an official Church inquiry into these matters.

Following Church protocol, I set up a diocesan commission over a year ago to inquire into the writings of Anne and to evaluate her reports of receiving messages from heaven. That work of evaluation is continuing and the outcome of it will be made public in due course.

I hope this statement is helpful in the clarification of these matters.

Yours sincerely in Christ,

Leo O'Reilly
Leo O'Reilly
Bishop of Kilmore.

October 11, 2004

Dear Friends,

I am very much impressed with the messages delivered by Anne who states that they are received from God the Father, Jesus, and the Blessed Mother. They provide material for excellent and substantial meditation for those to whom they are intended, namely to the laity, to bishops and priests; and sinners with particular difficulties. These messages should not be read hurriedly but reserved for a time when heartfelt recollection and examination can be made.

I am impressed by the complete dedication of Anne to the authority of the magisterium, to her local Bishop and especially to the Holy Father. She is a very loyal daughter of the Church.

Sincerely in Christ,

Philip M. Hannan
Archbishop Philip M. Hannan, (Ret.)
President of FOCUS Worldwide Network
Retired Archbishop of New Orleans

PMH/aac

106 Metairie Lawn Dr. • Metairie, LA 70001 • Phone(504) 840-9898 • Fax(504) 840-9818

Dr. Mark I. Miravalle, S.T.D.
Professor of Theology and Mariology, Franciscan University of Steubenville
313 High Street • Hopedale, OH 43976 • U.S.A.
740-937-2277 • mmiravalle@franciscan.edu

Without in any way seeking to anticipate the final and definitive judgment of the local bishop and of the Holy See (to which we owe our filial obedience of mind and heart), I wish to manifest my personal discernment concerning the nature of the messages received by "Anne," a Lay Apostle.

After an examination of the reported messages and an interview with the visionary herself, I personally believe that the messages received by "Anne" are of supernatural origin.

The message contents are in conformity with the faith and morals teachings of the Catholic Church's Magisterium and in no way violate orthodox Catholic doctrine. The phenomena of the precise manner of how the messages are transmitted (i.e., the locutions and visions) are consistent with the Church's historical precedence for authentic private revelation. The spiritual fruits (cf. Mt. 7:17-20) of Christian faith, conversion, love, and interior peace, based particularly upon a renewed awareness of the indwelling Christ and prayer before the Blessed Sacrament, have been significantly manifested in various parts of the world within a relatively brief time since the messages have been received and promulgated. Hence the principal criteria used by ecclesiastical commissions to investigate reported supernatural events (message, phenomena, and spiritual fruits) are, in my opinion, substantially satisfied in the case of "Anne's" experience.

The messages which speak of the coming of Jesus Christ, the "Returning King" do not refer to an imminent end of the world with Christ's final physical coming, but rather call for a spiritual receptivity to an ongoing spiritual return of Jesus Christ, a dynamic advent of Jesus which ushers in a time of extraordinary grace and peace for humanity (in ways similar to the Fatima promise for an eventual era of peace as a result of the Triumph of the Immaculate Heart of Mary, or perhaps the "new springtime" for the Church referred to by the words of the great John Paul II).

As "Anne" has received permission from her local ordinary, Bishop Leo O'Reilly, for the spreading of her messages, and has also submitted all her writings to the Congregation for the Doctrine of the Faith, I would personally encourage, (as the Church herself permits), the prayerful reading of these messages, as they have constituted an authentic spiritual benefit for a significant number of Catholic leaders throughout the world.

Mark Miravalle

Dr. Mark Miravalle
Professor of Theology and Mariology
Franciscan University of Steubenville
October 13, 2006

DIOCESE OF KILMORE

Tel: 049 4331496
Fax: 049 4361796
Email: bishop@kilmorediocese.ie
Website: www.kilmorediocese.ie

Bishop's House
Cullies
Cavan
Co. Cavan

To Whom It May Concern:

I hereby grant an Imprimatur for the books of Anne, a lay apostle, listed below which received the Nihil Obstat of Censor Deputatus Very Rev. John Canon Murphy, PP, VF, Bailieborough.

Volumes

Volume 1	*Thoughts on Spirituality*
Volume 2	*Conversations with The Eucharistic Heart of Jesus*
Volume 3	*God the Father speaks to His Children*
	The Blessed Mother speaks to Her Bishops and Priests
Volume 4	*Jesus the King*
	Heaven speaks to Priest
	Jesus speaks to Sinners
Volume 5	*Jesus the Redeemer*
Volume 6	*Heaven Speaks to Families*
Volume 7	*Greetings from Heaven*
Volume 8	*Resting in the Heart of the Saviour*
Volume 9	*Angels*
Volume 10	*Jesus Speaks to his Apostles*

Heaven Speaks Booklets

NB: The Heaven Speaks series of booklets are contained in the larger works called *Climbing the Mountain* and *Lessons in Love* and as such are included in this list of titles. The following have been published separately:

Heaven Speaks to Those Who Fear Purgatory
Heaven Speaks to Those Who Have Rejected God
Heaven Speaks to Those Who Struggle to Forgive
Heaven Speaks to Those Who Suffer from Financial Need
Heaven Speaks to Parents Who Worry About Their Children's Salvation

Books

Climbing the Mountain
Mist of Mercy
Serving in Clarity

Lessons in love
Whispers from the Cross
Transforming Grace
Monthly Message Book
Compilation of Heaven Speaks Booklets
Obedience/Priesthood Book *(taken from Serving in Clarity)*

Jesus Speaks to You Booklet *(taken from Volume Four)*
Jesus Speaks to Children *(taken from Volume Six)*
Mary Our Blessed Mother Speaks to Children *(taken from Volume Six)*

The Map

Given at Cullies, Cavan on 12th November 2013

_____
Leo O'Reilly, Bishop of Kilmore

Take Blowtorch! to the Next Level

If you are interested in taking your personal or group's spiritual journey, we offer the following resources which may be found on the web site: www.turnitintoablowtorch.com

Turn it Into a Blowtorch Personal Journal – the personal journal provides space for you to journal your spiritual journey during the 30 days and continuing beyond that. Each 'Day' is summarized so you easily take it with you without having to always carry the book. Using the journal offers you privacy and a means to reflect on the whole of the way Jesus is leading you.

Leader's Guide – a free facilitator's guide for prayer or church groups to take them through the 30 day program of spiritual renewal The Leader's Guide was developed by the author who has extensive experience in the development of adult learning programs which he has delivered to thousands of people.

Audio and Video Programs – audio and video program to complement the book will be released on a continuing basis. See either www.avanttpress.com or www.turnitintoablowtorch.com for links to those resources.

Blowtorch! Retreats– David is available on a limited basis to do Blowtorch! Retreats which are typically half day programs based on one of the chapters of the book. They are customized to the needs of the group. Full days are also available depending on circumstances. Use the contact us form on the Blowtorch web site to request availability.

Free Resources – please check the website for a list of available resources which will be added from time to time.

May God bless your spiritual journey and may Jesus Christ fill you with His Love and Mercy to overflowing as you grow in your personal dialogue with Him!

About the Author

David Leis is an award-winning consultant, author, speaker, trainer, executive coach, and college instructor. For over 30 years, he has spoken to and trained thousands of people in a wide variety of settings, from colleges to the Fortune 500 to small companies and non-profits around the globe.

His service to the Church has included developing a pre-marriage course used in several parishes, a marriage course, and a booklet on the Examination of Conscience. David has served in many roles in a number of parishes, has led hundreds of prayer group meetings, facilitated dozens of 2-3 day retreats, provided consulting to parish councils, is a 3rd Degree Knight of Columbus, was a CCD teacher, founded a men's fellowship group, led bible studies, and was a consultant to the Courage Ministry in New York City.

David is a graduate of West Point and the University of Southern California and has done coursework on an MBA and PhD. He served in the Army as an Airborne, Ranger, and Company Commander. Later, he worked as a Top 100 executive of Harris, a Fortune 500, and held management roles at RCA and GE. In addition to the writing he has done for the Church, David has authored an award winning training program for NATO, white papers on national security issues for which he was commended by former members of the US President's Cabinet, and training programs for many corporations on teamwork, leadership, strategic planning, diversity, consulting, and management.

David lives near Princeton, New Jersey, with his two sons and close to his daughter's family in Connecticut. He has donated his services to civic and religious organizations that serve the disabled and the poor.

www.ingramcontent.com/pod-product-compliance
Lightning Source LLC
LaVergne TN
LVHW051823080426
835512LV00018B/2700